Timeless Classics
**anny blatt**
from the Knit Collection™

# anny blatt

## Timeless Classics from the Knit Collection™

sixth&spring books

sixth&spring
books
233 Spring St.
New York, NY 10013

Editorial Director
Trisha Malcolm

Art Director
Chi Ling Moy

Copy Editor
Pat Harste

Graphic Designers
Doug Rosensweig
Caroline Wong

Technical Editors
Carla Scott
Pat Harste

Yarn Editor
Veronica Manno

Manager, Book Division
Michelle Lo

Production Manager
David Joinnides

President and Publisher, Sixth&Spring Books
Art Joinnides

Chairmen
Jay H. Stein
John E. Lehmann

Library of Congress Cataloging-in-Publication Data

Anny blatt : timeless classics from the knit collection /
[book editor, Trisha Malcolm].— 1st ed.
p.cm.
ISBN 1-931543-29-1
1. Knitting—Patterns. I. Malcolm, Trisha, 1960- II. Anny
Blatt (Yarn Company)

TT820.A65 2004
746.43'2041—dc21

                          2002044737

Printed in the U.S.A.

# "Only the best!"

Anny Blatt's long career spanned the same era as other celebrated French clothing designers such as Coco Chanel, Lanvin and Patou. She established her first knitwear studio in Deauville in the 1920s and then moved it to Paris in 1933. Anny Blatt designed her garments exclusively for the elegant clientele who frequented the posh resorts of Normandy, and approached each one of her designs by selecting the perfect pattern stitch to go with the finest quality yarn available. She also had an uncanny talent for predicting color and fiber trends and this, along with her powerful personality, made her famous. Her first creations, which included dresses, sweaters, twin sets and beach wear, are now very rare. However, a yellow silk beach dress from her 1934 collection is on display at the Musée de la Mode in Marseille.

After the end of World War II, the couture houses of Paris wanted to prove that Paris was still the fashion capital despite the devastation of war. Anny Blatt and other top designers such as Dior, Coco Chanel and Balenciaga, created a traveling fashion show. Since they only had remnants of fabric to work with and could not make full-sized apparel, they scaled their designs down to one-third of the normal size and dressed mannequins that were just 20" tall. The mannequins were even fully accessorized with small-scale jewelry by Van Cleef & Arpels, and little shoes, gloves and purses by Hermès. Anny Blatt's contribution to this momentous show was a magnificent wedding gown and a stunning coat and hat. A few years ago, this extraordinary traveling show—called "Le Petit Théâtre de la Mode" (The Little Theater of Fashion)—was exhibited at the Costume Institute of the Metropolitan Museum of Art in New York.

In 1968, Hervillier, a French spinning mill specializing in premier brushed mohair and other luxurious yarns, purchased the rights to the Anny Blatt name. From this point on, Anny Blatt became synonymous with fine yarns for hand knitting. In 1984, the company received the "Best Exporter of the Year" award, in the consumer goods category, from the government of France.

Pierre de Loye purchased Anny Blatt in 1991. This spinning mill was established in 1770 to produce silk, and had since specialized in producing top quality yarns. The company then moved to Avignon in the south of France.

Today, the company maintains the same uncompromising attitude towards quality developed by Anny Blatt who insisted on "only the best." The creative department is responsible for the unique, sophisticated and timeless designs that project an unforgettable visual statement for the person who wears them. The best fibers from the world over are selected for the yarns—angora, silk, kid mohair, camel, cashmere, Egyptian cotton, linen and extra fine merino wool for example— and these fibers are dyed and spun using the most advanced methods to create yarns in an amazing array of colors and textures. This is why the most discerning knitters knit with Anny Blatt yarns.

This book proudly presents a special collection of designs knit in sumptuous Anny Blatt yarns. Live in the lap of luxury and treat yourself to a little self indulgence—you won't be disappointed.

*Jean-Christophe Tarazona*
President, Anny Blatt USA

# contents

# soft & sumptuous

schiste

## STITCHES USED

**Double moss st, garter st.**

See explanation of sts on page 157.

**3-st cable at RHS:**

**Row 1:** CrK2/P1R.

**Row 2:** K1, P2.

Rep these 2 rows for 3-st cable at RHS.

**3-st cable at LHS:**

**Row 1:** CrP1/K2L.

**Row 2:** P2, K1.

Rep these 2 rows for 3-st cable at LHS.

**CrK2R:** Work 2nd st first, passing in front of first st, then K first st and drop both sts from LH needle.

**CrK2L:** K 2nd st first, behind first st, then K first st and drop both sts from LH needle.

**CrK2/1R:** Slip 1 st to cn and hold to back, K2, then K1 from cn.

**CrK1/2L:** Slip 2 sts to cn and hold to front, K1, then K2 from cn.

**CrK2/P1R:** Slip 1 st to cn and hold to back, K2, then P1 from cn.

**CrP1/K2L:** Slip 2 sts to cn and hold to front, P1, then K2 from cn.

## BACK

With 4 mm needles, cast on 135 (147/159/179) sts, and work in fancy pat foll chart.

Inc 1 st each side every 10th row 3 times, every 8th row 8 times = 157 (169/181/201) sts.

Work even until piece measures 34 cm or 13⅜" from beg.

**Armhole shaping:** Bind off 4 sts at beg of next 2 rows, 3 sts at beg of next 2 (4/6/8) rows, 2 sts at beg of next 4 (8/10/12) rows, dec 1 st each side every other row 4 (4/3/5) times = 121 (125/129/135) sts.

Work even until piece measures 54 (55/56/57) cm or 21¼ (21⅝/22/22⅜)" from beg.

**Shoulder shaping:** Bind off 11 (12/12/13) sts at beg of next 4 (2/6/6) rows, 10 (11/0/0) sts at beg of next 2 (4/0/0) rows. Place rem 57 sts on a holder for neck.

## FRONT

Work as for back.

## SLEEVES

With 4 mm needles, cast on 61 (65/67/71) sts and work in fancy pat foll chart. Inc 1 st each side every 4th (2nd/2nd/2nd) row 25 (4/12/18) times, every 6th (4th/4th/4th) row 2 (26/22/19) times = 115 (125/135/145) sts. Work even until piece measures 40 cm or 15¾" from beg.

**Cap shaping:** Bind off 3 sts at beg of next 2 (2/2/8) rows, 2 sts at beg of next 4 (4/4/42) rows, dec 1 st each side every other row 11 (6/1/0) times, bind off 2 sts at beg of next 24 (34/44/0) rows, bind off 3 sts at beg of next 2 (2/2/4) rows. Bind off rem 25 sts.

*(Continued on page 92)*

Cables make a sweater special, but kitten-soft angora makes it simply irresistible. Front, back and sleeves are kissed with an overall chevron pattern of cable twists. Finish the neck edge with a band of moss and garter stitches.

**SIZES**

Small (Medium/Large/X-Large)

**MATERIALS: LAINES ANNY BLATT**
Angora Super, Coloquinte 092: 11 (12/13/14) balls
**Knitting needles:** One pair each sizes 3½ and 4 mm (US 4 and 6)
Cable needle (cn)
St holders

**TENSION/GAUGE**

32 sts and 30 rows = 10 cm or 4" with 4 mm needles in fancy pat.

**SKILL LEVEL: ADVANCED**

surrey

## STITCHES USED

Garter st, st st, reverse st st, dc, tr, crab st.

See explanation of sts on page 157.

**Double Moss st:**

**Row 1:** *K1, P1*, rep from *to*.

**Rows 2 and 4:** K the knit sts and P the purl sts.

**Row 3:** *P1, K1*, rep from *to*.

Rep these 4 rows for pat.

**Double st:**

**Row 1:** K1.

**Row 2:** P1.

**Row 3:** K1 in row below.

Rep rows 2 and 3 for pat.

**Granite st:** Worked over an even number of sts.

**Row 1:** Knit.

**Row 2:** Purl.

**Row 3:** 1 selvage st, *P2tog*, rep from *to*, end 1 selvage st.

**Row 4:** 1 selvage st, *K1, K1 in strand between st just worked and next st on LH needle*, rep from *to*, end 1 selvage st.

Rep these 4 rows for pat.

**Eyelet pat:** Worked on 5 sts.

**Row 1:** K1, yo, K3tog, yo, K1.

**Rows 2 and 4:** Purl.

**Row 3:** K1, yo, SK2P (sl 1, K2tog, psso), yo, K1.

Rep these 4 rows for pat.

**Rope pat:** Worked over 3 sts.

**Row 1:** P1, K1, P1.

**Row 2:** K1, P1, K1.

**Row 3:** P1, K next st on LH needle and, leaving st on needle, K1 in st 2 rows below, then K1 in same st as before, P1.

**Row 4:** K1, P3tog, K1.

Rep these 4 rows for pat.

**Honeycomb pat:** Worked over a multiple of 8 sts, plus 1 selvage st each side.

**Rows 1, 2, 9 and 10:** With Victoria, col. Ivoire, knit.

**Rows 3, 5 and 7:** With Angora Super, col. Ivoire, 1 selvage st, *sl 1 purl-wise, K6, sl 1 P*, rep from *to*, end 1 selvage st.

**Rows 4, 6 and 8:** With Angora Super, col. Ivoire, 1 selvage st, *sl 1 purl-wise, P6, sl 1 P*, rep from *to*, end 1 selvage st.

**Rows 11, 13 and 15:** With Angora Super, col. Ivoire, 1 selvage st, *K3, sl 2 purlwise, K3*, rep from *to*, end 1 selvage st.

**Rows 12, 14 and 16:** With Angora Super, col. Ivoire, 1 selvage st, *P3, sl 2 purlwise, P3*, rep from *to*, end 1 selvage st.

Rep these 16 rows for pat.

**Fancy st pat:** Worked over a multiple of 4 sts, plus 1, plus 1 selvage st each side.

**Rows 1 and 7:** With Angora Super, col. Ivoire, knit.

**Rows 2 and 8:** With Angora Super, col. Ivoire, purl.

*(Continued on page 95)*

Haute couture is all about details and this exquisite sweater is no exception. Contrasts of colors, yarn textures and pattern stitches work together perfectly from the scalloped hem to the jewel neck.

## SIZES

Small (Medium/Large/X-Large)

## MATERIALS: LAINES ANNY BLATT

Angora Super d'Anny Blatt, Ivoire 271: 5 (5/6/6) balls, Cannelle 088: 2 (2/2/3) balls

Victoria d'Anny Blatt, Ivoire 271: 5 (5/6/6) balls, Cannelle 088: 3 (3/3/4) balls

**Knitting needles:** One pair each sizes 3½, 4 and 4½ mm (US 4, 6 and 7)

Crochet hook sizes 3½ mm and 4½ mm (US E/4 and G/6)

Bobbins

St holders

One button

## TENSION/GAUGE

23 sts and 32 rows to 10 cm or 4" square with 4 mm needles in Jacquard pat.

## SKILL LEVEL: ADVANCED

The classic belted jacket takes on a whole new look when worked in super-cozy kid mohair and a variety of easy rib patterns. Perfect for work or play, this timeless wardrobe staple also features handy pockets and front button closure.

## SIZES

Small (Medium/Large/X-Large)

## MATERIALS: LAINES ANNY BLATT

Kid Mohair d'Anny Blatt, Tourterelle 573: 12 (13/13/14) balls

**Knitting needles:** One pair each sizes 3½ and 5 mm (US 4 and 8)

Crochet hook size 4 mm (US F/5)

Stitch holder

Five buttons

## TENSION/GAUGES

26 sts and 35 rows to 10 cm or 4" square with 3½ mm needles in fancy K1/P1 rib.

17 sts and 28 rows to 10 cm or 4" square with 5 mm needles in fancy rib.

**SKILL LEVEL: INTERMEDIATE**

STITCHES USED

**K1/P1 rib, dc.**

See explanation of sts on page 157.

**Fancy K1/P1 Rib:** Worked on a multiple of 2 sts plus 1.

**Row 1 (RS):** P1, *K1, P1*, rep from *to*.

**Row 2:** *K1, sl 1*, rep from *to*, end K1.

Rep these 2 rows for fancy K1/P1 rib.

**Fancy Rib:** Worked on a multiple of 5 sts plus 2.

**Row 1 (RS):** *P2, sl 3 (wyib)*, rep from *to*, end P2.

**Row 2:** K2, *P3, K2*, rep from *to*.

Rep these 2 rows for fancy rib.

### BACK

With 3½ mm needles, cast on 139 (147/155/163) sts. Work in fancy K1/P1 rib for 5 cm or 2". Change to 5 mm needles and work in fancy rib, dec 47 (50/53/56) sts evenly across first row = 92 (97/102/107) sts. Work even until piece measures 10 cm or 4" from beg. Dec 1 st each side every 8th row 6 times, every 6th row once = 78 (83/88/93) sts. Work even until piece measures 32 cm or 12⅝" from beg. Inc 1 st each side every 10th row once, every 8th row 4 times = 88 (93/98/103) sts. Work even until piece measures 50 cm or 19⅝" from beg.

**Armhole shaping:** Bind off 3 sts at beg of next 2 rows, 2 sts at beg of next 4 (4/4/6) rows, dec 1 st each side every other row 2 (3/4/3) times = 70 (73/76/79) sts. Work even until piece measures 72 (73/74/75) cm or 28⅜ (28¾/29⅛/29½)" from beg.

**Shoulder and neck shaping:** Bind off 7 (7/8/8) sts at beg of next 4 (6/2/4) rows, 6 (0/7/7) sts at beg of next 2 (0/4/2) rows, AT THE SAME TIME, bind off center 20 (21/22/23) sts for back neck and, working both sides at once, bind off from each neck edge 5 sts once.

### RIGHT FRONT

With 3½ mm needles, cast on 69 (73/77/81) sts and work in fancy K1/P1 rib for 5 cm or 2". Change to 5 mm needles and work in fancy rib, beg with 1 selvage, sl 2 (0/3/1) sts, and dec 24 (25/26/27) sts evenly across first row = 45 (48/51/54) sts. Work even until piece measures 6 cm or 2⅜" from beg.

**Pocket placement:** Work first 8 (6/9/12) sts, sl next 27 sts to a holder for pocket opening but do not drop from needle, work these 27 sts (there are still 27 sts on holder), work rem 10 (15/15/15) sts. Work even until piece measures 10 cm or 4" from beg. Work decs at LHS as for back = 38 (41/44/47) sts. Work even until piece measures 32 cm or 12⅝" from beg. Work incs at LHS as for back = 43 (46/49/52) sts. Work even until piece measures 50 cm or 19⅝" from beg. Shape armhole at LHS as for back = 34 (36/38/40) sts. Work even until piece measures 60 (61/62/63) cm or 23⅝ (24/24⅜/24¾)" from beg.

*(Continued on page 98)*

glaucodot

sylvaine

## STITCHES USED

**K1/P1 rib.**

See explanation of sts on page 157.

**Fancy Pat:** Worked over a multiple of 26 sts.

**Row 1:** *[P1, K1] 3 times, P14, [K1, P1] 3 times*, rep from *to*.

**Row 2 and all WS rows:** K the knit sts and P the purl sts.

**Row 3:** *P1, yo, [K1, P1] twice, SKP (sl 1, K1, psso), P12, K2tog, [P1, K1] twice, yo, P1*, rep from *to*.

**Row 5:** *P2, yo, [K1, P1] twice, SKP, P10, K2tog, [P1, K1] twice, yo, P2*, rep from *to*.

**Row 7:** *P3, yo, [K1, P1] twice, SKP, P8, K2tog, [P1, K1] twice, yo, P3*, rep from *to*.

**Row 9:** *P4, yo, [K1, P1] twice, SKP, P6, K2tog, [P1, K1] twice, yo, P4*, rep from *to*.

**Row 11:** *P5, yo, [K1, P1] twice, SKP, P4, K2tog, [P1, K1] twice, yo, P5*, rep from *to*.

**Row 13:** *P6, yo, [K1, P1] twice, SKP, P2, K2tog, [P1, K1] twice, yo, P6*, rep from *to*.

**Row 15:** *P7, [K1, P1] twice, K1, P2, [K1, P1] twice, K1, P7*, rep from *to*.

**Row 17:** *P6, K2tog, [P1, K1] twice, yo, P2, yo, [K1, P1] twice, SKP, P6*, rep from *to*.

**Row 19:** *P5, K2tog, [P1, K1] twice, yo, P4, yo, [K1, P1] twice, SKP, P5*, rep from *to*.

**Row 21:** *P4, K2tog, [P1, K1] twice, yo, P6, yo, [K1, P1] twice, SKP, P4*, rep from *to*.

**Row 23:** *P3, K2tog, [P1, K1] twice, yo, P8, yo, [K1, P1] twice, SKP, P3*, rep from *to*.

**Row 25:** *P2, K2tog, [P1, K1] twice, yo, P10, yo, [K1, P1] twice, SKP, P2*, rep from *to*.

**Row 27:** *P1, K2tog, [P1, K1] twice, yo, P12, yo, [K1, P1] twice, SKP, P1*, rep from *to*.

Rep these 28 rows for fancy pat.

### BACK

With 3½ mm needles and Mérinos Icône, cast on 130 (138/146/154) sts and work in K1/P1 rib for 2 cm or ¾". Change to 4 mm needles and work in fancy pat foll chart.

### FRONT

Work as for back.

### SLEEVES

With 3½ mm needles and Mérinos Icône, cast on 64 (70/76/82) sts and work in K1/P1 rib for 2 cm or ¾". Change to 4 mm needles and work in fancy pat foll chart.

*(Continued on page 99)*

Knit a bold color palette of dramatically different yarns over a background pattern of ribbed lattice and you'll have art to wear! Styled with comfort in mind, this classic silhouette also features dropped shoulder sleeves and wide crew neck.

### SIZES

Small (Medium/Large/X-Large)

### MATERIALS: LAINES ANNY BLATT

Angora Super, Chutney 103: 3 balls, Miel 353: 3 balls, Icône 274: 2 balls

Kanpur, Icône 274: 3 balls, Miel 353: 3 balls, Chutney 103: 2 balls

Mérinos, Icône 274: 3 balls, Miel 353: 3 balls, Chutney 102: 2 balls

Pompons, Noir 383: 1 ball

**Knitting needles:** One pair each sizes 3½ and 4 mm (8) (US 4 and 6)

### TENSION/GAUGE

29 sts and 28.5 rows to 10 cm or 4" square with 4 mm needles in fancy pat.

**SKILL LEVEL: ADVANCED**

Wrap yourself in luxurious whisper-soft angora. This tie-front jacket is knit in a simple combination of stockinette stitch and double rib which makes it as easy to knit as it is to wear.

## SIZES
Small (Medium/Large/X-Large)

## MATERIALS: LAINES ANNT BLATT
Angora Super, Vert de Gris 598: 17 (18/19/20) balls
Knitting needles: One pair each sizes 3 and 3½ mm (US 3 and 4).

## TENSION/GAUGE
22 sts and 32 rows = 10 cm or 4" with 3½ mm needles in st st or K2/P2 rib.

## SKILL LEVEL: EASY

## STITCHES USED
K1/P1 rib, K2/P2 rib, st st.
See explanation of sts on page 157.

### BACK
With 3½ mm needles cast on 110 (118/130/142) sts. Work as foll: 18 (22/28/34) sts in K2/P2 rib beg with P2 (P2/K2/P2), then *20 sts in st st, 34 sts K2/P2 rib, 20 sts in st st and 18 (22/28/34 sts) K2/P2 rib beg with P2. Cont as established until piece measures 55 cm or 21⅝" from beg.

**Armhole shaping:** Bind off 4 (4/5/5) sts at beg of next 2 rows, 3 (3/4/4) sts at beg of next 2 (4/2/4) rows, 2 (2/3/3) sts at beg of next 6 (6/4/4) rows, 0 (0/2/2) sts at beg of next 0 (0/6/6) rows, 1 st at beg of next 4 rows = 80 (82/84/88) sts.

Work even until piece measures 77 (78/79/80) cm or 30¼ (30¾/31⅛/31½)" from beg.

**Neck shaping:** Bind off center 32 sts and work both sides at once until piece measures 78 (79/80/81) cm or 30¾ (31⅛/31½/31⅞)" from beg. Bind off rem 24 (25/26/28) sts each side for shoulders.

### RIGHT FRONT
With 3½ mm needles, cast on 102 (106/112/118) sts and work as foll: 10 sts K2/P2 rib beg with P2, then rep from * of back. Work even until piece measures 33 (34/35/36) cm or 13 (13⅜/13¾/14⅛)" from beg.

**Neck shaping:** Dec 1 st at RHS on next row, then every 2nd row 54 times and every 4th row 8 times. Work even until piece measures 55 cm or 21⅝" from beg. Shape armhole at LHS same as back. Work even until piece measures 78 (79/80/81) cm or 30¾ (31⅛/31½/31⅞)" from beg. Bind off rem 24 (25/26/28) sts for shoulder.

### LEFT FRONT
Work to correspond to right front, reversing shaping.

### SLEEVES
With 3½ mm needles, cast on 50 (54/58/62) sts and work in K2/P2 rib, beg with K2.
Inc 1 st each side (working inc sts into rib) every 8th (6th/6th/6th) row 15 (8/12/16) times, every 0 (8th/8th/8th) row 0 (9/6/3) times = 80 (88/94/100) sts.
Work even until piece measures 40 cm or 15¾" from beg.

**Cap shaping:** Bind off 2 (3/3/3) sts at beg of next 4 (2/2/2) rows, 0 (2/2/2) sts at beg of next 0 (4/6/10) rows, dec 1 st each side every other row 24 (22/19/16) times, bind off 2 sts at beg of next 2 (2/6/8) rows, 0 (3/3/3) sts at beg of next 2 rows. Bind off rem 20 sts.

### FRONT BANDS
With 3 mm needles, cast on 13 sts and work in K1/P1 rib for 171 (173/175/177) cm or 67⅜ (68/69/69¾)" from beg. Bind off all sts, working K2tog while binding off.

### BELTS (MAKE 2)
Work same as bands for 60 cm or 23⅝".

*(Continued on page 102)*

passy

# spring/summer

**gavaudun**

## STITCHES USED

**Reverse st st, dc, crab st.**

See explanation of sts on page 157.

**Cable Pat:** worked over 2 sts.

**Row 1:** K2.

**Row 2 and 4:** P2.

**Row 3:** Cr2R (K 2nd st first, passing in front of 1st st, then K 1st st).

**Fancy Pat No. 1:** worked over a multiple of 5 sts plus 3 for symmetry, plus 2 selvage. (See chart).

**Row 1:** 1 selvage *P3, K2*, rep from *to*, ending with P3, 1 selvage.

**Row 2:** K the knit sts and P the purl sts.

**Row 3:** 1 selvage, *P3, Cr2R*, rep from *to*, ending with P3, 1 selvage.

**Row 4:** 1 selvage, K3, *CrP2L (P 2nd st first, passing behind 1st st, the P 1st st).

Rep rows 3 and 4 for fancy pat no. 1.

**Fancy Pat No. 2 (Rosebud Pat):** worked over a multiple of 8 sts plus 1 for symmetry, plus 2 selvage. (See chart)

**Row 1:** 1 selvage, *K4, K1 tbl (through back lp), K3*, rep from *to*, ending with K1, 1 selvage.

**Rows 2 and 8:** P to end, working the tbl sts as P1 tbl.

**Row 3:** 1 selvage, *K2, work 1 fancy st to the right as foll: insert crochet hook under horizontal bar before the K1tbl 2 rows below, yrh, draw up a long lp, yrh, insert hook in same place, yrh and draw up a lp, yrh and pull through 3 lps on hook, place lp on RH needle, K2, K1tbl, work 1 fancy st to the left as foll: insert crochet hook under horizontal bar after the K1tbl 2 rows below and work as before, place lp on RH needle, K1*, rep from *to*, ending with 1 selvage.

**Row 4:** 1 selvage, P1, *P2tog, P2, P1 tbl, P2, 2tog, P1*, rep from *to*, ending with 1 selvage.

**Row 5:** 1 selvage, *K4, 1 bobble (work 4 sts in one st by K in front, back, front and back of st, pass the 1st 3 sts over the last st, place st on LH needle and P it), K3*, rep from *to*, ending with K1, 1 selvage.

**Row 6 and 12:** P to end.

**Row 7:** 1 selvage, K1 tbl, K3, rep from *to* in row 1, ending with K4, K1 tbl, 1 selvage.

**Row 9:** 1 selvage, K1 tbl, K2, work fancy st to the left, K1, rep from *to* in row 3, ending with K2, work fancy st to the right, K2, K1 tbl, 1 selvage.

**Row 10:** 1 selvage, P1 tbl, P2, P2tog, P1, rep from *to* in row 4, ending with P2tog, P2, P1 tbl, 1 selvage.

**Row 11:** 1 selvage, 1 bobble, K3, work from *to* of row 5, K4, 1 bobble, 1 selvage.

Rep these 12 rows for fancy pat no. 2.

*(Continued on page 103)*

What prettier way to accent a shapely buttoned V-neck vest than with a fanciful lattice pattern of dainty flowers? At each side, vertical columns of tiny cables create the figure-flattering shape.

**SIZES**

Small (Medium/Large)

**MATERIALS: LAINES ANNY BLATT**
Libertine, Gris Bleu 890: 11(11/12) balls

**Knitting needles:** One pair size 3½ mm (US E/4)
Crochet hook size 3½ mm (US E/4)
Seven buttons

**TENSION/GAUGES**

26 sts and 33 rows to 10 cm or 4" square with 3½ mm needles in fancy pat no. 1.
24 sts and 33 rows to 10 cm or 4" square with 3½ mm needles in fancy pat no. 2.

**SKILL LEVEL: INTERMEDIATE**

Black and white come together in perfect harmony to create a symphony of spiral motifs. Start with a sleeveless stockinette stitch pullover, then finish with decorative crochet chains that are sewn in place.

### SIZES

Small (Medium/Large)

### MATERIALS: LAINES ANNY BLATT

Kanpur, Blanc 050: 4 (4/5) balls, Noir 383: 2 balls

Knitting needles: One pair size 4 mm (US 6)

Crochet hook size 3 mm (UK 10) (US D/3)

### TENSION/GAUGE

23 sts and 30 rows to 10 cm or 4" square with 4 mm needles in st st.

### SKILL LEVEL: EASY

### STITCHES USED

**St st, dc.**

See explanation of sts on page 157.

### BACK

With 4 mm needles and col. Noir, cast on 106 (112/120) sts and work in st st, inc 1 st each end every 20 rows 3 times = 112 (118/126) sts, AT THE SAME TIME, when piece measures 7 cm or 2¾" from beg, cont with col. Blanc. Work even until piece measures 27 cm or 10⅝" from beg, ending with WS row.

**Armhole shaping:** Bind off 4 sts at beg of next 2 rows, 3 sts at beg of next 2 (2/4) rows, 2 sts at beg of next 6 (8/8) rows, dec 1 st each end every other row twice = 82 (84/86) sts. Work even until piece measures 46 (47/48) cm or 18⅛ (18½/18⅞)" from beg.

**Neck shaping:** Bind off center 16 sts for neck and working both sides at same time, bind off from each neck edge 8 sts once, 7 sts once, AT THE SAME TIME, when piece measures 47 (48/49) cm or 18½ (18⅞/19¼)" from beg, bind off from each shoulder edge 9 (9/10) sts once, 9 (10/10) sts once.

### FRONT

Work as for back until piece measures 39 (40/41) cm or 15⅜ (15¾/16⅛)" from beg.

**Neck shaping:** Bind off center 16 sts for neck and working both sides at same time, bind off from each neck edge 4 sts once, 3 sts once, 2 sts 3 times, 1 st twice, AT THE SAME TIME, when piece measures 47 (48/49) cm or 18½ (18⅞/9¼)" from beg, shape shoulders as for back.

### TO MAKE UP/FINISHING

See tips on page 157.

Sew shoulders and side seams. With RS facing, crochet hook and col. Blanc, work 2 rows dc around neck, armholes and lower edge of body. With col. Noir or Blanc, make chains various lengths, and work 1 row dc in each chain. Attach in spirals on front, foll diagram.

*(Continued on page 105)*

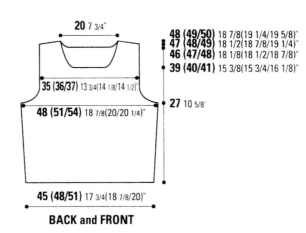

20 7 3/4"

48 (49/50) 18 7/8(19 1/4/19 5/8)"
47 (48/49) 18 1/2(18 7/8/19 1/4)"
46 (47/48) 18 1/8(18 1/2/18 7/8)"
39 (40/41) 15 3/8(15 3/4/16 1/8)"

35 (36/37) 13 3/4(14 1/8/14 1/2)"

27 10 5/8"

48 (51/54) 18 7/8(20/20 1/4)"

45 (48/51) 17 3/4(18 7/8/20)"

**BACK and FRONT**

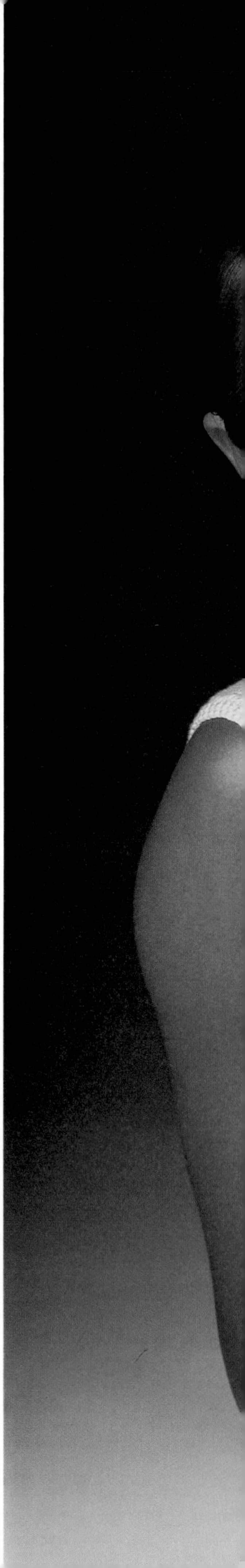

artouste

saumur

## STITCHES USED

**Garter st, reverse st st, dc, crab st.**

See explanation of sts on page 157.

**Double st:**

**Row 1:** K1.

**Row 2:** P1.

**Row 3:** K1, inserting needle in row below.

Rep rows 2 and 3 for Double st.

**Twist st pat:** Worked over 2 sts.

**Row 1:** Cr2R (K 2nd st on LH needle, passing in front of 1st st, then P 1st st.)

**Row 2:** Cr2L (P 2nd st on LH needle, passing behind 1st st, then P 1st st).

Rep these 2 rows for Twist st pat.

**Fancy st no. 1:** Worked on 5 sts.

**Row 1:** Yo, SKP (sl 1, K1, psso), K3.

**Row 2 and all even rows:** Purl.

**Row 3:** K1, yo, SKP, K2.

**Row 5:** K2, yo, SKP, K1.

**Row 7:** K3, yo, SKP.

**Row 8:** Purl.

Rep these 8 rows for Fancy st no. 1.

**Fancy st. no. 2:** Worked on 5 sts.

**Row 1:** K3, K2tog, yo.

**Row 2 and all even rows:** Purl.

**Row 3:** K2, K2tog, yo, K1.

**Row 5:** K1, K2tog, yo, K2.

**Row 7:** K2tog, yo, K3.

**Row 8:** Purl.

Rep these 8 rows for Fancy st no. 2.

**Fancy Purl st:** P1, wrapping yarn twice around needle.

**Fancy st no. 3:** Worked over a multiple of 6 sts plus 3.

**Rows 1 and 5:** Knit.

**Rows 2 and 6:** *1 Fancy Purl st*, rep from *to*

**Row 3:** *Cr6L (sl 6 Fancy Purl sts to RH needle letting yos drop, then sl sts back to LH needle; sl 3 sts to cn and hold to front of work, k3, k3 from cn)*, rep from *to*, end Cr3L (sl 3 Fancy Purl sts to RH needle letting yos drop, then sl sts back to LH needle; sl 2 sts to cn and hold to front of work, k1, k2 from cn).

**Rows 4 and 8:** Purl.

**Row 7:** Cr3R (sL 3 Fancy Purl sts to RH needle letting yos drop, then sl sts back to LH needle; sl 1 st to cn and hold to back of work, k2, k1 from cn), *Cr6R (sl 6 Fancy Purl sts to RH needle letting yos drop, then sl sts back to LH needle; sl 3 sts to cn and hold to back of work, k3, k3 from cn)*, rep from *to*.

Rep these 8 rows for Fancy st no. 3.

*(Continued on page 106)*

Heads will turn when you wear this twice-as-nice sleeveless top. The front is styled with a flattering scoop neck, while the back features a sexy V-neck and V-slit at the center bottom hem.

**SIZES**

Smal (Medium/Large/X-Large)

**MATERIALS: LAINES ANNY BLATT**

Libertine, Brume 064: 7 (8/8/9) balls

**Knitting needles:** One pair size 4 mm needles (US 6)

Cable needle (cn)

Crochet hook 3½ mm (US E/4)

Stitch holder

**TENSION/GAUGE**

24 sts and 33 rows to 10 cm or 4" square with 4mm needles in Fancy st no. 3 or rev st st.

**SKILL LEVEL: INTERMEDIATE**

Pretty in pink—a sweet windowpane pattern cardigan, knit using three beautiful contrasting textured yarns, is the perfect addition to your spring wardrobe. The modified V-neck allows you to layer it over any style top.

### SIZES

Small (Medium/Large)

### MATERIALS: LAINES ANNY BLATT

**Muguet, Rose 504:** 6 (6/7) balls

**Victoria, Rose 504:** 5 balls

**Pailettes, Blanc 050:** 1 ball

**Knitting needles:** One pair size 3½ mm needles (US 4)

Three buttons

### TENSION/GAUGE

24 sts and 38 rows to 10 cm or 4" square with 3½ mm needles in Fancy pat.

26 sts to 10 cm or 4" with 3½ mm needles in Sl St pat.

### SKILL LEVEL: INTERMEDIATE

### STITCHES USED

**Sl St pat**

**Row 1:** With Victoria, knit.

**Row 2:** With Victoria, *K1, sl, 1*, rep from *to*.

**Row 3:** With Muguet, knit.

**Row 4:** With Muguet, *sl 1, K1*, rep from *to*.

Rep these 4 rows fo Sl St pat.

**Fancy Pat:** Worked over a multiple of 16 sts.

**Rows 1, 3, 5, 7, 9, 11, 13 and 15:** *With Victoria, sl 1 st purlwise, P1, sl 1 st purlwise. With Muguet, K13*, rep from *to*.

**Rows 2, 4, 6, 8, 10, 12, 14, and 16:** K the knit sts and P the purl sts and the sl sts, matching colors.

**Rows 17-22:** Work in Sl St pat.

Rep rows 1- 22 for Fancy pat.

### BACK

With 3½ mm needles and Victoria, cast on 124 (132/138) sts. Work in Sl St pat for 2.5 cm or ⅞", then P 1 row on WS, dec 9 sts evenly across = 115 (123/129) sts. Work in Fancy pat, beg with 1 selvage st, then st 2 (14/11) of chart. When piece measures 30 cm or 11⅞" above Sl St pat, shape armholes.

**Armhole shaping:** Bind off 3 sts at beg of next 2 rows, 2 sts at beg of next 4 (6/8) rows, dec 1 st each side every other row twice = 97 (101/103) sts. **Note:** After 192 rows of Fancy pat have been worked, end with 6 (10/14) rows of Sl St pat. Work even until piece measures 50 (51/52) cm or 19⅝ (20/20½)" above Sl St pat.

**Shoulder shaping:** Bind off 6 (7/7) sts at beg of next 2 rows, 7 sts at beg of next 6 (4/2) rows, 8 sts at beg of next 0 (2/4) rows. Piece measures 52 (53/54) cm or 20½ (20⅞/21¼)" above Sl St pat. Bind off rem 43 sts for back neck.

### RIGHT FRONT

With 3½ mm needles and Victoria, cast on 60 (64/68) sts. Work in Sl St pat for 2.5 cm or ⅞", then P 1 row on WS, dec 4 (4/5) sts evenly across = 56 (60/63) sts. Work in Fancy pat, beg with 1 selvage st, then st 13 of chart. When piece measures 20 (21/22) cm or 7¾ (8¼/8⅝)" above Sl St pat, shape neck.

**Neck shaping:** Dec 1 st at RHS on next row, then every 10th row 4 times, every 8th row 5 times, AT THE SAME TIME, when piece measures same length as back to armhole, shape armhole at LHS as for back. When piece measures 43 (44/45) cm or 16⅞ (17⅜/17¾)" above Sl St pat, cont to shape neck by binding off at RHS 3 sts on next row, then every other row 2 sts twice, and 1 st 3 times. **Note:** After 192 rows of Fancy pat have been worked, end with 6 (10/14) rows of Sl St pat. When piece measures same length as back to shoulders, shape shoulder at LHS as for back.

*(Continued on page 108)*

**jullouville**

bicolore

## STITCHES USED

**St st.**

See explanation of sts on page 157.

**K1/P1 twisted rib:**

**Row 1:** *K1 through back loop (tbl), P1*, rep from *to*.

**Row 2:** K the knit sts and P the purl sts.

Rep these 2 rows for k1/p1 twisted rib.

**Single left slanting dec:** Sl 1, k1, psso.

**Single right slanting dec:** K2tog.

### EMBROIDERY

**Chain st, detached chain st (lazy daisy st).**

### CARDIGAN

### BACK

With col. Soufre and 3 mm needles, cast on 121 (129/137/143) sts. Work in K1/P1 twisted rib, beg with P1 (P1/P1/K1), for 3 cm or 1⅛". P one row on WS, inc 1 st = 122 (130/138/144) sts. Change to 3½ mm needles and work in st st until piece measures 34 cm or 13⅜" from beg.

**Armhole shaping:** Bind off 4 sts at beg of next 2 (2/4/4) rows, 3 sts at beg of next 2 (4/4/4) rows, 2 sts at beg of next 4 (4/2/4) rows, dec 1 st each side every other row 1 (1/2/2) times = 98 (100/102/104) sts. Work even until piece measures 54 (55/56/57) cm or 21¼ (21⅝/22/22⅜)" above rib.

**Shoulder and neck shaping:** Bind off 8 (9/10/9) sts at beg of next 2 rows, 9 (9/9/10) sts at beg of next 4 rows, AT THE SAME TIME, bind off center 46 sts and, working both sides at once, cont shoulder shaping.

### RIGHT FRONT

With col. Soufre and 3 mm needles, cast on 60 (64/68/71) sts and work in K1/P1 twisted rib, beg with K2, for 3 cm or 1⅛". Change to 3½ mm needles and work in st st. Shape neck when piece measures 32 (33/34/35) cm or 12⅝ (13/13⅜/13¾)" above rib.

**Neck shaping:** Work single left slanting dec at RHS (at 2 sts in from edge) on next row, then every other row 8 times, every 4th row 13 times, AT THE SAME TIME, when piece measures 34 cm or 13⅜" above rib, shape armhole at LHS as for back. When piece measures 54 (55/56/57) cm or 21¼ (21⅝/22/22⅜)" above rib, shape shoulder at LHS as for back.

### LEFT FRONT

Work as for right front, but in reverse, and beg rib with K1 (K1/K1/P1) and work right slanting dec at 2 sts in from LHS for neck dec.

*(Continued on page 109)*

---

Opposites make the most attractive twin set. Knit a scoop neck tank and a V-neck cardigan using two boldly contrasting colors. Switch colors to accent each with a stunning floral design embroidered in chain and lazy-daisy stitches.

### SIZES

Small (Medium/Large/X-Large)

### MATERIALS: LAINES ANNY BLATT

**Cardigan**

Louxor, Soufre 528: 7 (7/8/8) balls,
Noir 383: 1 ball

**Top**

Louxor, Noir 383: 5 (5/6/6) balls,
Soufre 528: 1 ball

Knitting needles: One pair each sizes 3 and 3½ mm (US 3 and 4)

Six black buttons

### TENSION/GAUGE

25 sts and 31 rows to 10 cm or 4" square with 3½ mm needles in St st.

### SKILL LEVEL: INTERMEDIATE

Look fashionably hot while staying super cool! Nothing beats the heat of summer like a sleeveless top that's worked in an airy ladder stitch. For bold contrast, a column of ribs transforms into an eye-catching braided diamond on both front and back.

SIZES

Small (Medium/Large/X-Large)

MATERIALS: LAINES ANNY BLATT

**Libertine, Gazon 246:** 9 (9/10/10) balls

**Knitting needles:** One pair size 3½

Cable needle (cn)

Crochet hook size 3 mm (US D/3)

TENSION/GAUGES

25 sts and 36 rows to 10 cm or 4" square with 3½ mm needles in rev st st.

37 sts braid pat with 3½ needles = 10 cm or 4" wide.

37 sts fancy pat (from the 1st to the 6th st, then rep from *to* 3 times, end with the 16th to 19th st of chart) with 3½ mm needles = 12.5 cm or 4⅞" wide.

SKILL LEVEL: ADVANCED

STITCHES USED

**Garter st, K3/P2 rib, rev st st, dc, crab st.**

See explanation of sts on page 157.

**Eyelet Pat:** worked over 4 sts.

**Row 1:** K1, yo, K2tog, K1.

**Rows 2 and 4:** Purl.

**Row 3:** K2, yo, K2tog, K1.

Rep these 4 rows for eyelet pat.

**Fancy Pat:** worked over a multiple of 9 sts plus 10, plus 1 selvage each side.

**Row 1:** 1 selvage, K2tog, K3, yo twice, *K3, K3tog, K3, yo twice*, rep from *to*, end with K3, K2tog, 1 selvage.

**Row 2:** 1 selvage, P4, *P1, K1, P7*, rep from *to*, end with P1, K1, P4, 1 selvage.

Rep these 2 rows for fancy pat.

**Braid Pat:** Beg on the 37th st, see chart.

**CrK3/P1R:** Sl 1 st to cn, hold to back of work, K next 3 sts, P1 from cn.

**CrP1/K3L:** Sl 3 sts to cn, hold to front of work, P next st, K3 from cn.

**Cr6R:** Sl 3 sts to cn, hold to back of work, K next 3 sts, K3 from cn.

**Cr6L:** Sl 3 sts to cn, hold to front of work, K next 3 sts, K3 from cn.

FRONT

With 3½ mm needles, cast on 130 (138/146/154) sts and work in garter st for 1 cm or ⅜". K one row on WS, inc 13 sts evenly across = 143 (151/159/167) sts. Cont as foll: 1 selvage, 4 sts eyelet pat, 11 (15/19/23) sts rev st st, 37 sts fancy pat (see gauge), 37 sts K3/P2 rib, beg with p2, 37 sts fancy pat (see gauge), 11 (15/19/23) sts rev st st, 4 sts eyelet pat, 1 selvage. Cont as established, dec 1 st each side (5 sts in from edge) every 6th row 3 times, every 4th row 7 times = 123 (131/139/147) sts. Work even until piece measures 17 cm or 6⅝" above garter st. Inc 1 st each side (5 sts in from edge) on next row, then every 6th row 9 times, AT THE SAME TIME, when piece measures 23 (24/25/26) cm or 9 (9⅜/9⅞/10¼)" above garter st, cont braid pat on the center 37 sts = 146 (154/162/170) sts. Work even until piece measures 33 cm or 13" above garter st.

**Armhole shaping:** Bind off 4 sts at beg of next 2 rows, 3 sts at beg of next 2 (4/4/4) rows, 2 sts at beg of next 6 (6/8/8) rows, dec 1 st each side every other row 1 (1/1/4) times, AT THE SAME TIME, when piece measures 35 (36/37/38) cm or 13¾ (14⅛/14½/15)" above garter st, work neck as foll:

**Neck shaping:** Divide work in half and working both sides at once, dec every other row at each neck edge (5 sts in from edge) as foll: work K3tog 9 times, K2tog 22 times. When piece measures 52 (53/54/55) cm or 20½ (20⅞/21¼/21⅝)" above garter st, bind off rem 19 (20/22/23) sts each side for shoulders.

*(Continued on page 112)*

prairie

# weekend

angelot

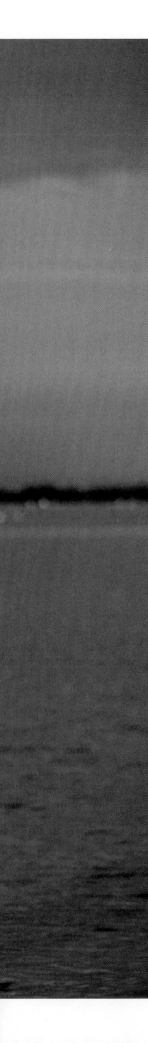

STITCHES USED

Dc, tr.

See explanation of sts on page 157.

**Eyelet pat:** Worked over a multiple of 12 sts plus 1 selvage st each side, see chart.

**Shell pat:**

**Rows 1 and 2:** Work dc.

**Row 3:** *1 dc, skip 2 sts, in next st work 5 tr, skip 2 sts*, rep from *to*.

BACK

Cast on 100 (108/114/126) sts and work in eyelet pat, beg with 1 selvage st and the 2nd (10th/7th/1st) st of chart.

Dec 1 st each side every 30th row 3 times and every 28th row 4 times = 86 (94/100/112) sts.

Work even until piece measures 74 cm or 29⅛" from beg. Inc 1 st each side on next row, then every 10th row 3 times = 94 (102/108/120) sts. Work even until piece measures 90 cm or 35⅜" from beg.

**Armhole shaping:** Bind off 2 sts at beg of next 2 rows and 1 st at beg of next 2 rows = 88 (96/102/114) sts.

Work even until piece measures 108 (109/110/111) cm or 42½ (43/43⅜/43¾)" from beg.

**Shoulder and neck shaping:** Bind off 8 (9/10/12) sts at beg of next 6 (4/4/4) rows, 0 (10/11/13) sts at beg of next 0 (2/2/2) rows, AT THE SAME TIME, bind off center 20 sts, and working both sides at once, bind off from each neck edge 10 sts once.

RIGHT FRONT

Cast on 50 (54/57/63) sts, and work in eyelet pat, beg with 1 selvage st and the 1st st of chart.

Work side decs, incs and armhole decs at LHS same as back.

Work even until piece measures 87 (88/89/90) cm or 34¼ (34⅝/35/35⅜)" from beg.

**Neck shaping:** Dec 1 st at RHS on next row, then every 4th row 12 times and every 2nd row 8 times.

Work even until piece measures 108 (109/110/111) cm or 42½ (43/43⅜/43¾)" from beg. Shape shoulder at LHS same as back.

LEFT FRONT

Work to correspond to right front, reversing shaping and beg eyelet pat same as back.

SLEEVES

Cast on 44 (48/52/56) sts and work in eyelet pat, beg with 1 selvage st and the 6th (4th/2nd/12th) st of chart. Inc 1 st each side every 8th row 8 (9/10/14) times, every 10th row 7 (6/5/1) times = 74 (78/82/86) sts. Work even until piece measures 50 (49/48/46) cm or 19⅝(19¼/18⅞/18⅛)" from beg.

**Cap shaping:** Bind off 5 (5/6/6) sts at beg of next 2 (6/2/6) rows, 4 (4/5/5) sts at beg of next 6 (2/6/2) rows. Bind off rem 40 sts.

*(Continued on page 113)*

Long, lacy and easy to wear, this simply styled sweater coat is the perfect fashion solution for a weekend away. Made in goes-with-everything mohair, you can easily dress it down for a walk on the beach or dress it up for dining out.

SIZES

Small (Medium/Large/X-Large)

MATERIALS: LAINES ANNY BLATT
Fine Kid, Lie de Vin 312: 7 (7/8/9) balls
Knitting needles: One pair size 4 mm (US 6)
Crochet hook size 3 mm (US D/3)
One snap

TENSION/GAUGE

19 sts and 29 rows = 10 cm or 4" with 4 mm needles in eyelet pat.

SKILL LEVEL: ADVANCED

Jazz up a basic stockinette stitch pullover beautifully by working a generous turtleneck and wide bands in a lovely eyelet rib pattern. Accent eyelets with single satin stitches using a colorful, contrasting yarn.

## SIZES

Small (Medium/Large/X-Large)

## MATERIALS: LAINES ANNY BLATT

Rustique, Bois de rose 054: 14 (15/16/17) balls

Flamenco, Impérial 275: 1 ball

Knitting needles: One pair each sizes 5½ and 6 mm (US 9 and 10)

## TENSION/GAUGE

16 sts and 20 rows = 10 cm or 4" with size 6 mm needles in st st and Rustique.

**SKILL LEVEL: INTERMEDIATE**

## STITCHES USED

**St st, K2/P2 rib.**

See explanation of sts on page 157.

**Fancy rib:** see chart

**Dec 1 st at 3 sts from RHS:** Work 3 sts in st st, K2tog, at LHS : 1 SKP, work 3 sts in st st

**Dec 2 sts at 3 sts from RHS:** Work 3 sts in st st, K3tog, at LHS : 1 SK2P, work 3 sts in st st

**M1 inc:** Insert LH needle into horizontal strand between last st worked and next st on LH needle and K through back loop of this strand.

## EMBROIDERY

**Satin st**

## BACK

With size 5½ mm needles sts and Bois de rose, cast on 70 (76/82/88) sts and work in fancy rib, beg and end with 1 selvage st and the 2nd (3rd/4th/1st) st of chart.

Work even until piece measures 11 cm or 4⅜" from beg. Cont in st st with 6 mm needles, inc 1 st each side at 2 sts from edge (using M1 inc) every 12th row once, every 10th row 2 times = 76 (82/88/94) sts.

Work even until piece measures 32 cm or 12⅝" from beg.

**Armhole shaping:** Bind off 2 (3/3/3) sts at beg of next 2 rows. Cont to dec as foll:

**Small:** Dec 1 st at 3 sts from edge every 2nd row 6 times = 60 sts.

**Medium:** Dec sts at 3 sts from edge every 2nd row: 2 sts once, 1 st 5 times = 62 sts.

**Large:** Dec sts at 3 sts from edge every 2nd row: 2 sts 2 times, 1 st 5 times = 64 sts.

**X-Large:** Dec sts at 3 sts from edge every 2nd row: 2 sts 3 times, 1 st 5 times = 66 sts.

Work even until piece measures 52 (53/54/55) cm or 20½ (20⅞/21¼/21⅝)" from beg.

**Shoulder and neck shaping:** Bind off 7 (8/8/9) sts at beg of next 4 (2/4/2) rows, 0 (7/0/8) sts at beg of next 0 (2/0/2) rows, AT THE SAME TIME, bind off center 22 sts for neck, and working both sides at once, bind off from each neck edge 5 sts once.

## FRONT

Work same as back until piece measures 46 (47/48/49) cm or 18⅛ (18½/18⅞/19¼)" from beg.

**Neck shaping:** Bind off center 16 sts for neck, and working both sides at once, bind off from each neck edge 3 sts once, 2 sts once and 1 st 3 times.

Work even until piece measures 52 (53/54/55) cm or 20½ (20⅞/21¼/21⅝)" from beg. Shape shoulders same as back.

*(Continued on page 114)*

aglanet

cachemire
rayé

Stripe it rich! Knit in luxurious cashmere, this snazzy set features a fun mix of horizontal pinstripes and wide vertical stripes. The short top features a flattering jewel neck that compliments the dramatic V-neck of the long cardigan.

SIZES

Small (Medium/Large/X-Large)

MATERIALS: LAINES ANNY BLATT

**Top**

**Cashmere 100%, Naturel 380:** 5 (5/6/6) balls, **Fauve 221:** 5 (5/6/6) balls

**Knitting needles:** One pair size 3½ mm (US 4)

**Cardigan**

**Cashmere 100%, Naturel 380:** 14 (14/15/15) balls, **Fauve 221:** 9 (9/10/10) balls

**Knitting needles:** One pair size 3 and 3½ mm (US 3 and 4)

Crochet hook size 3 mm (US C/2)

One button

TENSION/GAUGE

25 sts and 37 rows = 10 cm or 4" with larger needles in st st.

SKILL LEVEL: INTERMEDIATE

STITCHES USED

**K1/P1 rib, K2/P2 rib, st st, chain st.**

See explanation of sts on page 157.

**Striped st st no. 1:** * 2 rows Fauve, 2 rows Naturel *.

**Striped st st no. 2:** (See chart).

**Striped 2/2 rib:** * 2 rows Fauve, 2 rows Naturel *.

TOP

BACK

With smaller needles and Fauve, cast on 150(164/176/190) sts and work 18 rows in striped K2/P2 rib, beg with P1 (K2/K2/P1). Cont in striped st st no. 1 with larger needles, dec 38 (42/44/48) sts evenly spaced along 1st row (work 2 purl sts tog) = 112 (122/132/142) sts. Dec 1 st each side, at 2 in from edge, every 6 rows 3 times = 106 (116, 126, 136) sts.

Work even until piece measures 22 cm or 8⅝" from beg. Inc 1 st each side on next row, then every 20 row once = 110 (120/130/140) sts.

Work even until piece measures 32 (33/34/35) cm or 12⅝ (13/13⅜/13¾)" from beg.

**Armhole shaping:**

**Small:** Bind off 3 sts at beg of next 2 rows, 2 sts at beg of next 2 rows, dec 1 st each side every 2nd row once, every 4th row twice = 94 sts.

**Medium:** Bind off 3 sts at beg of next 4 rows, 2 sts at beg of next 2 rows, dec 1 st each side every 2nd row once, every 4th row twice, every 6th rows once = 96 sts.

**Large:** Bind off 4 sts at beg of next 2 rows, 3 sts at beg of next 4 rows, 2 sts at beg of next 2 rows, dec 1 st each side every 2nd row once, every 4th row twice, every 6th row once = 98 sts.

**X-Large:** Bind off 3 sts at beg of next 8 rows, 2 sts at beg of next 4 rows, dec 1 st each side every 2nd row twice, every 4th row twice = 100 sts.

Work even until piece measures 48 (50/52/54) cm or 19 (19 ⅝/20½/21¼)" from beg.

**Neck shaping:** Bind off center 16 sts and working both sides at same time, bind off from each neck edge, 4 sts once, 3 sts once, 2 sts twice, dec 1 st every 2nd row once, every 4th row once,AT SAME TIME, at 49 (51/53/55) cm or 19¼ (20/20¾/21⅝)" from beg, inc 1 st each side on next row, then every 4th row twice.

Work even until piece measures 53 (55/57/59) cm or 20⅞ (21⅝/22⅜/23¼)" from beg.

**Shoulder shaping:** Bind off from each shoulder edge 10 (10/10/11) sts twice, 9 (10/11/10) sts once.

FRONT

Work as for back until piece measures 37 (39/41/43) cm or 14½ (15⅜/16⅛/16⅞)" from beg.

*(Continued on page 115)*

Who said you had to sacrifice comfort for fashion? This stylish pullover has all the best details of a cozy sweatshirt. The hood and pouch pocket help keep you warm, and roomy sizing makes it easy to layer.

**SIZES**

Small (Medium/Large/X-Large)

**MATERIALS: LAINES ANNY BLATT**

Merinos, Prune 452: 14 (16/18/20) balls

Knitting needles: One pair size 5 mm (US 8)

**TENSION/GAUGE**

16 sts and 23 rows = 10 cm or 4" in st st with Mérinos double strand (center panel).

17 sts = 10 cm or 4" in center st st panel and rib.

**SKILL LEVEL: INTERMEDIATE**

**STITCH USED**

St st.

See explanation of sts on page 157.

**BACK**

The side diagonals are formed beg on the 35th row with 2 yos in center, the SKP at RHS, the K2tog at LHS.

With Mérinos double strand, cast on 35 (41/47/57) sts and work in st st foll chart for lower edge of back, then top of back.

Inc 1 st for curve as foll: at beg of the 3rd row and every 2nd row, work 1 yo each side of the center 35 (41/47/57) sts, beg with the 5th row then every 4th row, work 1 yo after the first st and before the last st, end with the 34th row = 81 (87/93/103) sts.

Cont to dec 1 st each side at 1 st from each edge (at RHS 1 SKP, at LHS K2tog), every 10th row twice = 77 (83/89/99) sts. Work 14 rows even then inc 1 st each side (using M1) every 8th row 3 times = 83 (89/95/105) sts.

Cont to foll chart for top of back.

**Armhole shaping:** Bind off 6 (4/5/6) sts at beg of next 2 (4/4/2) rows, 0 (0/0/7) sts at beg of next 0 (0/0/2) rows, dec 2 sts, at 3 sts from edge every 2nd row, (at RHS K3tog, at LHS: 1 SK2P) 3 times = 59 (61/63/67) sts. Work even until piece measures 54 (55/56/57) cm or 21¼ (21⅝/22/22⅜)" from beg.

**Neck and shoulder shaping:** Bind off center 17 sts for neck and working both sides at once, bind off from each neck edge 10 sts once, AT SAME TIME, bind off from each shoulder edge, 6 (6/7/8) sts 1 (2/1/1) times, 5 (0/6/7) sts once.

**FRONT**

Work same as back until piece measures 49 (50/51/52) cm or 19¼ (19⅝/20/20½ )" from beg.

**Neck and shoulder shaping:** Bind off center 13 sts for neck and working both sides at once, dec sts, at 2 sts from each neck edge, every 2nd row: 6 times (at RHS work K3tog, 2 sts; at LHS: 2 sts, 1 SK2P).

Cont to work decs at 1 st from edge as foll: work SKP at RHS, and K2tog at LHS, and the yos in center, these symbols are shown on border of the first size, and work in same way for all other sizes.

When piece measures 54 (55/56/57) cm or 21¼ (21⅝/22/22⅜)" from beg, shape shoulders same as back.

**SLEEVES**

With Mérinos double strand, cast on 13 (15/17/19) sts, and work in st st foll chart.

Work incs as foll : at beg of the 3rd row and every 2nd row : work 1 yo each side of center 13 (15/17/19) sts, at beg of the 5th row and every 4th row: work 1 yo after the first and before the last st, ending at the 22nd row = 41 (43/45/47) sts.

*(Continued on page 117)*

calybe

nathalie

## STITCHES USED

**Dc.**

See explanation of sts on page 157.

**Rib Pat:** Multiple of 2 sts plus 3.

**Row 1:** P1, *P1, yb, sl 1*, rep from *to*, end with P2.

**Row 2:** Purl.

Rep these 2 rows for rib pat.

**Fur st:** Crocheted on a base of 1 row dc.

Insert hook in 1 st, pull up a lp, *wrap yarn around index finger to form a lp (approx 3 cm or 1¼" long), yrh, pull up and lp with the strand which is behind index finger, yrh with the strand at base of lp, pull through 2 lps on hook, remove index finger from lp*, rep from *to*. To make the lps more regular, use a piece of cardboard instead of finger.

## BACK

With Lichen, cast on 103 (111/119/127) sts and work 1 row on WS as foll: P1, *K1, P1*, rep from *to*. Cont in rib pat, and at 15 and 25 cm or 5 ⅞" and 9⅞" from beg, inc 1 st each side at 1 st from edge, (working inc sts into pat) = 107 (115/123/131) sts. Work even until piece measures 33 cm or 13" from beg.

**Raglan shaping:** Bind off 3 sts at beg of next 2 rows, then dec each side on WS rows at 3 sts from edge as foll: **Small:** dec 1 st every 4th row twice, every 2nd row 35 times. **Medium:** dec 1 st every 2nd row 41 times. **Large:** dec 2 sts every 2nd row twice and 1 st every 2nd row 41 times. **X-Large:** every 2nd row: dec 2 sts 4 times and dec 1 st 41 times. Bind off rem 27 sts for neck.

**NOTE:** At beg of row, work P3 and P2tog for 1 dec, P3tog for 2 dec. At end of row, work P2tog tbl for 1 dec, P3tog tbl for 2 dec. On RS rows, work the first and last 3 sts as foll: P1, yb, sl 1, P1.

## FRONT

Work same as back until piece measures 33 cm or 13" from beg.

**Raglan and neck shaping:** Bind off 3 sts and beg of next 2 rows. Then on each WS row at 3 sts from edge, work as foll: **Small:** 1 st every 4th row twice, 1 st every 2nd row 31 times. **Medium:** 1 st every 2nd row 37 times. **Large:** every 2nd row, 2 sts twice and 1 st 37 times. **X-Large:** every 2nd row 2 sts 4 times and 1 st 37 times, AT THE SAME TIME, when piece measures 43 (44/45/46) cm or 16⅞ (17⅜/17¾/18⅛)" from beg, bind off center st for neck, and working both sides at once, dec 1 st at each neck edge, at 3 sts from edge, every 2nd row 11 times, every 4th row once, every 6th row once. Bind off rem 4 sts.

*(Continued on page 120)*

A figure-flattering raglan pullover is a wardrobe must. Work it in an easy slip-stitch rib and shape armholes with full-fashioned decreases. For a playful touch, trim the V-neck edge with faux fur yarn in a complimentary color.

**SIZES**

Small (Medium/Large/X-Large)

**MATERIALS: LAINES ANNY BLATT**

No. 5, Lichen 304: 15(16/17/18) balls
Huskye, Yéti 625: 1 ball
Knitting needles: One pair size 5 mm (US 8)
Crochet hook sizes 4 and 4½ mm (US E/4 and F/5)

**TENSION/GAUGE**

23 sts and 35 rows = 10 cm or 4" (unstretched) over rib pat.

**SKILL LEVEL: EASY**

corneille

## STITCHES USED

**Dc.**

See explanation of sts on page 157.

**24-st Diamond** (see chart).

**Cr10R:** Sl 5 sts to cn and hold to back, K5, then K5 from cn.

**K5/P2 rib :**

**Row 1:** *K5, P2*, rep from *to*.

**Row 2:** *K2, P5*, rep from *to*.

Rep these 2 rows for K5/P2 rib.

**Openwork Blocks:** Worked on a multiple of 4 sts plus 3 (see diagram). With crochet hook, ch 15.

**Row 1:** Ch 6, 1 dc in 9th ch from hook, sk 1 ch, 2 tr, in next ch work 1 tr, ch 3 and 1 dc.

**Row 2:** Ch 6, 1 dc in next ch-3 sp, work 3 tr, ch 3 and 1 dc. Rep row 2.

## BACK

With Rustique, cast on 76 (82/88/98) sts and work as foll: 26 (29/32/37) sts in K5/P2 rib, beg with K 5 (1/4/2) instead of 5, work 24 sts diamond, end 26 (29/32/37) sts in K5/P2 rib, beg with K 5.

Dec 1 st each side at 2 sts from each edge (at RHS work K2, SKP, at LHS work K2tog, K2), every 14th row twice = 72 (78/84/94) sts.

Work even until piece measures 30 cm or 11⅞" from beg. Inc 1 st each side on next row = 74 (80/86/96) sts.

Work even until piece measures 40 cm or 15¾" from beg.

**Armhole shaping:** Bind off 4 sts at beg of next 2 rows, 3 sts at beg of next 2 rows, 2 sts at beg of next 2 (4/4/6) rows, 1 st at beg of next 4 (2/4/4) rows = 52 (56/60/66) sts.

Work even until piece measures 62 (63/64/65) cm or 24⅜ (24¾/25⅛/25⅝)" from beg.

**Shoulder shaping:** Bind off 6 (7/8/9) sts at beg of next 2 (2/2/4) rows, 5 (6/7/0) sts at beg of next 2 (2/2/0) rows. Bind off rem 30 sts for neck.

## FRONT

Work same as back until piece measures 54 (55/56/57) cm or 21¼ (21⅝/22/22⅜)" from beg.

**Neck shaping:** Bind off center 20 sts, and working both sides at once, dec 2 st each neck edge at 2 sts from each edge every 2nd row 5 times (at RHS work to last 4 sts and K2tog, work 2 sts, at LHS : work the first 2 sts and 1 SKP).

Work even until piece measures 62 (63/64/65) cm or 24⅜ (24¾/25⅛/25⅝)" from beg. Shape shoulders same as back.

## SLEEVES

With Rustique, cast on 36 (36/38/38) sts and work as foll: 6 (6/7/7) sts in K5/P2 rib beg with P 1 (1/2/2), work 24 sts diamond, end 6 (6/7/7) sts in K5/P2 rib, beg with K5.

Inc 1 st each side at 2 sts from each edge (K in front and back of st), every 6th row 11 (9/9/7) times, every 4th row 1 (4/4/7) times = 60 (62/64/66) sts.

Work inc sts gradually into K5/P2 rib.

*(Continued on page 121)*

---

Diamonds are a girl's best friend...especially when they keep her toasty-warm. Knit a woolly pullover showcasing oversized cables and wide ribs. Trim sleeves with crochet using tweedy yarn, then complete the look with a coordinating crochet scarf.

### SIZES

Small (Medium/Large/X-Large)

Scarf width: 19 cm or 7⅜"

### MATERIALS: LAINES ANNY BLATT

**Pullover**

Rustique, Cannelle 088: 15 (17/19/20) balls

Chimere, Praline 450: 1 ball

Tweed'Anny, Marécage 357: 1 ball

Knitting needles: One pair size 6 mm (US 10)

Cable needle (cn)

Crochet hook size 5 mm (US H/7)

Shoulder pads

**Scarf**

Tweed'Anny, Marécage 357: 3 balls

Chimere, Praline 450: 2 balls

Flamenco, Tomette 566: 1 ball

Crochet hook size 5 mm (US H/7).

### TENSION/GAUGES

16 sts and 19 rows = 10 cm or 4" in Rustique over all sts.

24 sts of diamond motif = 15 cm or 5⅞" wide.

### SKILL LEVEL: INTERMEDIATE

les
ecrins

## STITCHES USED

Diamond motif (see chart for each size).

**CrK2/1R:** Sl 1 st to cn and hold to back, K2, K1 from cn.

**CrK1/2L:** Sl 2 sts to cn and hold to front, K1, K2 from cn.

**M1 purlwise on WS:** Insert LH needle into horizontal strand between last st worked and next st on LH needle, P this strand.

**K3/P1 rib:**

**Row 1:** K3, *P1, K3*, rep from *to*.

**Row 2:** K the knit sts and P the purl sts.

Rep row 2 for K3/P1 rib.

## EMBROIDERY

Chain st.

## BACK

With 2 strands Domino and 5½ mm needles, cast on 79 (79/87/95) sts and work in K3/P1 rib, beg with 1 selvage st, K2, *P1, K3*, rep from *to*, end with P1, K2, 1 selvage st. Cont as established until piece measures 3 cm or 1⅛" from beg, end with a RS row. On next WS, inc 7 (12/9/7) sts using M1 purlwise as foll:

**Small:** 1 selvage st, P14 inc 2 sts, K1, *P15 inc 1 st, K1*, rep from *to* twice more, P14 inc 2 sts, 1 selvage st = 86 sts.

**Medium:** 1 selvage st, P14 inc 3 sts, K1, *P15 inc 2 sts, K1*, rep from *to* twice more, P14 inc 3 sts, 1 selvage st = 91 sts.

**Large:** 1 selvage st, P18, K1, *P15 inc 3 sts, K1*, rep from *to* twice more, P18, 1 selvage st = 96 sts.

**X-Large:** 1 selvage st, P6 inc 1 st, K1, *P15 inc 1 st, K1*, rep from *to* 4 times more, P6 inc 1 st, 1 selvage st = 102 sts.

Cont with diamond motif, beg with 1 selvage st and the 1st (1st/1st/10th) st of chart corresponding to each size, until piece measures 54 cm or 21¼" from beg, after 5 diamonds have been completed, cont on RS in K3/P1 rib, binding off 4 (4/3/5) sts each side, and dec 5 (6/9/7) sts on the first row as foll:

**Small:** Bind off 4 sts, P1, K3, P1, K3, P2tog, *°°K3, P1°°, rep from °°to°° twice more, K3, P2tog*, rep from *to* twice more, K3, P1, K2, K2tog, P1, K3, P1, K3, P1, bind off last 4 sts = 73 sts. Cut yarn, cont in K3/P1 rib on WS.

**Medium:** Bind off 4 sts , K2,°°P1, K3°°, rep from °°to°° 3 times more, P1, K2, K2tog, P1, *K2tog, K2, P1, K3, P1, K3, P1, K2, K2tog, P1* rep from *to* once more, K2tog, K2,°°P1, K3°°, rep from °°to°° 3 times more, P1, K2, bind off last 4 sts = 77 sts. Cut yarn, cont in K3/P1 rib on WS.

**Large:** Bind off 3 sts, °°P1, K3°°, rep °°to°° 4 times more, *°°K2tog, K3°°, rep from °°to°° twice more, P1, K3*, rep from *to* twice more, °°P1, K3°°, rep from °°to°° twice more, P1, bind off last 3 sts = 81 sts. Cut yarn, cont in K3/P1 rib on WS.

*(Continued on page 122)*

Bold designer details are sure to make this sporty sweater coat a winter wardrobe favorite. Stitched in a traditional diamond cable-and-moss stitch combo, it is accented with contrasting chain-stitches and whimsical tassels on the collar.

### SIZES

Small (Medium/Large/X-Large)

### MATERIALS: LAINES ANNY BLATT

No. 5, Domino 166: 28 (30/32/34) balls

No. 4, Etain 196: 3 (3/4/4) balls

**Knitting needles:** One pair each sizes 4 and 5½ mm (US 6 and 9)

Cable needle (cn)

Crochet hook size 4mm (US F/5)

Six buttons

### TENSION/GAUGE

14.5 sts and 18.5 rows = 10 cm or 4" with 5½ mm needles and 2 strands No. 5 Domino in diamond motif.

**SKILL LEVEL: INTERMEDIATE**

Short and to the point. Straight forward styling accentuates the unique play of body-hugging ribs. Knit back and sleeves in plain double rib, work front in a traveling double rib pattern that creates a graphically bold chevron design.

SIZES

Small (Medium/Large/X-Large)

MATERIALS: LAINES ANNY BLATT

**100% Cachemire, Naturel 380:** 13 (15/17/19) balls

**Knitting needles:** One pair size 3½ mm (US 4)

Crochet hook size 3 mm (US D/3).

TENSION/GAUGE

30 sts and 32 rows = 10 cm or 4" with 3½ mm needles in K2/P2 rib.

SKILL LEVEL: ADVANCED

STITCHES USED

K2/P2 rib, dc, crab st.

See explanation of sts on page 157.

BACK

Cast on 142 (154/166/186) sts and work in K2/P2 rib, beg and end with P2 (K2/P2/K2) until piece measures 28 cm or 11" from beg.

**Armhole shaping:** Bind off 4 (4/5/5) sts at beg of next 2 rows, 3 (3/4/4) sts at beg of next 2 (4/2/4) rows, 2 (2/3/3) sts at beg of next 6 (6/4/4) rows, 0 (0/2/2) sts at beg of next 0 (0/6/8) rows, 1 st at beg of next 4 (6/6/6) rows = 112 (116/118/126) sts

Work even until piece measures 45 (46/47/48) cm or 17¾ (18⅛/ 18½/ 18⅞)" from beg.

**Neck shaping:** Bind off center 30 sts, and working both sides at once, dec 1 st at 2 sts from each edge, every 2nd row 4 times.

Work even until piece measures 46 (47/48/49) cm or 18⅛ (18½/18⅞/19¼)" from beg.

**Shoulder shaping:** Bind off from each shoulder edge 12 (13/13/14) sts 2 (3/2/1) times, 13 (0/14/15) sts 1 (0/1/2) times.

FRONT

Work same as back until piece measures 12 (13/14/15) cm or 4¾ (5⅛/5½/5⅞)" from beg. Cont as foll: work 40 (46/52/62) sts, P2 for first point, work 58 sts, P2 for 2nd point and work 40 (46/52/62) sts.

Work dec and inc foll chart and shifting towards the right or left every 2nd row 4 times, work 2 rows even over all sts and reverse the shifting 6 times in total. Cont in K2/P2 rib until piece measures 28 cm or 11" from beg.

Shape armholes same as back = 112 (116/118/126) sts.

Work even until piece measures 38 (39/40/41) cm or 15 (15⅜/15¾/16⅛)" from beg.

**Neck shaping:** Bind off center 22 sts, and working both sides at once, dec 1 st at each neck edge at 4 sts from edge, every 2nd row 8 times.

When same length as back to shoulder, shape shoulder same as back.

SLEEVES

Cast on 58 (62/70/74) sts and work in K2/P2 rib, inc 1 st each side every 4th row 12 (18/21/27) times, every 6th row 14 (10/8/4) times = 110 (118/128/136) sts.

Work even until piece measures 43 cm or 16⅞" from beg.

**Cap shaping:** Bind off 3 (3/4/4) sts at beg of next 2 rows, 2 (2/3/3) sts at beg of next 16 (20/2/6) rows, 0 (0/2/2) sts at beg of next 0 (0/36/32) rows, 1 (1/1/0) st at beg of next 12 (4/2/0) rows, 7 (2/3/3) sts at beg of next 4 (18/2/4) rows, 3 (3/4/4) sts at beg of next 2 rows. Bind off rem 26 sts.

TO MAKE UP/FINISHING

See tips on page 157.

Sew shoulder seams. Set in sleeves. Sew side and sleeve seams.

With crochet hook, work 1 row dc and 1 row crab st around neck.

*(Continued on page 125)*

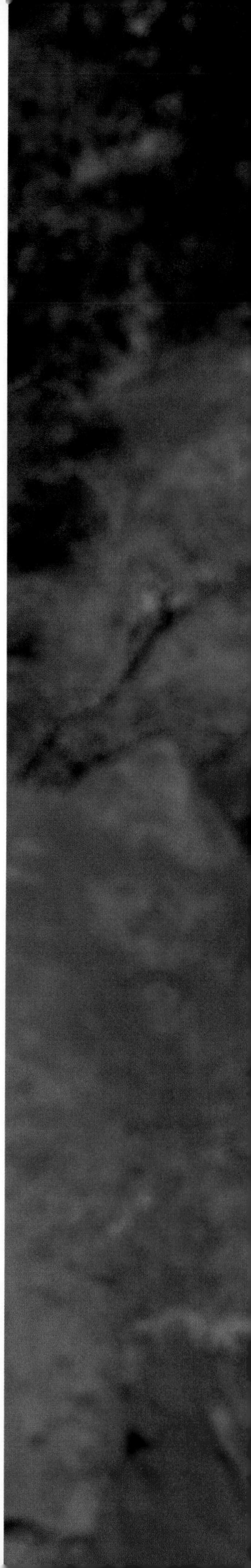

# carouge

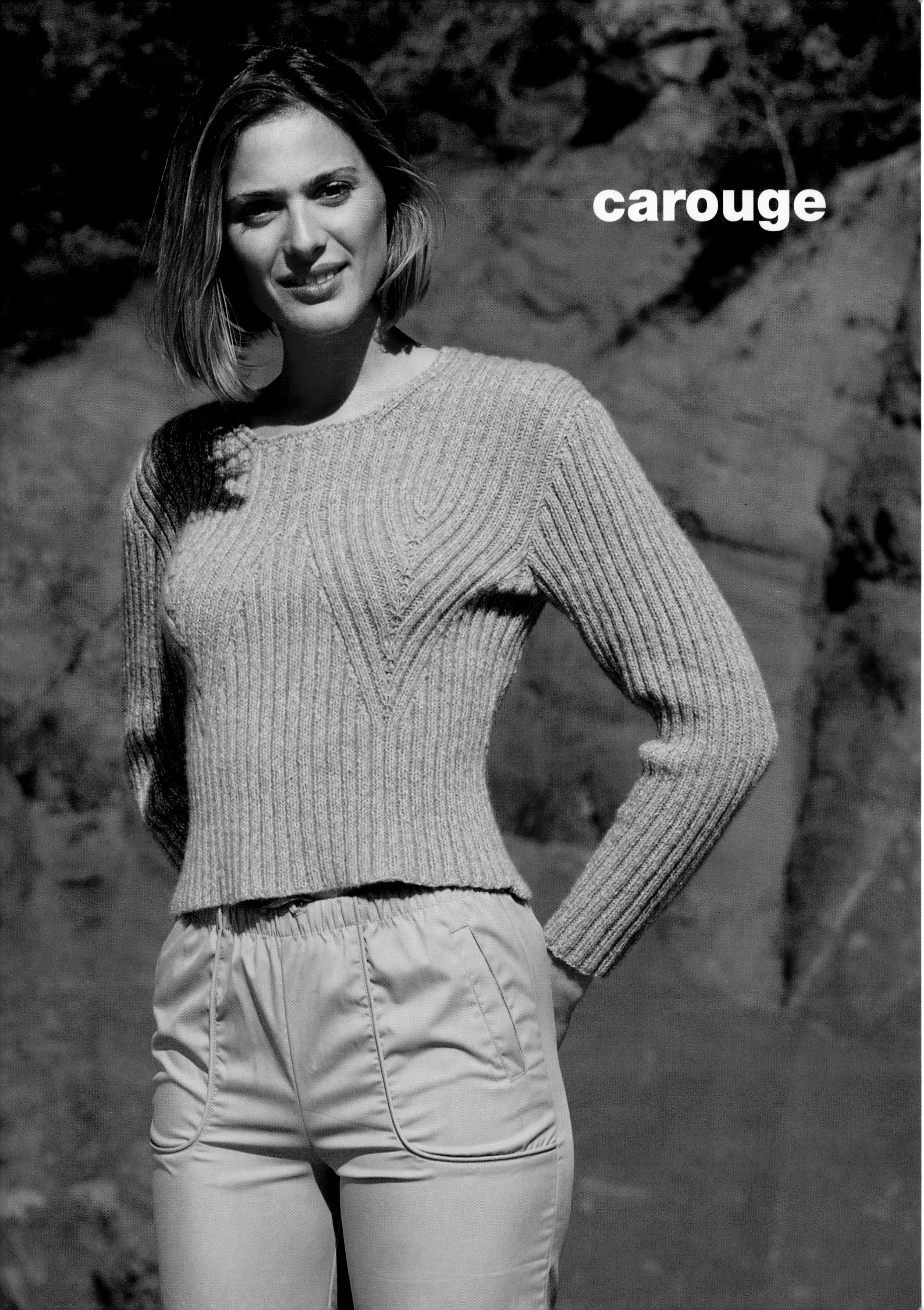

When the temperature drops, slip into a roomy, hip-length pullover in the softest of mohair yarns. Work body and sleeves in a striking eyelet pattern and the chill-chasing turtleneck in single rib.

## SIZES
Small (Medium/Large/X-Large)

## MATERIALS: LAINES ANNY BLATT
Kid Mohair, Quartz 475: 9 (10/10/11) balls

Knitting needles: One pair each sizes 3½ and 4½ mm (US 4 and 7)

## TENSION/GAUGE
20 sts and 21 rows = 10 cm or 4" with 4½ mm needles in fancy pat.

## SKILL LEVEL: ADVANCED

## STITCHES USED
**K1/P1 rib, st st.**
See explanation of sts on page 157.
**Fancy pat:** Worked on a multiple of 22 sts plus 1 selvage st each side (see chart).
Rep these 28 rows for fancy pat.
**SKP:** Sl 1, K1, psso.
**SK2P:** Sl 1, K2tog, psso.
**1 double dec:** Sl 2 sts tog to RH needle, K1, pass the 2 slipped sts over K st.
**K5tog:** Sl 2 sts tog to RH needle, K next 3 sts tog, pass the 2 slipped sts over the K3tog.
**3-st fancy st:** Yf, sl 3 sts to RH needle, bring yarn to back, sl 3 sts from RH needle back to LH needles and K them.

## BACK
With 4½ mm needles, cast on 106 (112/118/124) sts and work in K1/P1 rib for 2 cm or ¾", then cont as foll: 1 selvage st, 2 (0/1/2) sts in st st, 22 sts fancy pat foll chart, *4 (0/1/2) sts in st st, 22 sts fancy pat*, rep from *to* 3 (4/4/4) times, 2 (0/1/2) sts in st st, 1 selvage st. Cont as established until piece measures 64 (65/66/67) cm or 25⅛ (25⅝/26/26⅜)" from beg.
**Neck shaping:** Bind off center 20 sts, and working both sides at once, bind off from each neck edge 12 sts once. Work even until piece measures 65 (66/67/68) cm or 25⅝ (26/26⅜/26¾)" from beg. Bind off rem 31 (34/37/40) sts each side for shoulders.

## FRONT
Work same as back until piece measures 58 (59/60/61) cm or 22⅞ (23¼/23⅝/24)" from beg.
**Neck shaping:** Bind off center 14 sts, and working both sides at once, bind off from each neck edge 4 sts once, 3 sts twice, 2 sts twice, 1 st once. Work even until piece measures 65 (66/67/68) cm or 25⅝ (26/26⅜/26 ¾)" from beg. Bind off rem 31 (34/37/40) sts each side for shoulders.

## SLEEVES
With 4½ mm needles, cast on 46 (50/54/58) sts and work in K1/P1 rib for 2 cm or ¾", then cont as foll: 1 selvage st, 0 (1/2/3) sts in st st, 22 sts fancy pat, 0 (2/4/6) sts in st st, 22 sts fancy pat, 0 (1/2/3) sts in st st, 1 selvage st. Cont in pats as established, inc 1 st each side every 4th row 21 (21/20/20) times, every 2nd row 1 (1/2/2) times. Work even until piece measures 44 (43.5/43/42.5) cm or 17⅜ (17/16⅞/16⅝)" from beg. Bind off rem 90 (94/98/102) sts.

## TO MAKE UP/FINISHING
See tips on page 157.
Sew one shoulder seam.

*(Continued on page 126)*

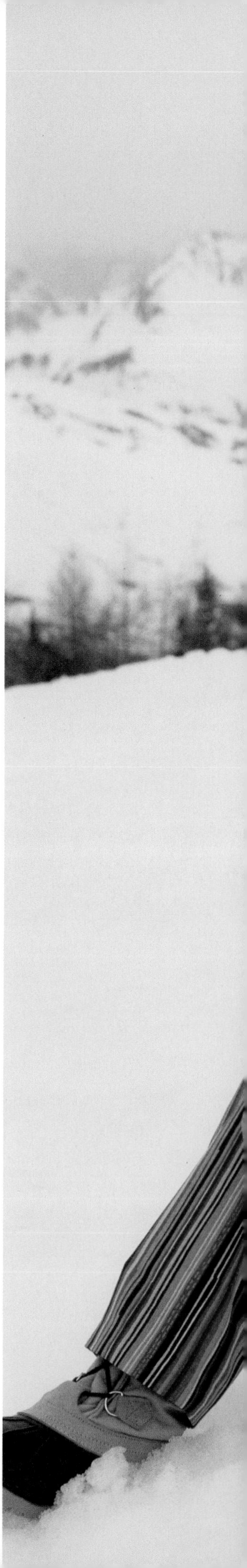

**bellecote**

Button up in something short and classy. Pattern this pretty cashmere cardigan in a sensational design of dazzling diamond cables and petite bobbles. Furry collar and cuffs worked in a matching color add fun fashion flair.

### SIZES

Small (Medium/Large/X-Large)

### MATERIALS: LAINE ANNY BLATT

Cachemir'Anny, Yeti 625:
14(15/16/17) balls

Huskye, Yeti 625: 1(1/1/1) ball

Knitting needles: One pair size 3½ mm (US 4)

Ten buttons

### TENSION/GAUGE

32 sts and 34 rows = 10 cm or 4" in fancy pat.

### SKILL LEVEL: INTERMEDIATE

### STITCHES USED

Garter st, st st.

See explanation of sts on page 157.

**Fancy pat (see chart):**

**Bobble:** *K1, K1tbl*, rep from *to* 2 times all in one st, turn, P 4, turn, K4tog.

**CrK1/P1L:** P the 2nd st first, passing behind the first st, then K first st and drop both sts from LH needle.

**CrK1/P1R:** P the 2nd st first, passing in front of the first st, then K first st and drop both sts from LH needle.

### BACK

With Cachemir'Anny, cast on 153 (163/173/183) sts and work 6 rows garter st, then cont in fancy pat, beg with the 15th (18th/13th/16th) st of chart. Work even until piece measures 30 (31/33/35) cm or 11⅞ (12¼/13/13¾)" from beg.

**Armhole shaping:** Bind off 4 sts at beg of next 2 rows, 3 sts at beg of next 2 (2/2/4) rows, 2 sts at beg of next 6 (6/8/8) rows, dec 1 st each side every other row 3 (4/4/3) times = 121 (129/135/141) sts. Work even until piece measures 50 (52/55/58) cm or 19⅝ (20½ /21⅝/22⅞)" from beg.

**Shoulder and neck shaping:** Bind off 11 (12/13/14) sts at beg of next 4 (6/6/6) rows, 10 sts at beg of next 2 (0/0/0) rows, AT THE SAME TIME bind off center 47 sts for neck, and working both sides at once, bind off from each neck edge 5 sts once.

### RIGHT FRONT

With Cachemir'Anny, cast on 77 (82/87/92) sts and work 6 rows garter st, then cont in fancy pat, beg with the 1st st of chart. Work even until piece measures 30 (31/33/35) cm or 11⅞ (12¼/13/13¾)" from beg.

**Armhole shaping:** Work decs at LHS same as back = 61 (65/68/71) sts. Work even until piece measures 40 (42/45/48) cm or 15¾ (16½/17¾/18⅞)" from beg.

**Neck shaping:** Bind off from RHS for neck 8 sts once, 5 sts once, 4 sts once, 3 sts once, 2 sts once, dec 1 st every other row 7 times. When piece measures 50 (52/55/58) cm or 19⅝ (20½ /21⅝/22⅞)" from beg, shape shoulder at side edge same as back.

### LEFT FRONT

Work to correspond to right front, reversing shaping.

### SLEEVES

With Cachemir'Anny, cast on 67 (67/73/73) sts and work 6 rows garter st, then cont in fancy pat, beg with the 18th (18th/15th/15th) st of chart, AT THE SAME TIME, inc 1 st each side every 6th (4th/4th/4th) row 8 (31/31/28) times, every 4th (0/0/2nd) row 19 (0/0/6) times = 121 (129/135/141) sts. Work even until piece measures 39 cm or 15⅜" from beg.

*(Continued on page 127)*

anatolie

**evening**

Special occasions call for something long, sleek and oh so chic. Every inch of this alluring ankle-length dress is designed to show off your figure from the fun flared hem to the body-hugging ribs and dramatic cable.

**SIZES**

Small (Medium/Large/X-Large)

**MATERIALS: LAINES ANNY BLATT**

Fine Kid, Iris 268: 12 (13/14/15) balls

Muguet, Iris 268: 1 ball

Knitting needles: One pair each sizes 5½ mm and 7 mm (US 9 and 10½)

Cable needle (cn)

St holders

**TENSION/GAUGES**

18½ sts and 22 rows = 10 cm or 4" using 5½ mm needles over all sts with 3 strands Fine kid held tog.

15 sts and 21 rows = 10 cm or 4" using 7 mm needles and Fine Kid single strand.

**SKILL LEVEL: INTERMEDIATE**

STITCHES USED

**St st**

See explanation of sts on page 157.

**Cr6R:** Slip 3 sts to cn and hold to back, K3, then K3 from cn.

FRONT

With Fine Kid single strand and 7 mm needles, cast on 170 (177/184/198) sts and work in st st for 6 rows, then dec 6 sts across row as foll :

**7th row:** K 24 (25/26/28) sts, *K2tog, K 22 (23/24/26) sts*, rep from *to* 5 times, end with K2tog, K 24 (25/26/28) sts = 164 (171/178/192) sts. Work even for 5 rows.

**13th row:** K 24 (25/26/28) sts, *K2tog, K 21 (22/23/25) sts*, rep from *to* 5 times, end with K2tog, K 23 (24/25/27) sts = 158 (165/172/186) sts. Work even for 5 rows.

**19th row:** K 24 (25/26/28) sts, *K2tog, K 20 (21/22/24) sts*, rep from *to* 5 times, end with K2tog, K 22 (23/24/26) sts = 152 (159/166/180) sts. Work even for 5 rows. 25th row: K 24 (25/26/28) sts, *K2tog, K 19 (20/21/23) sts*, rep from *to* 5 times, nd with K2tog, K 22 (23/24/26) sts = 146 (153/160/174) sts.

Cont these 6 decs every 4th row 10 times (there are a total of 84 decs) = 86 (93/100/114) sts. On the last row of st st (68th row) dec 10 (9/8/10) sts = 76 (84/92/104) sts.

Cont with 3 strands of Fine Kid held tog and 5½ mm needles and foll chart no. 1, working sts as foll: K 4 (8/12/16), P2, K64, P2, K 4 (8/12/16). Inc 1 st each side at 2 sts from edge every 20th row 4 times = 84 (92/100/112) sts. For clarity, only the 1st size is shown.

Cont foll chart no. 2, inc 2 sts over the center 28 K sts = 86 (94/102/114) sts.

Cont as established, keeping sts each side of center 28 sts in K4/P2 rib, until piece measures 72 cm or 28⅜" from beg. Dec 1 st (working P2tog) in the first and last group of P2, then work the same for the foll groups every 6th row = 78 (86/94/106) sts.

Work even until piece measures 83 cm or 32⅝" from beg. Dec 1 st each side at 3 sts from edge (P2tog) on next row, and every 6th row once more = 74 (82/90/102) sts.

Work even until piece measures 100 cm or 39⅜" from beg. Inc 1 st each side at 3 sts from edge on next row and every 6th row once more = 78 (86/94/106) sts.

Work even until piece measures 103 (104/105/106) cm or 40½ (41/41⅜/41¾)" from beg. Inc 1 st in each of the 4 groups of P2 = 86 (94/102/114) sts.

Work even until piece measures 113 cm or 44½" from beg.

**Armhole shaping:** Bind off 6 sts at beg of next 2 rows, 2 (3/4/4) sts at beg of next 4 (2/2/4) rows, 0 (2/2/2) sts at beg of next 0 (4/6/6) rows = 66 (68/70/74) sts.

*(Continued on page 128)*

calcite

The magic of black casts an elegant spell upon this classic cardigan. Work back bodice and cuffs in entrelac using contrasting textures. Embroider edges with sumptuous shades of ribbon yarn, then dot with brilliant faceted beads.

## SIZES

Small (Medium/Large/X-Large)

## MATERIALS: LAINES ANNY BLATT

Angora Super, Noir 383: 8 (9/10/11) 11 balls

Victoria Noir 383: 2 (2/3/3) balls, Dubai 167, Coloquinte 092, Pourpre 454, Magnetite 352, Iris 268, Rubis 511, Genepi 226: 1 ball each color

Feline, Noir 383: 1 ball

Gyps, Noir 383: 1(1/2/2) balls

Paillettes, Noir 383: 1 ball

Knitting needles: One pair each sizes 3½ mm and 4 mm (US 4 and 6)

Crochet hook size 2 mm (UK 14) (US B/1)

St holders

One button

94 faceted beads 5 mm in pink, red orange and violet

21 (21/24/24) black beads

## TENSION/GAUGE

21 sts and 30 rows = 10 cm or 4" using 4 mm needles and Angora Super in st st.

## SKILL LEVEL: ADVANCED

## STITCHES USED

Garter st, st st, dc.

See explanation of sts on page 157.

**Entrelacs:** Worked on a multiple of 6 sts.

**Base Triangles:** *Sl 1 st purlwise, P1, turn, K2, turn, sl 1 st purlwise, P2, turn, K3, turn, sl 1 st purlwise, P3, turn, K4, turn, sl 1 st purlwise, P4, turn, K5, turn, sl 1 st purlwise, P5. Place sts on a holder and rep from * without cutting yarn.

**1st row of rectangles (RS):** K2, turn, P2, turn, in the 1st st, work K2, 1 SKP, turn, sl 1 st purlwise, P2, turn, in the 1st st work K2, K1, 1 SKP, turn, sl 1 st purlwise, P3, turn, and cont as foll until all sts of 1st triangle have been worked. Place 6 sts on a holder.

*Without cutting yarn, pick up and K 6 sts along left side of triangle (then rectangle for the other rows), turn, P6, **turn, sl 1 st purlwise, K4, 1 SKP, turn, sl 1 st purlwise, P5** , rep from **to** until sts of 2nd rectangle have been worked.

Rep from * for each foll rectangle of triangle.

Along left side of last triangle (or rectangle), pick up and K 6 sts, turn, P2tog, P4, turn, sl 1 st purlwise, K4, turn, P2tog, P3, turn, sl 1 st purlwise, K3, turn, P2tog, P2, turn, sl 1 st purlwise, K2, turn, P2tog, P1, turn, sl 1 st purlwise, K1, turn, P2tog = 1 st on RH needle.

2nd row of rectangles: Keeping 1 st on needle, pick up and P 5 sts, turn, K6, then work same as 1st row of rectangles, beg from **, but reversing the K and P sts.

Pick up and P 6 sts along side of each foll rectangle, turn, K6, then rep from **, reversing the K and P sts.

## EMBROIDERY

Bullion st, stem st.

## BACK

Worked in 2 parts.

**1st part:** With Victoria col. Noir and 3½ mm needles, cast on 98 (106/116/128) sts and work in garter st for 1 cm or ⅜".

Cont in st st with Angora Super and 4 mm needles, dec 1 st each side at 3 sts from edges, every 12th row twice and every 10th row once = 92 (100/110/122) sts.

Work even until piece measures 15 cm or 5⅞" from beg. Inc 1 st each side at 3 sts from edges, on next row, then every 6th row 4 times and every 8th row twice = 106 (114/124/136) sts.

Work even until piece measures 31 cm or 12¼" from beg.

**Armhole shaping:** Bind off 4 (4/5/5) sts at beg of next 2 (4/2/2) rows, 3 (3/4/4) sts at beg of next 2 (2/2/4) rows, 2 (2/3/3) sts at beg of next 4 rows, 0 (0/2/2) sts at beg of next 0 (0/2/4) rows and 1 st at beg of next 2 rows = 82 (82/88/88) sts.

Work even until piece measures 34 (35/ 36/37) cm or 13⅜ (13¾/14⅛/14½)" from beg. Bind off all sts.

*(Continued on page 131)*

roche

# anemone

## STITCHES USED

K3/P3 Rib, st st, dc.

See explanation of sts on page 157.

**Moss st:**

**Row 1:** *K1, P1*, rep from *to*.

**Row 2:** K the purl sts and P the knit sts.

Rep row 2 for pat.

## EMBROIDERY

Chain st.

## BACK

With Mérinos col. Prune and 4 mm needles, cast on 101 (107) sts. Work in K3/P3 rib, beg with 1 selvage st and K3, for 25 cm or 9⅞", then cont in st st until piece measures 42 cm or 16½" from beg.

**Raglan shaping:** Bind off 3 sts at beg of next 2 rows, dec 1 st each side every other row 2 (3) times, every 4th row 5 (6) times = 81 (83) sts. Work rem of piece in 5 parts as foll:

**1st part:** Work in moss st on first 14 (15) sts on RHS, and dec 1 st each side on next row, then every other row 2 (3) times, then bind off 2 st at beg of next 2 rows. Bind off rem 4 sts.

**2nd part:** Work next 16 sts as foll: work in moss st, dec 1 st each side on next row, then every other row 3 times, then bind off 2 sts at beg of next 2 rows. Bind off rem 4 sts.

**3rd part:** Work next (center) 21 sts as foll: work in moss st, dec 1 st each side on next row, then every other row once, then bind off 2 sts at beg of next 6 rows. Bind off rem 5 sts.

**4th part:** Work as for 2nd part.

**5th part:** Work as for 1st part.

## FRONT

With Mérinos col. Prune and 4 mm needles, cast on 101 (107) sts. Work in K3/P3 rib, beg with 1 selvage and P3 for 25 cm or 9⅞". Cont with col. Aurore and st st and complete as for back.

## LEFT SLEEVE

With Mérinos col. Prune and 4 mm needles, cast on 50 (56) sts. Work in K3/P3 rib, beg with 1 selvage and K3, inc 1 st each side every 6th row 10 times, every 4th row 14 times = 98 (104) sts. Work even until piece measures 40 cm or 15¾" from beg.

**Raglan shaping:** Bind off 3 sts at beg of next 2 rows, 2 sts at beg of next 10 (12) rows, dec 1 st each side every other row 8 (9) times = 56 sts. Work even until piece measures 59 (60.5) cm or 23¼ (23¾)" from beg. Bind off from LHS 9 sts 4 times, 10 sts once. Bind off rem 10 sts. Work right sleeve to correspond, reversing raglan shaping.

*(Continued on page 134)*

Knit up something silky and sensational. Two shades of luxurious silk yarn create this festive saddle shoulder top. Worked in triple rib and stockinette stitch, it features a snazzy scalloped neck edge and dazzling chain-stitch motif on the bodice.

## SIZES

Small to Medium (Large to X-Large)

## MATERIALS: LAINES ANNY BLATT

Mérinos d'Anny Blatt, Prune 452: 8 (9) balls, Aurore 019: 2 balls

Kanpur d'Anny Blatt, Prune 452: 1 ball

Knitting needles: One pair 4 mm (US 6)

Crochet hook size 3½ mm (US E/4)

## TENSION/GAUGES

22 sts and 30 rows to 10 cm or 4" square with Mérinos and 4 mm needles in st st.

27 sts and 30 rows to 10 cm or 4" square with Mérinos and 4 mm needles in K3/P3 rib.

## SKILL LEVEL: INTERMEDIATE

You can always count on cables to make a twinset timeless. Adorn each piece with columns of dainty diamonds bedecked with perky bobbles. Trim edges with a variety of pretty crochet stitches.

## SIZES

Small (Medium/Large/X-Large)

## MATERIALS: LAINES ANNY BLATT

**Top**

Kanpur d'Anny Blatt, Glacier 231: 6 (6/7/7) balls

**Cardigan**

Kanpur d'Anny Blatt, Glacier 231: 11 (12/12/13) balls

Knitting needles: One pair 4 mm needles (UK 8) (US 6)

Cable needle (cn)

Crochet hook size 3 mm (UK 10) (US D/3)

Ten buttons

## TENSION/GAUGES

23 sts and 30 rows to 10 cm or 4" square with 4 mm needles in rev st st. 11 sts of Lozenge pat to 4 cm or 1½" wide with 4 mm needles.

**SKILL LEVEL: INTERMEDIATE**

STITCHES USED

**Garter st, rev st st, dc, crab st.**

See explanation of sts on page 157.

**Fancy Cable pat:** Worked over 2 sts.

**Row 1:** K2.

**Row 2:** P1, yrn, p1.

**Row 3:** K3, pass 1st st over the other 2 sts.

**Row 4:** P2.

Rep these 4 rows for pat.

**Lozenge pat:** Worked over 11 sts.

**Row 1:** P3, k5, p3.

**Rows 2, 16, 18, 20 and 22:** K the knit sts and P the purl sts.

**Row 3:** P2, CrK3R (sl 1 st to cn and hold to back of work, K2, K1 from cn), P1, CrK3L (sl 2 sts to cn and hold to front of work, k1, k2 from cn), P2.

**Rows 4 and 14:** K2, P2, K1, P1, K1, P2, K2.

**Row 5:** P1, CrK2/P1R (sl 1 st to cn and hold to back of work, K2, P1 from cn), K1, P1, K1, CrP1/K2L (sl 2 sts to cn and hold to front of work, P1, K2 from cn), P1.

**Rows 6 and 12:** K1, P3, K1, P1, K1, P3, K1.

**Row 7:** CrK3R, [P1, K1] twice, P1, CrK3L.

**Rows 8 and 10:** P2, [K1, P1] 3 times, K1, P2.

**Row 9:** K3, [P1, K1] 3 times, K2.

**Row 11:** CrP1/K2L, [P1, K1] twice, P1, CrK2/P1R.

**Row 13:** P1, CrP1/K2L, K1, P1, K1, CrK2/P1R, P1.

**Row 15:** P2, CrP1/K2L, P1, CrK2/P1R, P2.

**Rows 17 and 21:** P3, K2, 1 Bobble (work 4 sts in one st, turn, P4, turn, K4, turn, P4, turn, K4tog), K2, P3.

**Row 19:** P3, 1 Bobble, K3, 1 Bobble, P3.

Rep rows 3 - 22 for pat.

**Picot:** *1 dc, ch 3, 1 sc (US: sl st) in 1st ch st, 1 dc*, rep from *to*.

TOP

BACK

With 4 mm needles, cast on 113 (119/127/133) sts. Work in garter st for 2 cm or ¾", then K 1 row on WS, inc 8 (10/8/10) sts evenly across = 121 (129/135/143) sts. Work as foll: 1 selvage st, 1 st rev st st, 2 sts Fancy Cable pat, 13 (17/20/24) sts rev st st, *11 sts Lozenge pat, 8 sts rev st st*, rep from *to* 3 times more, work 11 sts Lozenge pat, 13 (17/20/24) sts rev st st, 2 sts Fancy Cable pat, 1 st rev st st, 1 selvage st. Cont in pat as established, dec 1 st each side (4 sts in from each edge) every 4th row 6 times, every other row 3 times = 103 (111/117/125) sts, AT THE SAME TIME, on 23rd row above garter st, replace the 2nd and 4th Lozenge pats with rev st st. Work even until piece measures 13 cm or 5⅛" above garter st. Inc 1 st each side (4 sts in from each edge) on next row, then every 6th row 8 times more = 121 (129/135/143) sts. Work even until piece measures 30 cm or 11⅞" above garter st.

(Continued on page 135)

semones

chili

STITCHES USED:

St st

See explanation of sts on page 157.

**Woven st:** worked over a multiple of 2 plus 1 selvage st each side.

**Rows 1 and 3:** Knit.

**Row 2:** 1 selvage st, *K1, yb, sl 1 purlwise*, rep from *to*, end with 1 selvage st.

**Row 4:** 1 selvage st, *yb, sl 1 purlwise, K1*, rep from *to*, end with 1 selvage st.

Rep these 4 rows for woven st.

**Border:** Work 6 rows st st, P 1 row for turning ridge, then 5 rows st st.

BACK

With Louxor and 3½ mm needles, cast on 132 (140/148/156) sts and work 12 rows of border, then work in woven st, inc 1 st each side every 18th row 3 times, every 16th row twice = 142 (150/158/166) sts. Work even until piece measures 23 cm or 9" above border.

**Armhole shaping:** Cast on 2 sts at beg of next 4 rows, 3 sts at beg of next 4 rows, 4 sts at beg of next 2 rows = 170 (178/186/194) sts. Work even until piece measures 45 (46/47/48) cm or 17¾ (18⅛/18½/18⅞)" above border.

**Shoulder and neck shaping:** Bind off 8 (9/9/10) sts at beg of next 4 (10/2/8) rows, 9 (10/10/11) sts at beg of next 10 (4/12/6) rows, AT THE SAME TIME, when piece measures 47 (48/49/50) cm or 18½ (18⅞/19¼/19⅝)" above border, bind off center 20 sts for neck and working both sides at once, bind off from each neck edge 14 sts once.

RIGHT FRONT

With Louxor and 3½ mm needles, cast on 81 (85/89/93) sts and work 12 rows of border, then work in woven st. Work side and armhole incs at LHS as for back.

**Note:** At 7 cm or 2¾" above border, work 2 buttonholes (bind off 3 sts, then cast on 3 sts on foll row), with the 1st one at 3 sts from front edge and the next one 17 sts over. Work even until piece measures 21 (22/23/24) cm or 8¼ (8⅝/9/9⅜)" above border. Reverse woven st (that is work RS rows on WS and vice versa) on 1 st at front edge, then cont to reverse 1 st more every 4th row 17 times for lapel. When piece measures 37 (38/39/40) cm or 14½ (15/15⅜/15¾)" above border, work as foll:

**Neck shaping:** Bind off from RHS 9 sts once, 6 sts once, 5 sts twice, 4 sts once, 3 sts once, 2 sts twice, 1 st 3 times. When piece measures 45 (46/47/48) cm or 17¾ (18⅛/18½/18⅞)" above border, work shoulder shaping at LHS as for back.

LEFT FRONT

Work to correspond to right front, reversing shaping and omitting buttonholes.

*(Continued on page 137)*

Woven and wonderful. Knit this boxy two-button jacket in a simple slip stitch pattern, then weave in a contrasting ribbon yarn to create the look of fabric. Scads of glittery paillettes add a touch of evening glitz.

SIZES

Small (Medium/Large/X-Large)

MATERIALS: LAINES ANNY BLATT

Louxor d'Anny Blatt, Chili 111: 12 (12/13/13) balls

Victoria d'Anny Blatt, Sanguine 534: 2 balls

Paillettes d'Anny Blatt, Noir 383: 1 ball

Knitting needles: One pair 3½ mm needles (US 4)

TENSION/GAUGE

28 sts and 44 rows to 10 cm or 4" square with Louxor and 3½ mm needles in woven st.

SKILL LEVEL: INTERMEDIATE

malachite

## STITCHES USED

St st, dc.

See explanation of sts on page 157.

**Fancy pat:** Multiple of 2 sts plus 2 selvage sts.

**Row 1:** With Ecru, 1 selvage st, *sl 1 purlwise, K1*, rep from *to*, end with 1 selvage st.

**Row 2:** With Ecru, purl.

**Row 3:** With Noir, 1 selvage st, *K1, sl 1 purlwise*, rep from *to*, end with 1 selvage st.

**Row 4:** With Noir, purl.

Rep these 4 rows for fancy pat.

## BACK

With Ecru, cast on 62 (68/74/82) sts and work in fancy pat, inc 1 st each side every 16th row once, every 14th row twice = 68 (74 st/80/88) sts. Work even until piece measures 27 cm or 10⅝" from beg.

**Armhole shaping:** Bind off 3 sts at beg of next 2 (4/4/4) rows 2 sts at beg of next 2 (2/4/6) rows, dec 1 st at bext of next 4 (2/2/2) rows = 54 (56/58/62) sts.

Work even until piece measures 49 (50/51/52) cm or 19¼ (19⅝/20½)" from beg.

**Shoulder shaping:** Bind off 7 (7/8/9) sts at beg of next 2 (4/2/2) rows, bind off 6 (0/7/8) sts at beg of next 2 (0/2/2) rows, leave rem 28 sts on a holder for neck.

## RIGHT FRONT

With Ecru, cast on 31 (34/37/41) sts and work in fancy pat, beg with 2 selvage sts instead of 1, and work incs at LHS same as back = 34 (37/40/44) sts.

Work even until piece measures 27 cm or 10⅝" from beg. Work decs at LHS for armhole same as back = 27 (28/29/31) sts.

Work even until piece measures 49 (50/51/52) cm or 19¼ (19⅝/20/20½)" from beg. Work decs at LHS for shoulder same as back, leave rem 14 sts on a holder for neck.

## LEFT FRONT

Work to correspond to right front, reversing shaping.

## SLEEVES

With Ecru, cast on 34 (34/36/36) sts and work in fancy pat until piece measures 10 cm or 4" from beg. Inc 1 st each side every 10th (8th/8th/6th) row 1 (4/1/9) times, every 8th (6th/6th/4th) row 7 (6/10/4) times = 50 (54/58/62) sts.

Work even until piece measures 46 cm or 18⅛" from beg.

**Cap shaping:** Bind off 3 sts at beg of next 2 rows, 2 sts at beg of next 4 rows, dec 1 st each side every 4th (2nd/2nd/2nd) row 7 (1/2/3) times, every 0 (4th/4th/4th) row 0 (6/5/4) times, bind off 2 sts at beg of next 2 (4/6/8) rows, 3 sts at beg of bext 2 rows. Bind off rem 12 sts.

*(Continued on page 138)*

A busy lifestyle demands flexible fashion and this classy zip-front jacket takes you from a day at the office to a night on the town without missing a beat. An ever-popular houndstooth check lends timeless appeal to the military silhouette.

## SIZES

Small (Medium/Large/X-Large)

## MATERIALS: LAINES ANNY BLATT

Rustique, Ecru 182: 7 (8/8/9) balls, Noir 383: 7 (8/8/9) balls
**Knitting needles:** One pair size 7 mm (US 10½)
Crochet hook size 5 mm (US H/7)
Stitch holders
Zipper

## TENSION/GAUGE

14 sts and 21 rows = 10 cm or 4" in fancy pat.

**SKILL LEVEL: INTERMEDIATE**

You'll sparkle like the stars in the midnight sky when you wear this heavenly top. The stunning step rib pattern gives it rich texture and the easy styling makes it perfect for pairing with slacks or a skirt.

## SIZES
Small (Medium/Large/X-Large)

## MATERIALS: LAINES ANNY BLATT
Muguet, Souris 543: 6(7/8/9) balls
Knitting needles: One pair each sizes 3½ and 4mm (UK 9 and 8) (US 4 and 6)

## TENSION/GAUGE
23 sts and 32 rows = 10 cm or 4" with 4mm needles in st st and rev st st.

## SKILL LEVEL: EASY

### STITCHES USED

**St st, rev st st, K2/P2 rib**

See explanation of sts on page 157.

*....* Rep the sts between the *'s as many times as indicated or to end.

**K4/P4 rib:**

**Row 1:** *K4, P4*, rep from *to*.

**Row 2:** *K4, P4*, rep from *to*.

Rep these 2 rows for K4/P4 rib.

### BACK

Cast on 108 (114/120/126) sts and work foll chart until piece measures 34 (35/36/37) cm or 13⅜ (13¾/14⅛/14½)" from beg.

**Armhole shaping:** Bind off 4 sts at beg of next 2 rows, 3 sts at beg of next 2 rows, 2 sts at beg of next 2 (2/4/4) rows, dec 1 st each side every other row 2 (3/2/3) times = 86 (90/94/98) sts. Work even until piece measures 54 (56/58/60) cm or 21¼ (22/22⅞/23⅝)" from beg.

**Shoulder and neck shaping:** Bind off 11 (12/13/14) sts at beg of next 4 rows, AT THE SAME TIME, bind off center 42 sts for neck and work both sides at once.

### FRONT

Work same as back until piece measures 51 (53/55/57) cm or 20 (20⅞/21⅝/22⅜)" from beg.

**Neck shaping:** Bind off center 20 sts for neck, and working both sides at once, bind off from each neck edge 5 sts once, 3 sts once, 2 sts once, 1 st once. When piece measures 54 (56/58/60) cm or 21¼ (22/22⅞/23⅝)" from beg, shape shoulders same as back.

### SLEEVES

Cast on 64 (66/68/70) sts and work foll chart, inc 1 st each side every 4th row 5 (6/5/4) times, every 2nd row 0 (0/2/4) times = 74 (78/82/86) sts. Work even until piece measures 9 cm or 3½" from beg.

**Cap shaping:** Bind off 3 sts at beg of next 2 rows, 2 sts at beg of next 4 rows, dec 1 st each side every other row 20 (22/24/26) times, bind off 3 sts at beg of next 2 rows. Bind off rem 14 sts.

### TO MAKE UP/FINISHING

See tips on page 157.

Sew one shoulder seam.

With 3½mm needles, pick up and k 76 sts along front neck and 52 sts along back neck = 128 sts. Work as foll (as front): 12 sts K2/P2 rib beg with K2, 52 sts K4/P4 rib beg with K2, 20 sts K2/P2 rib beg with P2, 36 sts K4/P4 rib beg with P4, 8 sts K2/P2 rib beg with K2. Cont as established until band measures 12 cm or 4¾" from beg. Bind off all sts. Sew 2nd shoulder and neckband seam. Set in sleeves. Sew side and sleeve seams.

*(Charts and schematics continued on page 139)*

léto

**sayoun**

## STITCHES USED

**St st, dc.**

See explanation of sts on page 157.

**Jacquard pat:** See charts. Take care to twist yarns on WS at each col. change to prevent holes.

## BACK

With Muguet and 4 mm needles, cast on 130 (138/146/154) sts. Work in Jacquard pat no. 1, beg with 1 selvage st, then st 1 and row 1 of chart.

**Note:** Rep rows 7-42 once, then rows 7-34, then work Jacquard pat no. 2, beg with 1 selvage st and st 1 of chart, working rows 1-42 once, then rep rows 7-42, AT SAME TIME, dec 1 st each side each side every 8th row 5 times, every 6th row twice = 116 (124/132/140) sts. Work even until piece measures 21 cm or 8¼" from beg. Inc 1 st each side of next row, then every 8th row 4 times, every 6th row twice = 130 (138/146/154) sts. Work even until piece measures 38 cm or 15" from beg.

**Armhole shaping:** Bind off 4 sts at beg of next 2 (2/4/4) rows, 3 sts at beg of next 2 (4/4/6) rows, 2 sts at beg of next 4 (4/2/2) rows, dec 1 st each side every other row 1 (1/2/2) times. Work even until piece measures 53 (54/55/56) cm or 20⅞ (21¼/21⅝/22)" from beg.

**Neck shaping:** Bind off center 18 sts and, working both sides at once, bind off from each neck edge 6 sts once, 5 sts once, 4 sts once, 3 sts once, 2 sts once, 1 st once. Work even until piece measures 58 (59/60/61) cm or 22⅞ (23¼/23⅝/24)" from beg. Bind off rem 23 (24/25/26) sts each side for shoulders.

## FRONT

Work as for back until piece measures 48 (49/50/51) cm or 18⅞ (19¼/19⅝/20)" from beg.

**Neck shaping:** Bind off center 16 sts and working both sides at once, bind off from each neck edge 5 sts once, 4 sts once, 3 sts twice, 2 sts twice, 1 st 3 times. Work even until piece measures 58 (59/60/61) cm or 22⅞ (23¼/23⅝/24)" from beg. Bind off rem 23 (24/25/26) sts each side for shoulders.

## SLEEVES

With Muguet and 4 mm needles, cast on 82 (88/94/100) sts. Work in Jacquard pat no. 3, beg with 1 selvage st and st 1 (2/3/4) of chart, AT SAME TIME, inc 1 st each side every other row 10 times, every 4th row once = 104 (110/116/122) sts. Work even until piece measures 9 cm or 3½" from beg.

**Cap shaping:** Bind off 3 sts at beg of next 2 rows, 2 sts at beg of next 22 (28/34/40) rows, dec 1 st each side every other row 11 (8/5/2) times, bind off 2 sts at beg of next 2 rows, 3 sts at beg of next 2 rows. Bind off rem 22 sts.

*(Continued on page 141)*

---

All that glitters is pure elegance, especially when you start with basic black. Knit the jacquard pattern first, then sew on rows of sparkling crystal beads and light-catching paillettes. Trim the plunging scoop neck and hems simply with single crochet.

### SIZES

Small (Medium/Large/X-Large)

### MATERIALS: LAINES ANNY BLATT

**Muguet d'Anny Blatt, Noir 383:** 3 (3/4/4) balls

**Louxor d'Anny Blatt, Noir 383:** 4 (4/5/5) balls

**Antique d'Anny Blatt, Argent 016:** 5 (5/6/6) balls

**Knitting needles:** One pair size 4 mm (US 6)

Crochet hook size 3½ mm (US E/4)

156 black paillettes

156 black beads

300 crystals

### TENSION/GAUGE

27 sts and 29 rows to 10 cm or 4" square with 4 mm needles in Jacquard pat no. 1 or no. 2.

### SKILL LEVEL: INTERMEDIATE

blanc
neige

## STITCHES USED

Garter st, st st, dc, crab st.

See explanation of sts on page 157.

**Cord st:** Worked over 5 sts

**Row 1:** P2, K1, P2.

**Row 2:** K the knit sts and P the purl sts.

**Row 3:** P2, 1 fancy st (insert the RH needle between the K st and the next P st but two rows below, K1, then without dropping the st from LH needle, P and K the st), P2.

**Row 4:** K2, P3tog, K2.

Rep these 4 rows for cord st.

**Fancy pat no. 1:** Worked over a multiple of 14 sts, plus 1, plus 1 selvage st each side. Note: The number of sts are different except for rows 7 and 12 which are a multiple of 14.

**Row 1:** With Louxor, 1 selvage st, *K1, SKP (sl 1, K1, psso), K9, K2tog*, rep from *to*, end K1, 1 selvage st.

**Row 2:** With Louxor, 1 selvage st, P1, *P2tog, P7, P2tog tbl, P1*, rep from *to*, end 1 selvage st.

**Row 3:** With Louxor, 1 selvage st, *K1, SKP, K2, yo, K3, K2tog, rep from *to*, end K1, 1 selvage st.

**Row 4:** With Louxor, 1 selvage st, P1, *P2tog, P2, in yo work (K1, P1, K1, P1, K1), P1, P2tog tbl, P1*, rep from *to*, end 1 selvage st.

**Row 5:** With Louxor, 1 selvage st, *K1, SKP, K6, K2tog*, rep from *to*, end K1, 1 selvage st.

**Row 6:** With Louxor, 1 selvage st, P1, *P2tog, P7*, rep from *to*, end with 1 selvage st.

**Row 7:** With Louxor, 1 selvage st, *K2, [yo, K1] 6 times*, rep from *to*, end K1, 1 selvage st.

**Row 8:** With Louxor, purl.

**Rows 9 and 10:** With Muguet, knit.

**Row 11:** With Muguet, purl.

**Row 12:** With Muguet, knit.

Rep these 12 rows for fancy pat.

**Fancy pat no. 2:** Worked over a multiple of 6 sts, plus 1, plus 1 selvage st each side. Note: the number of sts are different in every row.

**Row 1:** 1 selvage st, *K3, SK2P (sl 1, K2tog, psso), K2*, rep from *to*, end K1, 1 selvage st.

**Row 2 and all WS rows:** Purl.

**Row 3:** 1 selvage st, *K3, work 3 sts in 1 as foll: (K1, do not drop st from needle, K1 in same st but one row below then K same st on needle, drop sts from LH needle), K2*, rep from *to*, end K1, 1 selvage st.

**Row 5:** 1 selvage st, *SK2P, K5*, rep from *to*, end SK2P, 1 selvage st.

**Row 7:** 1 selvage st, *work 3 sts in 1, K5*, rep from *to*, end work 3 sts in 1, 1 selvage st.

Rep these 8 rows for fancy pat no. 2.

*(Continued on page 142)*

White on white delight. This lacy cardigan, boasting dainty peek-a-boo eyelets, is knit with two contrasting textured yarns. Other pretty details include soft scalloped hems and pearl button closure, making it a must-have sweater for summer evenings out.

**SIZES**

Small (Medium/Large/X-Large)

**MATERIALS: LAINES ANNY BLATT**

Louxor d'Anny Blatt, Blanc 050: 8 (9/9/10) balls

Muguet d'Anny Blatt, Blanc 050: 2 (2/2/3) balls

Knitting needles: One pair each size 3 and 3½ mm (US 3 and 4)

Crochet hook size 3 mm (UK 10) (US D/3)

Seven buttons

Two shoulder pads

**TENSION/GAUGE**

37 sts and 39 rows to 10 cm or 4" square with Louxor and 3½ mm needles in Fancy pat no. 1 or 2.

**SKILL LEVEL: ADVANCED**

**duet**

axis

## STITCH USED

**Fancy pat:** Worked on an even number of sts.

**Row 1:** Knit.

**Row 2:** *K1, P1*, rep from *to*.

Rep these 2 rows for fancy pat.

## BACK

With col. Gaïa, cast on 123 (131/139/149) sts and work in fancy pat, beg with K1, until piece measures 7 cm or 2¾" from beg. Work stripes as foll: 2 rows col. Ultraviolet, 6 rows col. Gaïa, 2 rows col. Coloquinte, 6 rows col. Gaïa, 2 rows col. Améthyste, 6 rows col. Gaïa, 2 rows col. Ultraviolet, then work with col. Gaïa to end of piece, AT SAME TIME, when piece measures 38 cm or 15" from beg, work as foll:

**Raglan shaping:** Bind off 3 sts at beg of next 2 rows. Work dec each side at 2 sts from each edge. Note: At RHS: single (double) dec: K2, 1 SKP (1 SK2P). At LHS: single (double) dec: work to last 4 (5) sts and K2tog (K3tog), K2.

**X-Small:** 1 single dec every 4th row twice and 1 single dec every 2nd row 38 times.

**Small:** 1 single dec every 2nd row 44 times.

**Medium:** Every 2nd row: 1 double dec 3 times and 1 single dec 42 times.

**Large:** Every 2nd row: 1 double dec 6 times and 1 single dec 41 times.

**All sizes:** Bind off rem 37 sts for neck.

## FRONT

Work same as back, but beg with P1.

Work even until piece measures 38 cm or 15" from beg.

**Raglan shaping:** Bind off 3 sts at beg of next 2 rows. Work decs at 2 sts from each edge:

**X-Small:** 1 single dec every 4th row twice and 1 single dec every 2nd row 33 times.

**Small:** 1 single dec every 2nd row 39 times.

**Medium:** Every 2nd row: 1 double dec 3 times and 1 single dec 37 times.

**Large:** Every 2nd row: 1 double dec 6 times and 1 single dec 36 times. AT THE SAME TIME, when piece measures 59 (60/61/62) cm or 23¼ (23⅝/24/24⅜)" from beg, work as foll:

**Neck shaping:** Bind off center 15 sts, and working both sides at once, bind off from each neck edge : 4 sts twice, 3 sts twice and 2 sts once.

## RIGHT SLEEVE

With col. Gaïa, cast on 60 (64/68/74) sts and work in fancy pat, inc 1 st each side every 6th row 21 times = 102 (106/110/116) sts, AT THE SAME TIME, when piece measures 7 cm or 2¾" from beg, work stripes same as back, then work with col. Gaïa to end of piece.

Work even until piece measures 42 cm or 16½" from beg.

**Raglan shaping:** Bind off 3 sts at beg of next 2 rows. Work decs at 2 sts from each edge:

*(Continued on page 144)*

Whether he's a sportsman or a spectator he'll love the good looks and comfort fit of this raglan-sleeve pullover. An easy broken rib stitch in variegated and solid color yarns create the uniquely spirited stripe pattern.

### SIZES

X-small (Small/Medium/Large)

### MATERIALS: LAINES ANNY BLATT

No. 5, Gaïa 250: 9 (10/11/12) balls
Ultraviolet 592: 2 balls
Coloquinte 092 and Améthyste 009: 1 ball each
Knitting needles: One pair size 4½ mm (US 7)

### TENSION/GAUGE

23 sts and 32 rows = 10 cm or 4" with 4½ mm needles in fancy pat.

### SKILL LEVEL: INTERMEDIATE

cap ferrat    st. tropez

## WOMAN'S PULLOVER

### STITCHES USED

**K1/P1 rib, reverse st st**

See explanation of sts on page 157.

**8-st cable and 12-st cable:** See charts.

**1 elongated st:** on RS, sl 1, on WS work P1 tbl.

**Cr6R:** Sl 3 sts to cn and hold to back, K3, K3 from cn.

**Cr6L:** Sl 3 sts to cn and hold to front, K3, K3 from cn.

**Cr8R:** Sl 4 sts to cn and hold to back, K4, K4 from cn.

**Cr8L:** Sl 4 sts to cn and hold to front, K4, K4 from cn.

**Bobble:** Work 5 sts in one st (K1, P1, K1, P1, K1), turn, P5, turn, K5, turn P2tog, P1, P2tog, turn, sl the first 2 sts tog to RH needle, K the 3rd st and pass the 2 slipped sts over the K st.

### BACK

With 10 mm needles and double strand, cast on 57 (61/65) sts and work 4 cm or 1½" in K1/P1 rib. Inc 11 sts on next row and work as foll: 7 (9/11) sts reverse st st, 8-st cable, 2 sts reverse st st, 1 elongated st, 7 sts reverse st st with 1 bobble on the center st on the 7th row, then the foll every 6th row, 1 elongated st, 2 sts reverse st st, 12-st cable, 2 sts reverse st st, 1 elongated st, 7 sts reverse st st with bobbles, 1 elongated st, 2 sts reverse st st, 8-st cable, 7 (9/11) sts reverse st st = 68 (72/76) sts.

**Note:** The elongated sts correspond to the K sts of K1/P1 rib.

Work even until piece measures 39 cm or 15⅜" from beg.

**Armhole shaping:** Bind off 3 sts at beg of next 2 (4/2) rows, 2 sts at beg of next 2 (0/4) rows = 58 (60/62) sts. Work even until piece measures 64 (64/65) cm or 25⅛ (25⅛/25⅝)" from beg.

**Shoulder and neck shaping:** Bind off 10 sts at beg of next 2 rows, 7 (8/9) sts at beg of next 2 rows, AT THE SAME TIME bind off center 10 sts for neck, and working both sides at once, bind off 7 sts from each neck edge once.

### FRONT

Work same as back until piece measures 56 (56/57) cm or 22 (22/22⅜)" from beg.

**Neck shaping:** Bind off center 10 sts for neck, and working both sides at once, bind off from each neck edge 3 sts once, 2 sts once, 1 st twice. When piece measures 64 (64/65) cm or 25⅛ (25⅛/25⅝)" from beg, shape shoulders same as back.

### SLEEVES

With 10 mm needles and double strand, cast on 28 sts and work 4 cm or 1½" in K1/P1 rib. Inc 5 sts on next row and work as foll: 2 sts reverse st st, 8-st cable, 2 sts reverse st st, 1 elongated st, 7 sts reverse st st with bobbles, 1 elongated st, 2 sts reverse st st, 8-st cable, 2 sts reverse st st = 33 sts.

*(Continued on page 145)*

Outdoor fun means dressing warm and this cozy pair fills the bill. For her, a quick-knit cowl neck pullover that's patterned with chunky chain cables and big bobbles. For him, an easy-knit V-neck sweater worked in an interesting broken rib stitch.

### Woman's pullover

**SIZES**
Small (Medium/Large)

**MATERIALS: LAINES ANNY BLATT**
Rustique, Mousse 363: 34(36/38) balls
Knitting needles: One pair each sizes 10 and 12 mm (US 15 and 17)
Cable needle (cn)

**TENSION/GAUGE**
12 sts and 13.5 rows = 10 cm or 4" with 10 mm needles and double strand over all sts.
8-st cable = 5 cm or 2" wide.
12-st cable = 9 cm or 3½" wide.

**SKILL LEVEL: ADVANCED**

### Man's pullover

**SIZES**
Small (Medium/Large)

**MATERIALS: LAINES ANNY BLATT**
Merinos, Camel 137: 15(17/19) balls
Knitting needles: One pair each sizes 3 and 3 ½ mm (US 3 and 4)

**TENSION/GAUGE**
30 sts and 32.5 rows = 10 cm or 4" with 3½ mm needles in fancy pat.

**SKILL LEVEL: EASY**

cannes

boulogne

## WOMAN'S SWEATER

### STITCHES USED

**St st, reverse st st.**

See explanation of sts on page 157.

**Fancy pat:**

**Row 1:** Knit.

**Row 2:** *K1, P1*, rep from *to*.

Rep these 2 rows.

**Woven st:**

**Row 1 and 3:** Knit.

**Row 2:** 1 selvage st, *K1, yarn to back, sl 1 purlwise*, rep from *to*, end with 1 selvage st.

**Row 4:** 1 selvage st, *yarn to back, sl 1 purlwise, K1*, rep from *to*, end with 1 selvage st.

Rep these 4 rows.

**Cable no. 1 and no. 2:** See charts.

**Cr6R:** Slip 3 sts to cn and hold to back, K3, K3 from cn.

**Cr6L:** Slip 3 sts to cn and hold to front, K3, K3 from cn.

### BACK

With No. 4, cast on 137 (147/157/175) sts and work as foll: *10 sts cable no. 1 twice, 19 sts cable no. 2, 10 sts cable no. 1 twice, 19 sts cable no. 2, 10 sts cable no. 1 twice, 19 sts cable no. 2 and 10 sts cable no. 1 twice* (5 sts reverse st st, then rep from *to* same as 1st size and end with 5 sts reverse st st/10 sts cable no. 1, then rep from *to* same as 1st size and end with 10 sts cable no. 1/19 sts cable no. 1, beg with the 2nd st of chart, then rep from *to* same as 1st size and end with 19 sts cable no. 1, beg with the 1st st of chart). Work even until piece measures 21 cm or 8¼" from beg. Work 2 rows woven st, dec 10 (10/10/14) sts on first row = 127 (137/147/161) sts. Work 4 rows woven st with Victoria and 4 rows with Kanpur.

Cont in fancy pat with No. 4 until piece measures 44 cm or 17⅜" from beg.

**Armhole shaping:** Bind off 4 sts at beg of next 2 (2/2/4) rows, 3 sts at beg of next 2 (4/4/4) rows, 2 sts at beg of next 4 (4/8/8) rows and 1 st at beg of next 2 (4/4/4) rows = 103 (105/107/113) sts. Work even until piece measures 63 (64/65/66) cm or 24¾ (25⅛/25⅝/26)" from beg.

**Shoulder shaping:** Bind off 7 (7/7/8) sts at beg of next 6 (4/2/4) rows, 8 (8/8/9) sts at beg of next 2 (4/6/4) rows. Bind off rem 45 sts for neck.

### POCKET LININGS (MAKE 2)

With No. 4, cast on 34 sts and work in st st for 11.5 cm or 4½". Place sts on a holder.

### FRONT

Work as for back until piece measures 21 cm or 8¼" from beg. Work 2 rows woven st, dec 10 (10/10/14) sts on first row = 127 (137/147/161) sts. Work 4 rows woven st with Victoria and 4 rows with Kanpur.

*(Continued on page 147)*

Cozy up to texture for two. Her pretty polo neck pullover—trimmed with extra-wide bands of braided and eccentric cables—compliments his handsome crew neck pullover worked in an impressive pattern of various combinations of the chain cable.

### Woman's sweater

**SIZES SIZES**

Small (Medium/Large/X-Large)

**MATERIALS: LAINES ANNY BLATT**

No. 4, Opale 405: 15 (15/16/17) balls

Victoria, Raisin 501: 1 ball

Kanpur, Ecorce 180: 1 ball

Knitting needles: One pair size 3½ mm (US 4)

Cable needle (cn)

St holders

Three buttons

**TENSION/GAUGE**

25 sts and 36 rows = 10 cm or 4" with 3½ mm needles and No. 4 in fancy pat.

### Man's sweater

**SIZES**

X-Small (Small/Medium/Large)

**MATERIALS: LAINES ANNY BLATT**

No. 5, Opale 405: 18 (19/20/21) balls

Knitting needles: One pair each sizes 3½ and 4 mm ( (US 4 and 6)

Cable needle (cn)

**TENSION/GAUGE**

23 sts and 29 rows = 10 cm or 4" with 4 mm needles in st st and cables.

**SKILL LEVEL FOR BOTH: ADVANCED**

antre

atrium

## WOMAN'S SWEATER

### STITCHES USED

**St st.**

See explanation of sts on page 157.

**6-st Cable:** See chart.

**CrK4R:** Slip 2 sts to cn and hold to back, K next 2 sts, then K 2 sts from cn.

**CrK4L:** Slip 2 sts to cn and hold to front, K next 2 sts, then K 2 sts from cn.

**16-st Fancy Cable:** See chart.

**CrK2/P2R:** Slip 2 sts to cn and hold to back, K next 2 sts, then P2 from cn.

**CrP2/K2L:** Slip 2 sts to cn and hold to front, P next 2 sts, then K 2 sts from cn.

**M1 inc:** Insert LH needle into horizontal strand between last st worked and next st on LH needle and K through back loop of this strand.

### BODY

Worked in one piece from right sleeve to left sleeve.

Cast on 54 (60/66) sts and work as foll: 10 (13/16) sts in st st, working the last st tbl, 16 sts fancy cable, 2 sts reverse st st, 16 sts fancy cable, 10 (13/16) sts in st st working the first st tbl.

Inc 1 st each side every 8th row 9 times, every 6th row 8 times, every 2nd row 5 times, inc 2 sts 10 times = 138 (144/150) sts. Work 2 rows even then cast on 39 sts at beg of next 2 rows, work in 6-st cable (at RHS beg with 1 selvage st, at LHS end with 1 selvage st) = 216 (222/228) sts.

Work even until piece measures 58 (60/62) cm or 22⅞ (23⅝/24⅜)" from beg. Work each of the center 2 sts tog with 1 st of fancy cable, work 2 rows then place 107 (110/113) sts at LHS on a holder and cont on 107 (110/113) sts on RHS for back, dec 1 st for neck at 2 sts from edge of fancy cable (work 1 SKP) every 2nd row 4 times = 103 (106/109) sts. Work even until piece measures 80 (82/84) cm or 31½ (32¼/33)" from beg. Work incs at neck edge at 2 sts from edge of fancy cable 4 times = 107 (110/113) sts, then place sts on a 2nd holder.

Work 107 (110/113) sts from holder on LHS and dec 1 st at neck each at 2 sts from edge of fancy cable (work K2tog) every 2nd row 10 times = 97 (100/103) sts.

Work even until piece measures 75 (77/79) cm or 29½ (30¼/31⅛)" from beg. Inc 1 st at neck at 2 sts from edge of fancy cable 10 times = 107 (110/113) sts, then work 2 rows more and join the 2 parts adding 2 sts in center = 216 (222/228) sts.

Work even until piece measures 89 (93/97) cm or 35 (36⅝/38¼)" from beg. Bind off 39 sts at beg of next 2 rows = 138 (144/150) sts. Work 2 rows even, then dec 2 sts each side every 2nd row 10 times, dec 1 st every 2nd row 5 times, every 6th row 8 times, every 8th row 9 times = 54 (60/66) sts.

*(Continued on page 151)*

Knit a dynamic duo using two time-honored yarns. Angora gives an ultra-feminine touch to this stylish dolman sleeve cable top. Fine merino wool lends a rugged look to this handsome V-neck pullover stitched in eye-catching mosaic diamonds.

### Woman's sweater

**SIZES**
Small (Medium/Large)

**MATERIALS: LAINES ANNY BLATT**
Angora Super, Platine 443: 10 (11/12) balls
Knitting needles: One pair size 4 mm (US 6)
Cable needle (cn)
St holders

**TENSION/GAUGE**
25 sts and 30 rows = 10 cm or 4" over all sts.
16 sts fancy cable = 6 cm or 2⅜" wide.

**SKILL LEVEL: ADVANCED**

### Man's sweater

**SIZES**
Small (Medium/Large)

**MATERIALS: LAINES ANNY BLATT**
Merinos, Noir 383: 10 (12/13) balls,
Patine 443: 8 (10/11) balls
Knitting needles: One pair each sizes 2½ and 3 mm (US 2 and 3)

**TENSION/GAUGE**
26 sts and 51 rows = 10 cm or 4" using size 3 mm needles in fancy pat.

**SKILL LEVEL: INTERMEDIATE**

Dress your favorite guy in fabulous Fair Isle style. This terrific turtleneck pullover has all the features that a man loves: easy fit, great graphics in earth-tone hues. Work in stockinette stitch following the charted pattern; trim edges in double rib.

SIZES

Small (Medium/Large)

MATERIALS: LAINES ANNY BLATT

**Cachemir'Anny, Vert de Gris 598:** 10 (11/12) balls

**Camel 137:** 2 (2/2) balls

**Ecru 182, Bronze 061, Boisè 060, Dubai 167** and **Miel 353:** 1 ball each

**Knitting needles:** One pair each sizes 3, 3½, 4 and 4½ mm (US 3, 4, 6 and 7).

TENSION/GAUGES

23 sts and 32 rows = 10 cm or 4" with 4 mm needles in st st.

23 sts and 25 rows = 10 cm or 4" with 4½ mm needles in jacquard.

SKILL LEVEL: INTERMEDIATE

STITCHES USED

**St st, K2/P2 rib, jacquard (see chart).**

See explanation of sts on page 157.

BACK

With 3 mm needles and Vert de Gris, cast on 124 (130/136) sts and work in K2/P2 rib for 3 cm or 1⅛" from beg. Change to 4 mm needles and cont in st st, inc 1 st on first row = 125 (131/137) sts. Work even until piece measures 17 cm or 6⅝" from beg. Change to 4½ mm needles and cont in jacquard, beg with the 7th (4th/7th) st of chart. Work even until piece measures 37 cm or 14½" from beg. Change to 4 mm needles and cont in st st with Vert de Gris until piece measures 41 cm or 16⅛" from beg.

**Armhole shaping:** Bind off 3 sts at beg of next 2 rows, 2 sts at beg of next 2 rows, dec 1 st each side every other row twice = 111 (117/123) sts. Work even until piece measures 65 (66/67) cm or 25⅝ (26/26⅜)" from beg.

**Neck and shoulder shaping:** Bind off center 27 sts for neck, and working both sides at once, bind off from each neck edge 8 sts once, AT THE SAME TIME bind off from each shoulder edge 11(12/13) sts twice, 12(13/14) sts once.

FRONT

Work same as back until piece measures 61 (62/63) cm or 24 (24⅜/24¾)" from beg.

**Neck shaping:** Bind off center 15 sts for neck, and working both sides at once, bind off from each neck edge 4 sts once, 3 sts once, 2 sts twice, dec 1 st every other row 3 times. When piece measures 65 (66/67) cm or 25⅝ (26/26⅜)" from beg, shape shoulder same as back.

SLEEVES

With 3 mm needles and Vert de Gris, cast on 52 (54/56) sts, and work in K2/P2 rib for 5 cm or 2". Change to 4 mm needles and work in st st, inc 4 sts on 1st row = 56 (58/60) sts. Cont to inc 1 st each side every 6th row 9 (7/5) times, every 4th row 19 (22/25) times = 112 (116/120) sts, AT THE SAME TIME, when piece measures 23 cm or 9" from beg (there are 76 (80/86) sts), change to 4½ mm needles and cont in jacquard, beg with the 7th (5th/3rd) st of chart. When piece measures 43 cm or 16⅞" from beg, change to 4 mm needles and cont in st st with Vert de Gris. Work even until piece measures 51 cm or 20" from beg.

**Cap shaping:** Bind off 2 sts at beg of next 0 (4/12) rows, 3 sts at beg of next 6 (8/4) rows, 5 sts at beg of next 2 (0/0) rows, 7 sts at beg of next 2 rows. Bind off rem 70 sts.

*(Continued on page 154)*

dijon

amazone          aucuba

## WOMAN'S SWEATER

### STITCHES USED

St st, reverse st st.

See explanation of sts on page 157.

**18 sts cable:** See chart.

**Cr4/5L:** Slip 5 sts to cn and hold to front, K next 4 sts, then K5 from cn.

**Cr5/4R:** Slip 4 sts to cn and hold to back, K next 5 sts, then K4 from cn.

### BACK

Cast on 52 (56/60/64) sts and work sts as foll: 13 (15/17/19) sts in st st, 4 sts reverse st st, 18 sts cable, 4 sts reverse st st, 13 (15/17/19) sts in st st.

Work even until piece measures 37 cm or 14½" from beg.

**Armhole shaping:** Bind off 3 sts at beg of next 2 rows, 2 sts at beg of next 2 (2/2/4) rows, 1 st at beg of next 2 (4/4/6) rows = 40 (42/42/44) sts.

Work even until piece measures 57 (58/58/60) cm or 22⅜ (22⅞/22⅞/23⅝)" from beg.

**Shoulder shaping:** Bind off 4 (4/4/5) sts at beg of next 2 (4/4/2) rows, 3 (0/0/4) sts at beg of next 2 (0/0/2) rows. Cont on rem 26 sts for collar as foll: 4 sts reverse st st, 18 sts in st st, 4 sts reverse st st.

Work even until piece measures 69 (70/70/72) cm or 27⅛ (27½/27½/28⅜)" from beg. Bind off.

### FRONT

Work as for back.

### SLEEVES

Cast on 26 sts, and work sts as foll: 4 sts reverse st st, 18 sts cable, 4 sts reverse st st.

Work even until piece measures 8 cm or 3⅛" from beg. Inc 1 st each side on next row, then every 16th (12th/8th/6th) 2 (3/5/6) times = 32 (34/38/40) sts.

Work even until piece measures 45 cm or 17¾" from beg.

**Cap shaping:** Bind off 3 (3/3/4) sts at beg of next 2 rows, 2 sts at beg of next 4 (6/10/10) rows, dec 1 st each side every other row 6 (5/3/3) times.

**Note:** AT THE SAME TIME, after the 3rd cable crossing, cont in st st over these 18 sts. Bind off rem 6 sts.

### TO MAKE UP/FINISHING

See tips on page 157.

Sew shoulder and collar seams. Set in sleeves.

Sew side and sleeve seams.

*(Continued on page 155)*

---

Pair up in two dramatically different cable fashions. An amplified double cable plays center stage on this roomy, rolled neck sweater. The clean-cut lines of this classic turtleneck pullover allow the overall pattern of cabled diamonds to radiate.

### Woman's sweater

**SIZES**

Small (Medium/Large/X-Large)

**MATERIALS: LAINES ANNY BLATT**
Tangara, Madone 371: 18 (20/22/24) balls

**Knitting needles:** One pair size 9 mm (US 13)

Cable needle (cn)

**TENSION/GAUGE**

9 sts and 13 rows = 10 cm or 4" in St st.

**SKILL LEVEL: INTERMEDIATE**

### Man's sweater

**SIZES**

Small (Medium/Large)

**MATERIALS: LAINES ANNY BLATT**
Merinos, Lin 307: 20 (21/22) balls

**Knitting needles:** One pair size 3½ mm (US 4)

Cable needle (cn)

Stitch holders

**TENSION/GAUGE**

32 sts and 41 rows= 10 cm or 4" in fancy pat.

**SKILL LEVEL: ADVANCED**

*(Continued from page 13)*

# schiste

TO MAKE UP/FINISHING

See tips on page 157.

Sew one shoulder seam.

With 3 ½ mm needles work 114 sts from neck holders,

and work double moss st for 2 cm or ¾", then work 4 rows garter st. Bind off all sts.

Sew 2nd shoulder and neckband seam.

Set in sleeves. Sew side and sleeve seams.

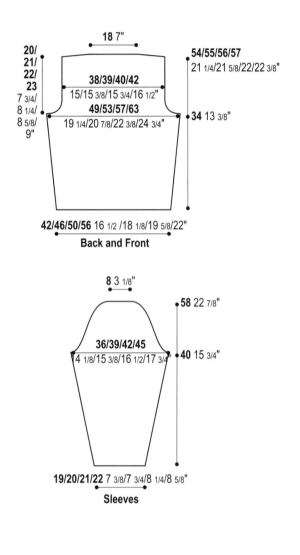

**18** 7"

**20/
21/
22/
23**
7 3/4/
8 1/4/
8 5/8/
9"

**54/55/56/57**
21 1/4/21 5/8/22/22 3/8"

**38/39/40/42**
15/15 3/8/15 3/4/16 1/2"

**49/53/57/63**
19 1/4/20 7/8/22 3/8/24 3/4"

**34** 13 3/8"

**42/46/50/56** 16 1/2 /18 1/8/19 5/8/22"

**Back and Front**

**8** 3 1/8"

**58** 22 7/8"

**36/39/42/45**
4 1/8/15 3/8/16 1/2/17 3/4"

**40** 15 3/4"

**19/20/21/22** 7 3/8/7 3/4/8 1/4/8 5/8"

**Sleeves**

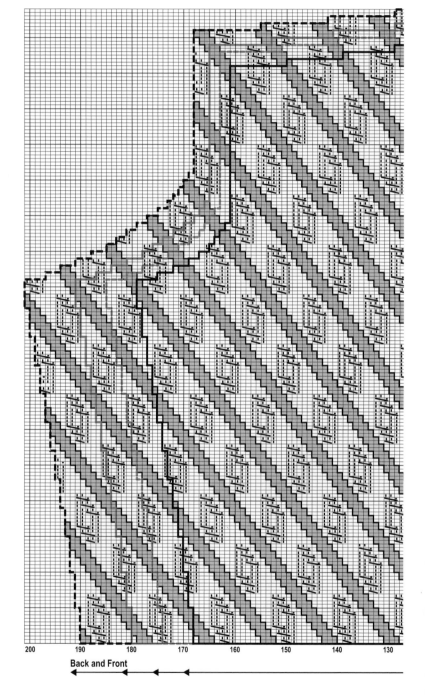

200   190   180   170   160   150   140   130

**Back and Front**

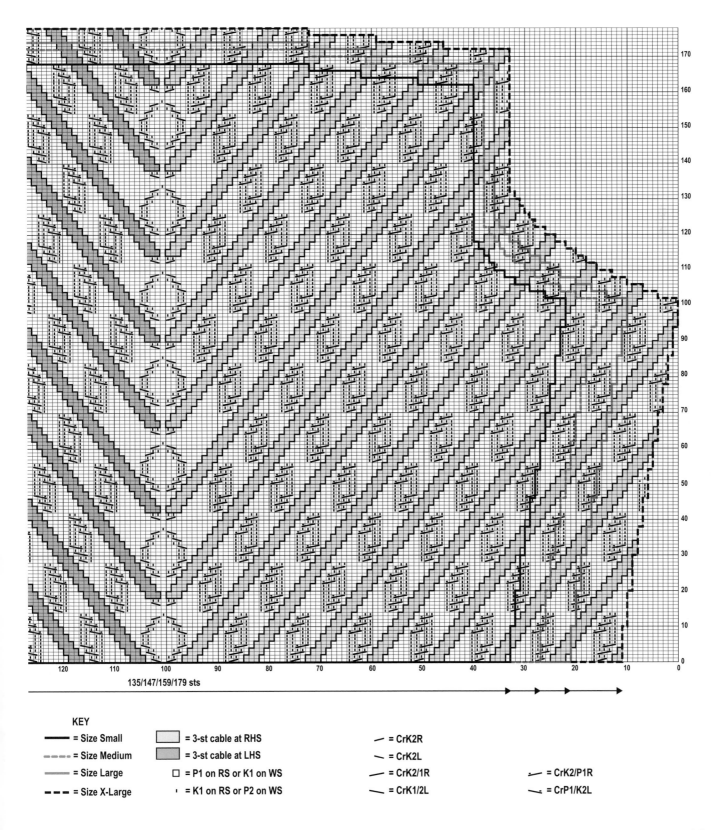

135/147/159/179 sts

**KEY**

| | | |
|---|---|---|
| ——— = Size Small | ▨ = 3-st cable at RHS | ⟋ = CrK2R |
| – – – = Size Medium | ▩ = 3-st cable at LHS | ⟍ = CrK2L |
| ——— = Size Large | ☐ = P1 on RS or K1 on WS | ⟋ = CrK2/1R |
| – – – = Size X-Large | ' = K1 on RS or P2 on WS | ⟍ = CrK1/2L |

⟋ = CrK2/P1R
⟍ = CrP1/K2L

*(Continued from page 93)*

# schiste

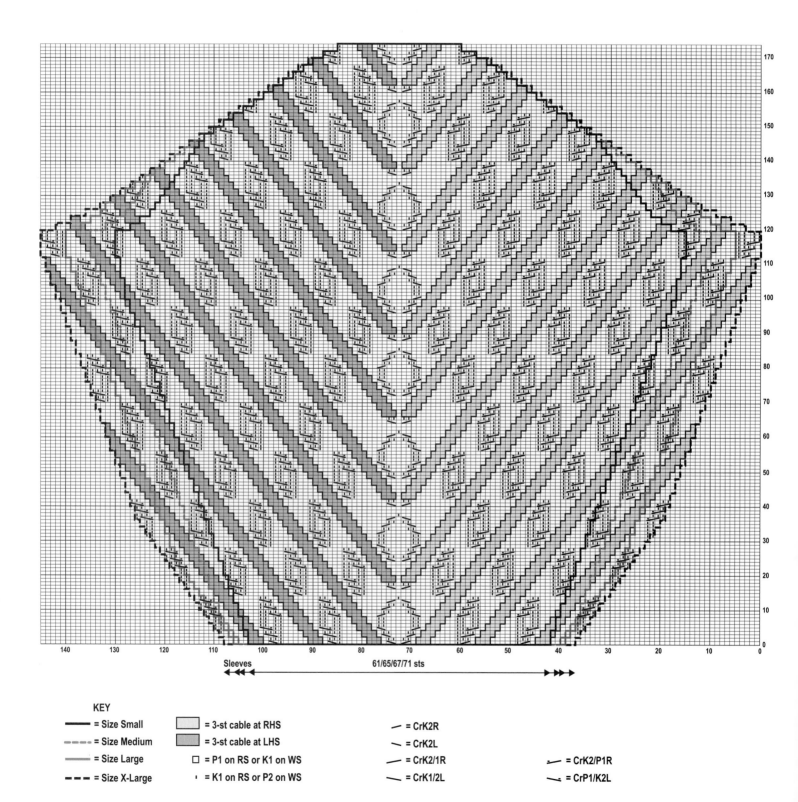

Sleeves
61/65/67/71 sts

170
160
150
140
130
120
110
100
90
80
70
60
50
40
30
20
10
0

140  130  120  110  100  90  80  70  60  50  40  30  20  10  0

**KEY**

—— = Size Small

- - - - = Size Medium

—— = Size Large

- - - = Size X-Large

⬜ = 3-st cable at RHS

⬛ = 3-st cable at LHS

☐ = P1 on RS or K1 on WS

╎ = K1 on RS or P2 on WS

╱ = CrK2R

╲ = CrK2L

╱ = CrK2/1R

╲ = CrK1/2L

╱ = CrK2/P1R

╲ = CrP1/K2L

*(Continued from page 15)*

# surrey

**Row 3:** With Victoria, col. Ivoire, 1 selvage st, *K2, sl 1 purlwise, K1*, rep from *to*, end K1, 1 selvage st.

**Rows 4 and 6:** With Victoria, col. Ivoire, 1 selvage st, K1, *K1, sl 1 purlwise, K2*, rep from *to*, end 1 selvage st.

**Row 5:** With Victoria, col. Ivoire, 1 selvage st, *P2, sl 1 purlwise, P1*, rep from *to*, end P1, 1 selvage st.

**Row 9:** With Victoria, col. Ivoire, 1 selvage st, *sl 1 purlwise, K3*, rep from *to*, end sl 1 purlwise, 1 selvage st.

**Rows 10 and 12:** With Victoria, col. Ivoire, 1 selvage st, sl 1 purlwise, *K3, sl 1 P*, rep from *to*, end 1 selvage st.

**Row 11:** With Victoria, col. Ivoire, 1 selvage st, *sl 1 purlwise, P3*, rep from *to*, end sl 1 purlwise, 1 selvage st. Rep these 12 rows for pat.

**Jacquard pat:** See chart. Take care to twist yarns on WS at each color change to prevent holes. K first row of color change on RS rows, and P first row of color change on WS rows. Use separate bobbins for motifs.

**SKP:** Sl 1, K1, psso.

### FRONT

Begun in 5 parts.

**First part:** With 4 mm needles and Victoria, cast on 10 (13/17/20) sts as foll: 6 sts with col. Ivoire and 4 (7/11/14) sts with col. Cannelle. Work the col. Ivoire sts in Eyelet pat with 1 selvage st at LHS, and work the col. Cannelle sts in Double Moss st, AT THE SAME TIME, add sts at RHS every other row as foll: 4 sts once, 3 sts once and 2 sts once = 19 (22/26/29) sts. Place sts on a holder.

**Second part:** With 4 mm needles and Victoria, col. Cannelle, cast on 8 sts. Work in Double Moss st, adding sts each side every other row as foll: 4 sts once, 3 sts once and 2 sts once = 26 sts. Place sts on a holder.

**Third part:** Work as for second part.

**Fourth part:** Work as for second part, but with Victoria, col. Ivoire.

**Fifth part:** Work as for first part, but in reverse, and working all sts with Victoria, col. Ivoire.

Join all 5 parts, adding 2 sts between all parts = 124 (130/138/144) sts. Work in Jacquard pat, foll chart.

**Note:** Work the 5 sts of Eyelet pat and 1 selvage st as far as armhole with Victoria, col. Cannelle; these sts do not appear on chart, AT SAME TIME, dec 1 st each side (6 sts in from each edge) on next row, then every 6th row 3 times more, every 4th row 5 times = 106 (112/120/126)

sts. Work even until piece measures 17 cm or 6⅝" from beg. Inc 1 st each side (6 sts in from each edge) on next row, then every 8th row 4 times, every 6th row 4 times = 124 (130/138/144) sts. Work even until piece measures 36 cm or 14⅛" from beg.

**Armhole shaping:** Bind off 5 sts at beg of next 2 rows, 4 sts at beg of next 2 rows, 3 sts at beg of next 2 (2/2/4) rows, 2 sts at beg of next 2 (4/6/6) rows, dec 1 st each side every other row 1 (1/2/1) times = 94 (96/98/100) sts. Work even until piece measures 46 (47/48/49) cm or 18⅛ (18½/18⅞/19¼)" from beg.

**Neck shaping:** Bind off center 14 sts and, working both sides at once, bind off from each neck edge 4 sts once, 3 sts once, 2 sts twice, dec 1 st at each neck edge every other row once, every 4th row twice. Work even until piece measures 56 (57/58/59) cm or 22 (22⅜/22⅞/23¼)" from beg. Bind off rem 26 (27/28/29) sts each side for shoulders.

### BACK

Work as for front, omitting neck shaping, until piece measures 50 (51/52/53) cm or 19⅝ (20/20½/20⅞)" from beg. Divide work in half and, working both sides at once with separate balls of yarn, work even until piece measures 56 (57/58/59) cm or 22 (22⅜/22⅞/23¼)" from beg. Bind off sts each side for shoulders. Place marker 21 sts from center opening on each side.

### SLEEVES

With 3½ mm needles and Victoria, col. Ivoire, cast on 49 (53/57/63) sts. Work 2 rows in garter st, then cont in Fancy st pat, beg with 1 selvage st and st 4 (2/4/1) of chart. Cont in pat as established until piece measures 7cm or 2¾" from beg. P 1 row on WS, inc 9 sts evenly across = 58 (62/66/72) sts. Change to 4 mm needles and, with col. Ivoire throughout, work as foll: With Victoria, 1 selvage st, 5 sts Eyelet pat; with Angora Super, 1 (3/5/8) sts in st st; with Victoria, 2 sts rev st st, 1 Double st, 8 sts rev st st, 1 Double st, 2 sts rev st st; with Angora Super, 16 sts in st st; with Victoria, 2 sts rev st st, 1 Double st, 8 sts rev st st, 1 Double st, 2 sts rev st st; with Angora Super, 1 (3/5/8) sts in st st; with Victoria, 5 sts Eyelet pat, 1 selvage st. Cont in pat as established, inc 1 st each side (working inc sts 6 sts in from each edge and into st st with Angora Super) every 6th row 13 times, every 4th row 5 times = 94 (98/102/108) sts. Work even until piece measures 32 cm or 12⅝" above Fancy st pat.

*(Continued on page 96)*

(Continued from page 95)

# surrey

**Cap shaping:** Bind off 3 sts at beg of next 2 rows, 2 sts at beg of next 6 (10/14/20) rows, dec 1 st each side every other row 23 (21/19/16) times, bind off 2 sts at beg of next 2 rows, 3 sts at beg of next 2 rows. Bind off rem 20 sts.

## TO MAKE UP/FINISHING

See tips on page 157.

With 3½ mm needles and Victoria col. Ivoire, pick up and K 122 (130/136/142) sts evenly along lower edge of front. K 1 row on WS. Bind off all sts. Work in same way along lower edge of back. Sew shoulder seams. Work in same way around neck edge, but pick up 106 sts (66 sts along front neck edge and 20 sts along each side of back neck). Sew side seams. Sew sleeve seams. Set sleeves into armholes. With crochet hook and Victoria col. Ivoire, work 1 row dc and 1 row crab st along lower edges of body and sleeves, and around neck, including opening at center back neck. Work a loop buttonhole at corner of back neck opening and sew button on opposite corner.

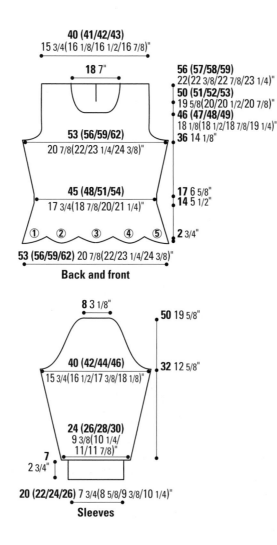

**Back and front**

40 (41/42/43)
15 3/4(16 1/8/16 1/2/16 7/8)"

18 7"

56 (57/58/59)
22(22 3/8/22 7/8/23 1/4)"

50 (51/52/53)
19 5/8(20/20 1/2/20 7/8)"

46 (47/48/49)
18 1/8(18 1/2/18 7/8/19 1/4)"

36 14 1/8"

53 (56/59/62)
20 7/8(22/23 1/4/24 3/8)"

45 (48/51/54)
17 3/4(18 7/8/20/21 1/4)"

17 6 5/8"
14 5 1/2"

① ② ③ ④ ⑤

2 3/4"

53 (56/59/62) 20 7/8(22/23 1/4/24 3/8)"

**Sleeves**

8 3 1/8"

50 19 5/8"

40 (42/44/46)
15 3/4(16 1/2/17 3/8/18 1/8)"

32 12 5/8"

24 (26/28/30)
9 3/8(10 1/4/11/11 7/8)"

7
2 3/4"

20 (22/24/26) 7 3/4(8 5/8/9 3/8/10 1/4)"

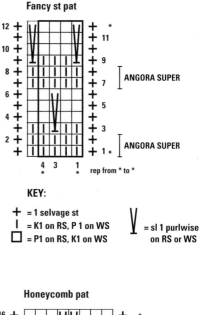

**Fancy st pat**

12 · · · · · · · · · · *
· · · · · · · 11
10 · · · · · · ·
· · · · · · · 9
8 · · · · · · · ] ANGORA SUPER
· · · · · · · 7
6 · · · · · · ·
· · · · · · · 5
4 · · · · · · ·
· · · · · · · 3
2 · · · · · · ·
· · · · · · · 1 * ] ANGORA SUPER

4 3 1
*            * rep from * to *

**KEY:**

+ = 1 selvage st

| = K1 on RS, P 1 on WS

□ = P1 on RS, K 1 on WS

V = sl 1 purlwise on RS or WS

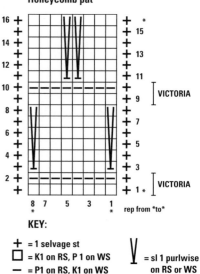

**Honeycomb pat**

16 · · · · · · · · · · *
· · · · · · · 15
14 · · · · · · ·
· · · · · · · 13
12 · · · · · · ·
· · · · · · · 11
10 · · — — — — · · ·
· · · · · · · 9 ] VICTORIA
8 · · · · · · ·
· · · · · · · 7
6 · · · · · · ·
· · · · · · · 5
4 · · · · · · ·
· · · · · · · 3
2 · · · · · · ·
· · · · · · · 1 * ] VICTORIA

8 7 5 3 1
*              * rep from *to*

**KEY:**

+ = 1 selvage st

□ = K1 on RS, P 1 on WS

— = P1 on RS, K 1 on WS

V = sl 1 purlwise on RS or WS

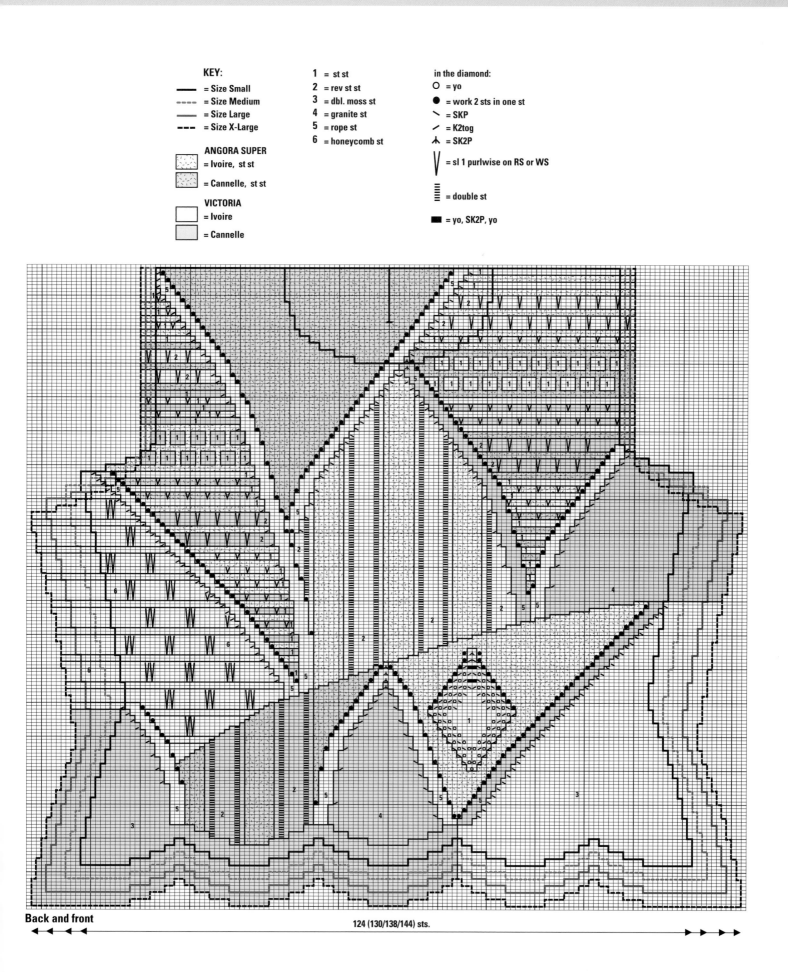

KEY:

—— = Size Small
----- = Size Medium
—— = Size Large
- - - = Size X-Large

**ANGORA SUPER**
= Ivoire, st st
= Cannelle, st st

**VICTORIA**
= Ivoire
= Cannelle

1 = st st
2 = rev st st
3 = dbl. moss st
4 = granite st
5 = rope st
6 = honeycomb st

in the diamond:
O = yo
● = work 2 sts in one st
╲ = SKP
╱ = K2tog
人 = SK2P

V = sl 1 purlwise on RS or WS

= double st

■ = yo, SK2P, yo

**Back and front**

124 (130/138/144) sts.

(Continued from page 16)

# glaucodot

**Neck shaping:** Bind off 5 (6/7/8) sts at RHS on next row, then cont to bind off at same edge every other row 3 sts once, 2 sts once, dec 1 st every other row twice. When piece measures 72 (73/74/75) cm or 28⅜ (28¾/29⅛/29½)" from beg, shape shoulder at LHS as for back. Sl sts from pocket holder to 5 mm needles and work in fancy rib for 14 cm or 5½". Change to 3½ mm needles and work in K1/P1 rib for 5 cm or 2". Bind off in rib.

## LEFT FRONT

Work as for right front, reversing shaping and placement of pocket.

## SLEEVES

With 3½ mm needles, cast on 61 (67/73/79) sts. Work in fancy K1/P1 rib for 5 cm or 2". Change to 5 mm needles and work in fancy rib, dec 21 (23/25/27) sts on first row = 40 (44/48/52) sts. Inc 1 st each side every 8th row 6 times, every 6th row 7 times = 66 (70/74/78) sts. Work even until piece measures 40 cm or 15¾" from beg.

**Cap shaping:** Bind off 3 sts at beg of next 0 (0/2/2) rows, 2 sts at beg of next 2 (4/2/4) rows, dec 1 st each side every other row 24 (22/21/20) times, bind off 2 sts at beg of next 0 (2/4/2) rows, 3 sts at beg of next 0 (0/0/2) rows. Bind off rem 14 sts.

## BELT

With 3½ mm needles, cast on 17 sts and work in fancy K1/P1 rib for 115 cm or 45⅜". Bind off in rib.

## BUTTONHOLE BAND

With 3½ mm needles, cast on 13 sts and work in fancy K1/P1 rib for 60 (61/62/63) cm or 23⅝ (24/24⅜/24¾)", making 5 buttonholes (by binding off 3 sts for each buttonhole, then casting on 3 sts over bound-off sts on foll row), with the first one at 2 (3/4/5) cm or ¾ (1⅛/1½/2)" from beg and the other 4 spaced 14 cm or 5½" apart.

Work a 2nd band in same way, omitting buttonholes.

## TO MAKE UP/FINISHING

See tips on page 157.

Sew buttonhole band along right front and button band along left front. Sew pocket seams. Sew shoulder seams. Set in sleeves. Sew side and sleeve seams. With 3½ mm needles, pick up and k 129 (133/137/141) sts around neck edge. Work in fancy K1/P1 rib, inc 1 st each side (at 2 sts in from edges) every 4th row 5 times, every other row 11 times = 161 (165/169/173) sts. Bind off. With crochet hook, work belt loops at each waist seam as foll: ch 16, then work 1 row sc. Sew on buttons.

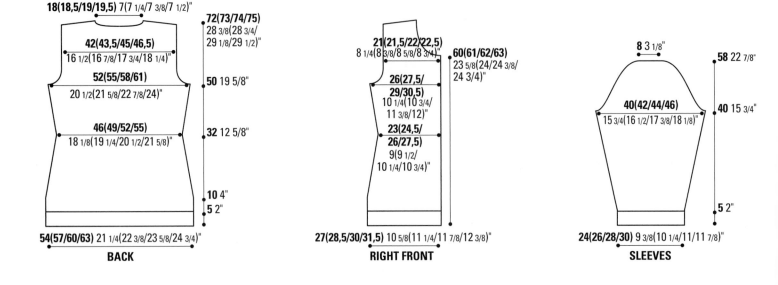

*(Continued from page 19)*

# sylvaine

### TO MAKE UP/FINISHING

See tips on page 157.

Sew one shoulder seam. With 3½ mm needles and

Mérinos Icône, pick up and K110 sts evenly around neck

edge and work in K1/P1 rib for 2 cm or ¾". Bind off in rib.

Sew 2nd shoulder and neckband seam. With center of

bound-off sts of sleeve at shoulder seam, sew top of

sleeve to front and back. Sew side and sleeve seams.

*(Continued on page 100)*

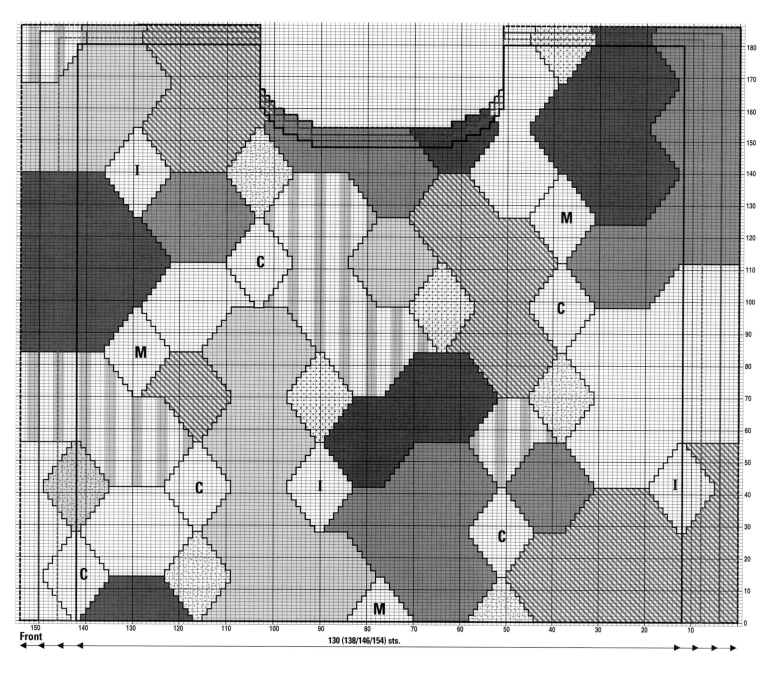

**Front**

130 (138/146/154) sts.

**KEY**

| | |
|---|---|
| ——— | = Size Small |
| ••••• | = Size Medium |
| ——— | = Size Large |
| - - - - | = Size X-Large |

**Fancy Pat**
**MÉRINOS**
= col. Miel
= col. Icône
= col. Chutney

**ANGORA SUPER**
= col. Miel
= col. Icône
= col. Chutney

**KANPUR**
**+ POMPONS col. Noir**
= col. Miel
= col. Icône
= col. Chutney

**KANPUR**
**M** = col. Miel
**I** = col. Icône
**C** = col. Chutney

*(Continued from page 99)*

# sylvaine

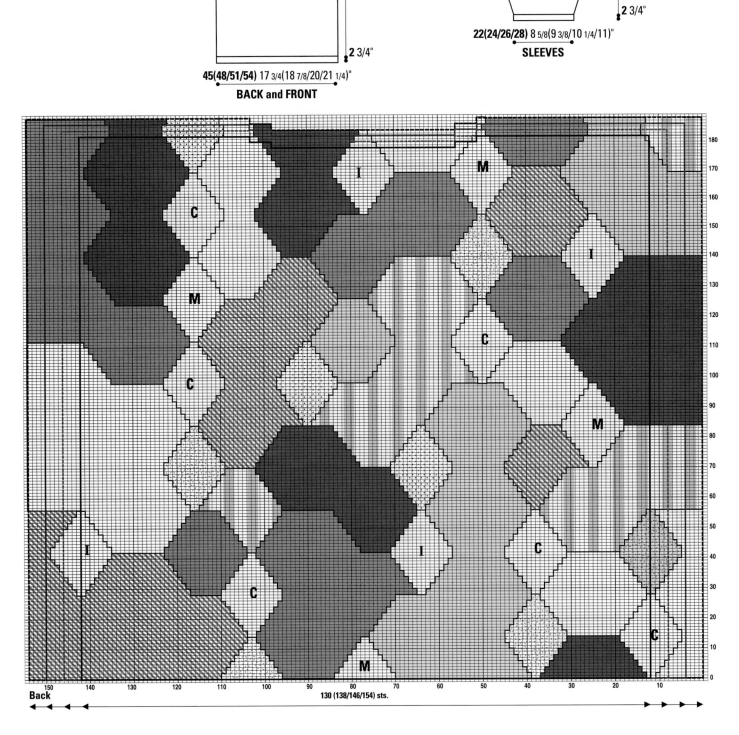

**18** 7"

**63(64/65/66)**
24 3/4(25 1/8/2
5 5/8/26)"

**52(53/54/55)**
20 1/2(20 7/8/
21 1/4/21 5/8)"

**2 3/4"**

**45(48/51/54)** 17 3/4(18 7/8/20/21 1/4)"
**BACK and FRONT**

**50(52/54/56)** 19 5/8(20 1/2/21 1/4/22)"
**46**
18 1/8"

**2 3/4"**

**22(24/26/28)** 8 5/8(9 3/8/10 1/4/11)"
**SLEEVES**

**Back**
150   140   130   120   110   100   90   80   70   60   50   40   30   20   10
**130 (138/146/154) sts.**

180
170
160
150
140
130
120
110
100
90
80
70
60
50
40
30
20
10
0

**Fancy pat**
The WS rows do not appear on chart.
Work these rows as k the knit sts and p the purl sts.

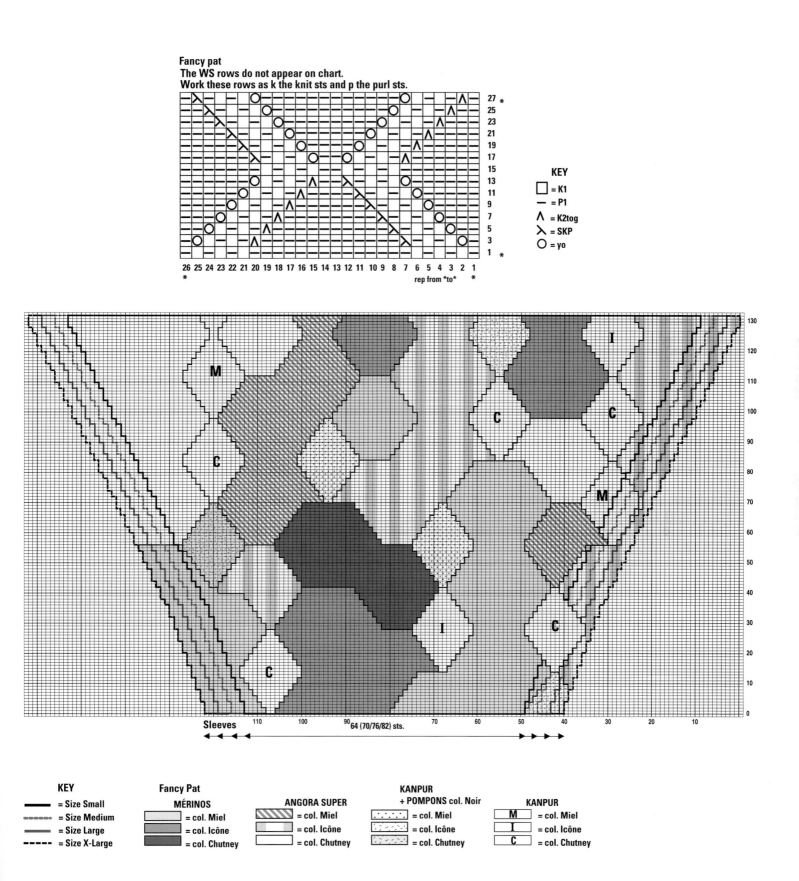

**KEY**

☐ = K1

— = P1

∧ = K2tog

✕ = SKP

○ = yo

26 25 24 23 22 21 20 19 18 17 16 15 14 13 12 11 10 9 8 7 6 5 4 3 2 1

\*                                                                    rep from *to*     \*

**Sleeves**

64 (70/76/82) sts.

**KEY**

—— = Size Small

∙∙∙∙∙∙ = Size Medium

—— = Size Large

– – – – = Size X-Large

**Fancy Pat**
**MÉRINOS**

= col. Miel

= col. Icône

= col. Chutney

**ANGORA SUPER**

= col. Miel

= col. Icône

= col. Chutney

**KANPUR**
**+ POMPONS** col. Noir

= col. Miel

= col. Icône

= col. Chutney

**KANPUR**

M = col. Miel

I = col. Icône

C = col. Chutney

*(Continued from page 20)*

# passy

### TO MAKE UP/FINISHING

See tips on page 157.

Sew side seams, (leaving 4 cm or 1½" unsewn at 29 (30/31/32) cm or 11⅜ (11⅞/12¼/12⅝)" from lower edge of right side for belt loop opening).

Sew shoulder seams. Set in sleeves. Sew side and sleeve seams.

Sew on front bands, then belts.

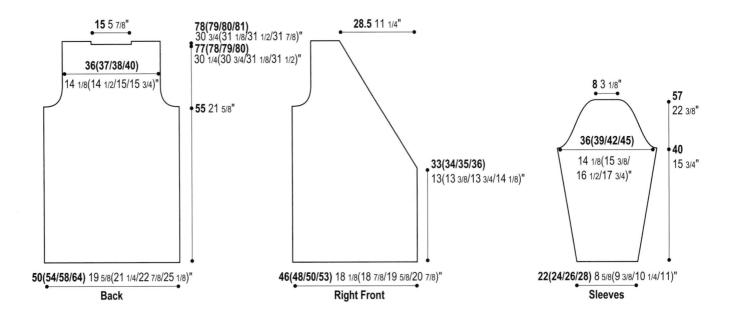

**15** 5 7/8"

**78(79/80/81)**
30 3/4(31 1/8/31 1/2/31 7/8)"
**77(78/79/80)**
30 1/4(30 3/4/31 1/8/31 1/2)"

**28.5** 11 1/4"

**36(37/38/40)**
14 1/8(14 1/2/15/15 3/4)"

**55** 21 5/8"

**33(34/35/36)**
13(13 3/8/13 3/4/14 1/8)"

**50(54/58/64)** 19 5/8(21 1/4/22 7/8/25 1/8)"
**Back**

**46(48/50/53)** 18 1/8(18 7/8/19 5/8/20 7/8)"
**Right Front**

**8** 3 1/8"

**57** 22 3/8"

**36(39/42/45)**
14 1/8(15 3/8/16 1/2/17 3/4)"

**40** 15 3/4"

**22(24/26/28)** 8 5/8(9 3/8/10 1/4/11)"
**Sleeves**

*(Continued from page 25)*

# gavaudun

### BACK

With 3½ mm needles, cast on 125 (133/141) sts and work as foll: 1 selvage, 24 (28/32) sts in fancy pat no. 1, beg with P 4 (3/2) before the 1st 2 K sts, 2 sts cable, 3 sts reverse st st, 65 sts fancy pat no. 2 , beg with the 1st st of chart, 3 sts reverse st st, 2 sts cable, 24 (28/32) sts fancy pat no. 1, beg with P3 before the 1st 2 K sts, 1 selvage. Cont in pats as established, dec 1 st in each group of P sts of fancy pat no. 1 and in P3 each side of fancy pat no. 2, every 16th row twice = 105 (109/113) sts. Work even until piece measures 15 cm or 5⅞" from beg. Inc 1 st (by P 2 sts in one) in each group of P sts as before, on next row, then every 16th row once more = 125 (133/141) sts. Work even until piece measures 29 cm or 11⅜" from beg, ending with a WS row.

**Armhole shaping:** Bind off 4 sts at beg of next 2 rows, 3 sts at beg of next 4 rows, 2 sts at beg of next 4 (6/8) rows, dec 1 st each end every other row 2 (3/4) times = 93 (95/97) sts. Work even until piece measures 47 (48/49) cm or 18½ (8⅞/19¼)" from beg.

**Shoulder and neck shaping:** Bind off 8 (9/9) sts at beg of next 2 (6/4) rows, 9 (0/10) sts at beg of next 4 (0/2) rows, AT THE SAME TIME, when piece measures 48 (49/50) cm or 18⅞ (19¼/19⅝)" from beg, bind off center 13 sts for neck and working both sides at same time, bind off from each neck edge 14 sts once.

### RIGHT FRONT

With 3½ mm needles, cast on 3 sts. Work in fancy pat no. 2, beg with the 4th st of chart, and inc 1 st at RHS every other row 10 times, AT THE SAME TIME, cast on at LHS 4 sts once, 5 sts twice, 6 sts once, 29 (33/37) sts once (Note: work fancy pat no. 2 over the first 32 sts, then 3 sts in reverse st st, 2 sts cable, 24 (28/32) sts fancy pat no. 1, beg with P3 before the first K sts, ending with 1 selvage. After all incs have been worked, work decs and incs in fancy pat no. 1 and armholes decs at LHS as for back.) When piece measures 33 (34/35) cm or 13 (13⅜/13¾)" from beg, end with a WS row and work as foll:

**Neck shaping:** Bind off from RHS 2 sts 10 times. Work even until piece measures 49 (50/51) cm or 19¼ (19⅝/20)" from beg. Shape shoulder at LHS as for back.

### LEFT FRONT

Work to correspond to right front, beg fancy pat no. 2 with 5th st of chart and reversing shaping.

### TO MAKE UP/FINISHING

See tips on page 157.

Sew shoulder seams. With RS facing and 3½ mm needles, pick up 28 sts from point A to B (see schematics) on right front, 40 sts from B to C, 40 sts along back neck, 40 sts from C to B and 28 sts from B to A = 176 sts. K one row on WS. Bind off all sts. Sew side seams. With RS facing and 3½ mm crochet hook, work 2 rows dc and 1 row crab st along outside edge of vest, working 7 button loops on 2nd dc row along right front (by ch 2, sk 2 sts), with the first one just below neck shaping, the last at end of point at lower edge, and 5 others spaced evenly between. Work crochet edging around each armhole in same way. Sew on buttons.

*(Continued from page 103)*

# gavaudun

**Fancy Pat N°1**

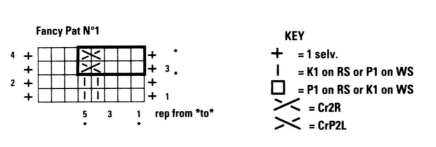

**KEY**

+ = 1 selv.

| = K1 on RS or P1 on WS

□ = P1 on RS or K1 on WS

⤬ = Cr2R

⤫ = CrP2L

**Fancy Pat N°2 (Rosebud Pat)**

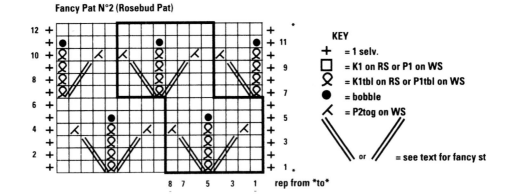

**KEY**

+ = 1 selv.

□ = K1 on RS or P1 on WS

Ⴍ = K1tbl on RS or P1tbl on WS

● = bobble

⤵ = P2tog on WS

\\\ or /// = see text for fancy st

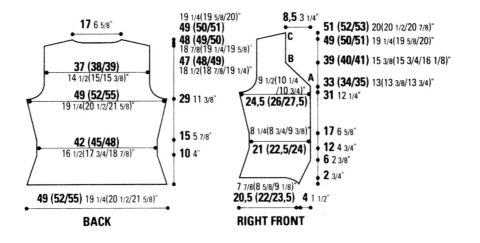

**BACK**

**RIGHT FRONT**

*(Continued from page 26)*

# artouste

**Key**

chain with col. Noir

chain with col. Blanc

*(Continued from page 29)*

# saumur

## FRONT

With 4 mm needles, cast on 119 (127/133/141) sts. Work in garter st for 1,5 cm or ½", then work as foll: 1 selvage sts, 5 sts Fancy st no. 2, 4 (5/6/6) sts rev st st, [2 sts Twist st pat, 3 (3/3/4) sts rev st st] twice, 2 sts Twist st pat, [6 (7/8/9] sts rev st st, 1 Double st] twice, 1 (2/2/2) sts rev st st, 45 sts Fancy st no. 3, 1 (2/2/2) sts rev st st, [1 Double st, 6 (7/8/9) sts rev st st] twice, [2 sts Twist st pat, 3 (3/3/4) sts rev st st] twice, 2 sts Twist st pat, 4 (5/6/6) sts rev st st, 5 sts Fancy st no. 1, 1 selvage st. Cont in pat as established, dec 1 st each side (working decs 6 sts in from each edge) every 12th row once, every 10th row 3 times = 111 (119/125/133) sts. Work even until piece measures 16 cm or 6¼" above garter st. Inc 1 st each side (6 sts in from each edge) on next row, then every 14th row once, every 12th row twice = 119 (127/133/141) sts. Work even until piece measures 31 cm or 12¼" above garter st.

**Armhole shaping:** Bind off 4 sts at beg of next 2 rows, 3 sts at beg of next 2 (4/4/6) rows, 2 sts at beg of next 4 (4/6/6) rows, dec 1 st each side every other row twice = 93 (95/97/99) sts. Work even until piece measures 43 (44/45/46) cm or 16⅞ (17⅜/17¾/18⅛)" above garter st.

**Neck shaping:** Bind off center 13 sts for back neck and working both sides at once, bind off from each neck edge 4 sts once, 3 sts once, 2 sts 3 times, dec 1 st each neck edge every other row twice. Work even until piece measures 50 (51/52/53) cm or 19⅝ (20/20½/20⅞)" above garter st.

**Shoulder shaping:** Bind off from each shoulder edge 8 sts 2 (1/0/0) times, 9 sts 1 (2/3/2) times, 10 sts 0 (0/0/1) times.

## BACK

Begin in 2 parts.

**First Part:** With 4 mm needles, cast on 46 (50/53/57) sts. Work in garter st for 1.5 cm or ½", then cont as foll: 4 sts garter st, Cr2L (k 2nd st on LH needle, passing behind 1st st, then k 1st st), Cr3L, 1 (2/2/2) sts rev st st, [1 Double st, 6 (7/8/9) sts rev st st] twice, [2 sts Twist st pat, 3 (3/3/4) sts rev st st] twice, 2 sts Twist st pat, 4 (5/6/6) sts rev st st, 5 sts Fancy st no. 1, 1 selvage st. Cont in pat as established, inc at RHS (4 sts in from edge, working inc sts into Fancy st. no. 3) every other row: 2 sts once, 1 st 11 times. Work even until piece measures 8 cm or 3⅛" above garter st. Place sts on holder.

**Second Part:** Work as for first part, but in reverse. Reverse pat placement as foll: 1 selvage st, 5 sts Fancy st no. 2, 4 (5/6/6) sts rev st st, 2 sts Twist st pat, [3 (3/3/4) sts rev st st, 2 st Twist st pat] twice, [6 (7/8/9) sts rev st st, 1 Double st] twice, 1 (2/2/2) sts rev st st, Cr5L (sl 5 Fancy Purl sts to RH needle letting yos drop, then sl sts back to LH needle; sl 3 sts to cn and hold to front of work, k2, k3 from cn), 4 sts garter st.

**Note:** Work same decs at side edge (at LHS for first part, and at RHS for second part) as for front.

Pick up sts of first part from holder and cont on all sts, inc 1 st at center, and cont working decs, inc and armhole shaping at side edges as for back. Work even until piece measures 38 (39/40/41) cm or 15 (15⅜/15¾/16⅛)" above garter st.

**Neck shaping:** Bind off center st and, working both sides at once, dec 1 st at each neck edge every other row 21 times, AT THE SAME TIME, when piece measures 50 (51/52/53) cm or 19⅝ (20/20½/20⅞)" above garter st, shape shoulder as for front.

## TO MAKE UP/FINISHING

See tips on page 157.

Sew one shoulder seam. With 4 mm needles, pick up and k136 sts around neck edge (64 sts on front and 36 sts on each back neck edge). K 1 row on WS. Bind off all sts. With crochet hook, work 1 row dc and 1 row crab st around neck. With 4 mm needles, pick up and k 104 (108/112/116) sts around armhole edge. K 1 row on WS. Bind off all sts. With crochet hook, work 1 row dc and 1 row crab st. Sew rem shoulder seam. Sew side seams.

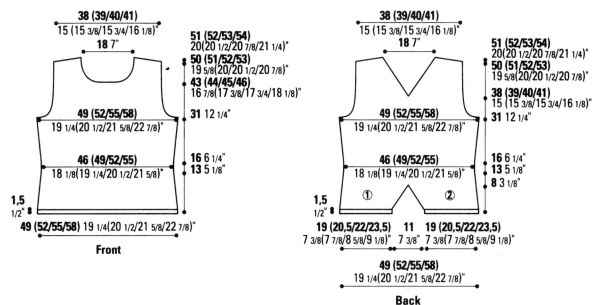

**38 (39/40/41)**
15 (15 3/8/15 3/4/16 1/8)"

**18** 7"

**51 (52/53/54)**
20(20 1/2/20 7/8/21 1/4)"

**50 (51/52/53)**
19 5/8(20/20 1/2/20 7/8)"

**43 (44/45/46)**
16 7/8(17 3/8/17 3/4/18 1/8)"

**49 (52/55/58)**
19 1/4(20 1/2/21 5/8/22 7/8)"

**31** 12 1/4"

**46 (49/52/55)**
18 1/8(19 1/4/20 1/2/21 5/8)"

**16** 6 1/4"
**13** 5 1/8"

**1,5**
1/2" **8**

**49 (52/55/58)** 19 1/4(20 1/2/21 5/8/22 7/8)"

**Front**

**38 (39/40/41)**
15 (15 3/8/15 3/4/16 1/8)"

**18** 7"

**51 (52/53/54)**
20(20 1/2/20 7/8/21 1/4)"

**50 (51/52/53)**
19 5/8(20/20 1/2/20 7/8)"

**38 (39/40/41)**
15 (15 3/8/15 3/4/16 1/8)"

**49 (52/55/58)**
19 1/4(20 1/2/21 5/8/22 7/8)"

**31** 12 1/4"

**46 (49/52/55)**
18 1/8(19 1/4/20 1/2/21 5/8)"

**16** 6 1/4"
**13** 5 1/8"
**8** 3 1/8"

**1,5**
1/2" **8**

① ②

**19 (20,5/22/23,5)** **11** **19 (20,5/22/23,5)**
7 3/8(7 7/8/8 5/8/9 1/8)" 7 3/8" 7 3/8(7 7/8/8 5/8/9 1/8)"

**49 (52/55/58)**
19 1/4(20 1/2/21 5/8/22 7/8)"

**Back**

### Fancy st no. 1

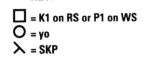

rep from *to*

**KEY:**

□ = K1 on RS or P1 on WS
○ = yo
⅄ = SKP

### Fancy st no. 2

rep from *to*

**KEY:**

□ = K1 on RS or P1 on WS
○ = yo
⅄ = K2tog

### Fancy st no. 3

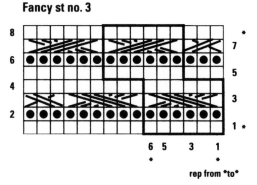

rep from *to*

**KEY:**

□ = K1 on RS or P1 on WS
● = fancy purl st
= Cr3R
= Cr3L
= Cr6R
= Cr6L

(Continued from page 30)

# jullouville

## LEFT FRONT

Work as for right front, but in reverse.

## SLEEVES

With 3½ mm needles and Victoria, cast on 60 (64/70) sts. Work in Sl St pat for 2.5 cm or ⅞", then P 1 row on WS, dec 5 sts evenly across = 55 (59/65) sts. Work in Fancy pat, beg with 1 selvage st, then st 8 (6/3) of chart, inc 1 st each side (working inc into pat) every 8th row 17 times = 89 (93/99) sts. Work even until piece measures 38 cm or 15" above Sl St pat.

**Cap shaping:** Bind off 3 sts at beg of next 2 rows, 2 sts at beg of next 0 (0/6) rows, dec 1 st each side every other row 25 (29/26) times, every 4th row 2 (0/0) times, bind off 2 sts at beg of next 2 rows, 3 sts at beg of next 2 rows. Bind off rem 19 sts.

## TO MAKE UP/FINISHING

See tips on page 157.

On the fronts, back and sleeves, sew paillettes at each intersection of pat (see photo). Sew shoulder seams. With 3½ mm needles and Victoria, pick up and K 172 (174/176) sts along right front edge as foll: 58 (60/62) sts from A to B (see schematics), 62 sts from B to C, 28 sts from C to D and 24 sts to center back neck. Purl 1 row on WS, then work in Sl St pat. Work 3 buttonholes on 6th row (by binding off 2 sts for each buttonhole on first row, and castng on 2 sts over bound-off sts on foll row), with the first buttonhole 17 (18/19) sts from edge, and 2 others spaced 17 (18/19) sts apart. When band measures 2.5 cm or ⅞", bind off all sts in pat.

Work in same way on left front and back, omitting buttonholes. Set in sleeves. Sew side and sleeve seams. Sew on buttons.

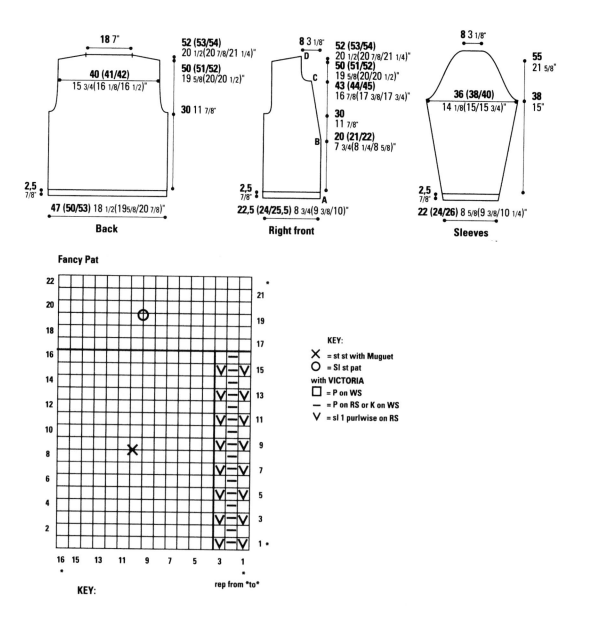

**Back**

18 7"

52 (53/54) 20 1/2(20 7/8/21 1/4)"

40 (41/42) 15 3/4(16 1/8/16 1/2)"

50 (51/52) 19 5/8(20/20 1/2)"

30 11 7/8"

2,5 7/8"

47 (50/53) 18 1/2(195/8/20 7/8)"

**Right front**

8 3 1/8"

52 (53/54) 20 1/2(20 7/8/21 1/4)"

50 (51/52) 19 5/8(20/20 1/2)"

43 (44/45) 16 7/8(17 3/8/17 3/4)"

30 11 7/8"

20 (21/22) 7 3/4(8 1/4/8 5/8)"

2,5 7/8"

22,5 (24/25,5) 8 3/4(9 3/8/10)"

**Sleeves**

8 3 1/8"

55 21 5/8"

36 (38/40) 14 1/8(15/15 3/4)"

38 15"

2,5 7/8"

22 (24/26) 8 5/8(9 3/8/10 1/4)"

**Fancy Pat**

**KEY:**
X = st st with Muguet
O = Sl st pat
**with VICTORIA**
□ = P on WS
— = P on RS or K on WS
V = sl 1 purlwise on RS

rep from *to*

KEY:

*(Continued from page 33)*

# bicolore

### SLEEVES

With col. Soufre and 3 mm needles, cast on 72 (76/82/86) sts. Work in K1/P1 twisted rib for 3 cm or 1⅛". P one row on WS, inc 10 sts evenly across = 82 (86/92/96) sts. Change to 3½ mm needles and work in st st, inc 1 st each side every 4th row 3 times, every other row 5 times = 98 (102/108/112) sts. Work even until piece measures 8 cm or 3⅛" above rib.

**Cap shaping:** Bind off 3 sts at beg of next 2 rows, 2 sts at beg of next 16 (20/26/30) rows, dec 1 st each side every other row 15 (13/10/8) times, bind off 2 sts at beg of next 2 rows, 3 sts at beg of next 2 rows. Bind off rem 20 sts.

### TO MAKE UP/FINISHING

See tips on page 157.

With col. Noir, embroider fronts foll diagram. Sew shoulder seams. Set in sleeves. Sew side and sleeve seams. With RS facing, Soufre and 3 mm needles, pick up and K 192 (196/198/202) sts along right front edge and one half back neck (96/100/102/106) sts from A to B (see schematics), 70 sts from B to C and 26 sts along one half back neck). Work in K1/P1 twisted rib, beg with K2, for 2 cm or ¾". Bind off sts in rib. **Note:** On the 4th row, make 6 buttonholes (binding off 3 sts for each buttonhole, then cast on 3 sts over bound-off sts on foll row) with the first 3 sts from lower edge, and the other 5 spaced 15 (16/16/17) sts apart. Along left front, pick up and K 193 (197/199/203) sts along one half back neck and left front edge (27 sts along 2nd half back neck, 70 sts from C to B and 96/100/102/106) sts from B to A). Work in K1/P1 twisted rib, beg with P1, for 2 cm or ¾". Bind off in rib. Sew ends of band tog at center back neck. Sew on buttons.

### TOP

### BACK

With col. Noir and 3 mm needles, cast on 112 (120/126/134) sts. Work in K1/P1 twisted rib for 3 cm or 1⅛". Change to 3½ mm needles and work in st st, dec 1 st each side every 20th row once, every 18th row once = 108 (116/122/130) sts. Work even until piece measures 15 cm or 5⅞" above rib. Inc 1 st each side on next row, then every 12th row 3 times, every 10th row once = 118 (126/132/140) sts. Work even until piece measures 33 cm or 13" above rib.

**Armhole shaping:** Bind off 5 sts at beg of next 2 (2/4/4) rows, 4 sts at beg of next 4 (4/2/4) rows, 3 sts at beg of next 2 (4/4/4) rows, 2 sts at beg of next 2 (2/4/2) rows, dec 1 st each side every other row 2 (2/1/2) times = 78 (80/82/84) sts. Work even until piece measures 47 (48/49/50) cm or 18½ (18⅞/19¼/19⅝)" above rib.

**Neck shaping:** Bind off center 18 sts for back neck and working both sides at once, bind off from each neck edge 5 sts once, 4 sts once, 3 sts once, 2 sts twice. Work even until piece measures 51 (52/53/54) cm or 20 (20½/20⅞/21¼)"above rib. Bind off rem 14 (15/16/17) sts each side for shoulders.

### FRONT

Work as for back until piece measures 35 (36/37/38) cm or 13¾ (14⅛/14½/15)" above rib.

**Neck shaping:** Bind off center 14 sts for back neck and, working both sides at once, bind off from each neck edge 4 sts once, 3 sts twice, 2 sts 3 times, 1 st twice. Work even until piece measures 51 (52/53/54) cm or 20 (20½/20⅞/21¼)" above rib. Bind off rem 14 (15/16/17) sts each side for shoulders.

### TO MAKE UP/FINISHING

See tips on page 157.

With col. Soufre, embroider fronts foll diagram. Sew one shoulder seam. With RS facing, 3 mm needles and col. Noir, pick up and K184 sts around neck edge (66 sts on back and 118 sts on front). Work in K1/P1 twisted rib for 2 cm or ¾". Bind off in rib. Sew rem shoulder and neckband seam. With RS facing, size 3 mm needles and col. Noir, pick up and K 124 (130/134/140) sts evenly around each armhole edge and work as for neckband. Sew side seams, including armhole bands.

*(Continued on page 110)*

*(Continued from page 109)*

# bicolore

**30 (31/32/33)** 11 7/8(12 1/4/12 5/8/13)"

**20** 7 3/4"

**51 (52/53/54)**
20(20 1/2/20 7/8/21 1/4)"

**47 (48/49/50)**
18 1/2(18 7/8/19 1/4/19 5/8)"

**35 (36/37/38)**
13 3/4(14 1/8/14 1/2/15)"

**33** 13"

**46 (49/52/55)**
18 1/8(19 1/4/20 1/2/21 5/8)"

**42 (45/48/51)**
16 1/2(17 3/4/18 7/8/20)"

**15** 5 7/8"

**12** 4 3/4"

**3** 1 1/8"

**44 (47/50/53)** 17 3/8(18 1/2/19 5/8/20 7/8)"
**Back and Front**

**KEY:**

━━━ = Size Small

••••• = Size Medium

──── = Size Large

─ ─ ─ = Size X-Large

**Embroidery in color Soufre**

∼ = chain st

◯ = detached chain st

**Top**

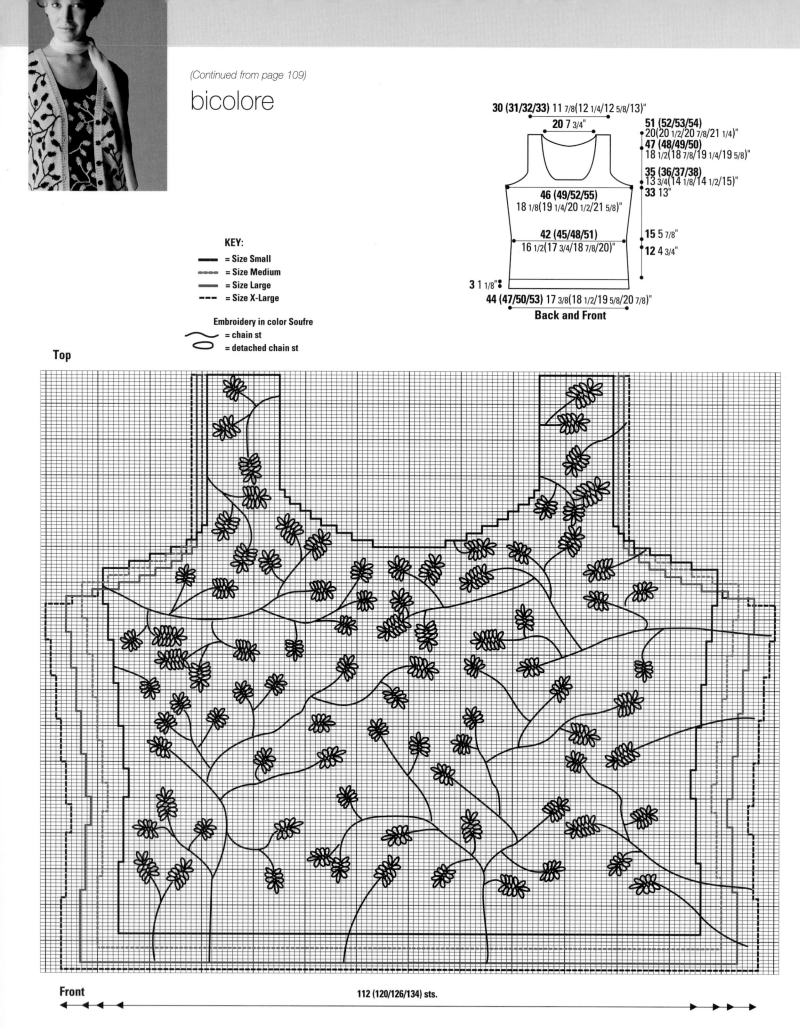

**Front**

**112 (120/126/134) sts.**

# Cardigan

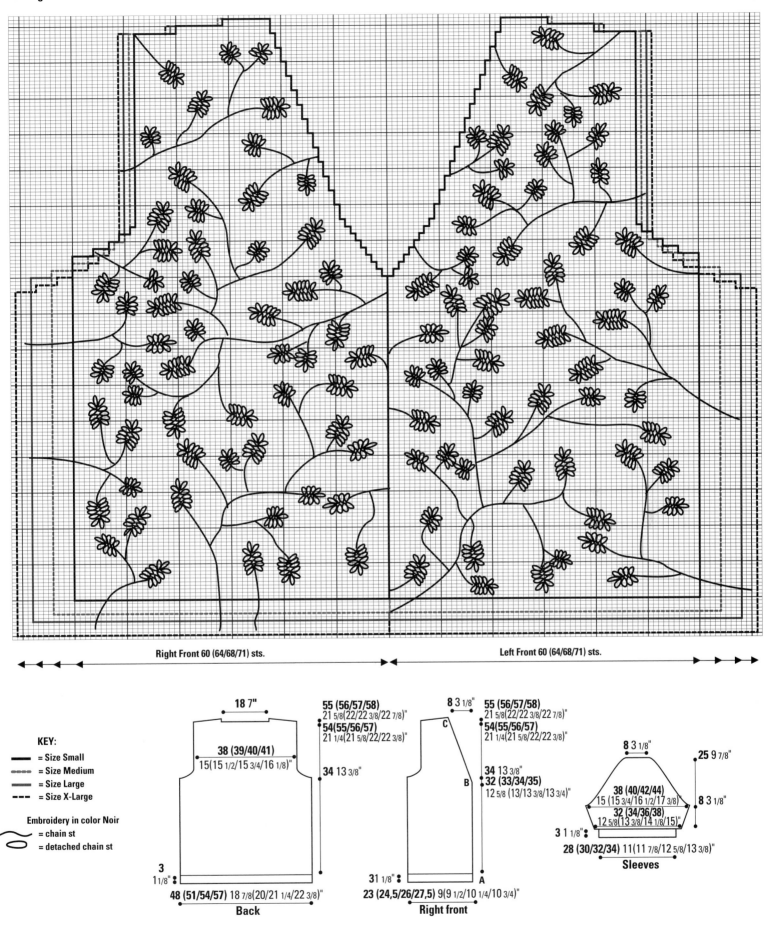

**KEY:**

— = Size Small

---- = Size Medium

━ = Size Large

--- = Size X-Large

Embroidery in color Noir

∼ = chain st

∽ = detached chain st

Right Front 60 (64/68/71) sts.

Left Front 60 (64/68/71) sts.

**18** 7"

**55 (56/57/58)** 21 5/8(22/22 3/8/22 7/8)"

**54(55/56/57)** 21 1/4 (21 5/8/22/22 3/8)"

**38 (39/40/41)** 15(15 1/2/15 3/4/16 1/8)"

**34** 13 3/8"

**3** 1/8"

**48 (51/54/57)** 18 7/8(20/21 1/4/22 3/8)"

**Back**

**8** 3 1/8"

C

**55 (56/57/58)** 21 5/8(22/22 3/8/22 7/8)"

**54(55/56/57)** 21 1/4 (21 5/8/22/22 3/8)"

B

**34** 13 3/8"

**32 (33/34/35)** 12 5/8 (13/13 3/8/13 3/4)"

**31** 1/8"

**23 (24,5/26/27,5)** 9(9 1/2/10 1/4/10 3/4)"

A

**Right front**

**8** 3 1/8"

**25** 9 7/8"

**38 (40/42/44)** 15 (15 3/4/16 1/2/17 3/8)"

**8** 3 1/8"

**32 (34/36/38)** 12 5/8(13 3/8/14 1/8/15)"

**3** 1 1/8"

**28 (30/32/34)** 11(11 7/8/12 5/8/13 3/8)"

**Sleeves**

(Continued from page 34)

# prairie

## BACK

Work as for front until piece measures 33 (34/35/36) cm or 13 (13⅜/13¾/14⅛)" above garter st. Work braid pat over center 37 sts. When piece measures 45 (46/47/48) cm or 17¾ (18⅛/18½/18⅞)" above garter st, work as foll:

**Neck shaping:** Divide work in half and working both sides at once, dec every other row at each neck edge (5 sts in from edge) as foll: work 2 rows even, then K3tog twice on next row, then every other row: K3tog and K2tog on same row 12 times. When piece measures 52 (53/54/55) cm or 20½ (20⅞/21¼/21⅝)" above garter st, bind off rem 19 (20/22/23) sts each side for shoulders.

## TO MAKE UP/FINISHING

See tips on page 157.

Sew shoulder seams. With 3½ mm needles, pick up and K 110 (116/122/128) sts evenly around each armhole edge. K one row on WS, then bind off all sts. Beg at center front, pick up 54 sts along one side of front neck and 36 sts along one side of back neck = 90 sts. K one row and bind off. Work in same way along other side of neck. Sew side seams. With 3 mm crochet hook, work 1 row dc and 1 row crab st around each armhole and around neck.

**Fancy Pat**

19  17  15  13  11  9  7  5  3  1
rep from *to*

**KEY:**
+ = 1 selvage
I = K1 on RS or P1 on WS
— = K1 on WS
O = yo
⟍ = K2tog
⋏ = K3tog

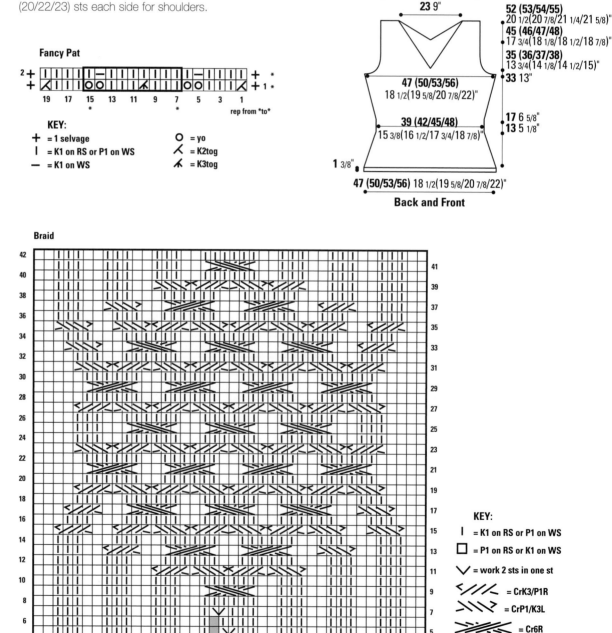

36 (37/38/39) 14 1/8(14 1/2/15/15 3/8)"
23 9"
52 (53/54/55) 20 1/2(20 7/8/21 1/4/21 5/8)"
45 (46/47/48) 17 3/4(18 1/8/18 1/2/18 7/8)"
35 (36/37/38) 13 3/4(14 1/8/14 1/2/15)"
33 13"
47 (50/53/56) 18 1/2(19 5/8/20 7/8/22)"
17 6 5/8"
13 5 1/8"
39 (42/45/48) 15 3/8(16 1/2/17 3/4/18 7/8)"
1 3/8"
47 (50/53/56) 18 1/2(19 5/8/20 7/8/22)"

**Back and Front**

**Braid**

**KEY:**
I = K1 on RS or P1 on WS
☐ = P1 on RS or K1 on WS
∨ = work 2 sts in one st
⟋⟋⟋ = CrK3/P1R
⟍⟍⟍ = CrP1/K3L
⟋⟋ = Cr6R
⟍⟍ = Cr6L
▨ = st which does not exist

*(Continued from page 39)*

# angelot

### TO MAKE UP/FINISHING

See tips on page 157.

Sew shoulder seams. Set in sleeves. Sew side and sleeve seams.

Along coat and lower edge of sleeves, work 2 rows dc, then along lower edge of body work 1 row more dc, along fronts and lower edge of sleeves work 1 row shell pat. Sew snap to top of neck.

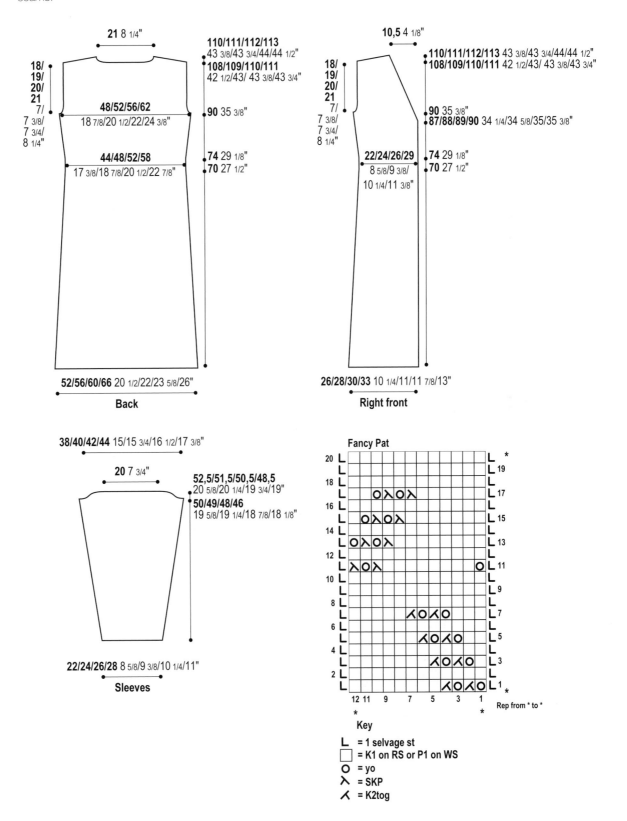

**Back**

21 8 1/4"

110/111/112/113 43 3/8/43 3/4/44/44 1/2"
108/109/110/111 42 1/2/43/ 43 3/8/43 3/4"

18/19/20/21 7/ 7 3/8/ 7 3/4/ 8 1/4"

48/52/56/62 18 7/8/20 1/2/22/24 3/8"

90 35 3/8"

44/48/52/58 17 3/8/18 7/8/20 1/2/22 7/8"

74 29 1/8"
70 27 1/2"

52/56/60/66 20 1/2/22/23 5/8/26"

**Right front**

10,5 4 1/8"

110/111/112/113 43 3/8/43 3/4/44/44 1/2"
108/109/110/111 42 1/2/43/ 43 3/8/43 3/4"

18/19/20/21 7/ 7 3/8/ 7 3/4/ 8 1/4"

90 35 3/8"
87/88/89/90 34 1/4/34 5/8/35/35 3/8"

22/24/26/29 8 5/8/9 3/8/ 10 1/4/11 3/8"

74 29 1/8"
70 27 1/2"

26/28/30/33 10 1/4/11/11 7/8/13"

**Sleeves**

38/40/42/44 15/15 3/4/16 1/2/17 3/8"

20 7 3/4"

52,5/51,5/50,5/48,5 20 5/8/20 1/4/19 3/4/19"
50/49/48/46 19 5/8/19 1/4/18 7/8/18 1/8"

22/24/26/28 8 5/8/9 3/8/10 1/4/11"

**Fancy Pat**

Rep from * to *

### Key

L = 1 selvage st
☐ = K1 on RS or P1 on WS
O = yo
人 = SKP
人 = K2tog

*(Continued from page 40)*

# aglanet

### SLEEVES

With size 5½ mm needles and Bois de rose, cast on 36 (38/40/42) sts and work in fancy rib, beg and end with 1 selvage st and 3rd (2nd/1st/4th) st of chart.

Work even until piece measures 11 cm or 4⅜" from beg. Cont in st st with 6 mm needles, inc 1 st each side at 2 sts from edge (using M1 inc), every 8th (6th/6th/4th) row 1 (7/3/15) times, every 6th (4th/4th/0) rows 8 (4/10/0) times = 54 (60/66/72) sts.

Work even until piece measures 42 cm or 16½" from beg.

**Cap shaping:** Bind off 2 (3/3/3) sts at beg of next 2 rows. Cont to dec as foll:

**Small:** Dec sts at 3 sts from edge every 2nd row: 1 st 17 times, bind off 3 sts at beg of next 2 rows.

**Medium:** Dec sts at 3 sts from edge every 2nd row: 2 sts 2 times, 1 st 15 times, bind off 3 sts at beg of next 2 rows.

**Large:** Dec sts at 3 sts from edge every 2nd row: 2 sts 2 times, 1 st 12 times, 2 sts 3 times, bind off 3 sts at beg of next 2 rows.

**X-Large:** Dec sts at 3 sts from edge every 2nd row: 2 sts 2 times, 1 st 9 times, 2 sts 6 times, bind off 3 sts at beg of next 2 rows.

Bind off rem 10 sts.

### TO MAKE UP/FINISHING

See tips on page 157.

Sew one shoulder seam.

**Collar:** With 5½ mm needles and Bois de rose, pick up 80 sts around neck (34 sts along back, 46 sts along front), and work as foll : K 1 row on WS, then work 20 rows in K2/P2 rib, beg and end with 1 selvage st, 25 rows in K2/P2 fancy rib, beg with 1 selvage st and the 1st st of chart, end with 1 selvage st, then bind off all sts.

Sew 2nd shoulder and collar seam.

Set in sleeves. Sew side and sleeve seams.

**Embroidery:** With Flamenco work satin st in fancy rib, inserting needle into the eyelets (see photo).

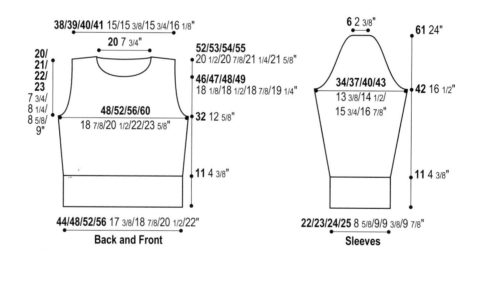

**Back and Front**

**Sleeves**

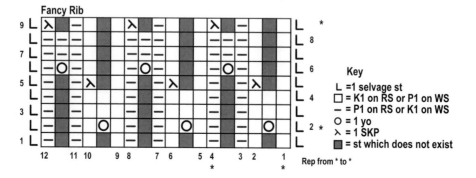

Fancy Rib

Key
L =1 selvage st
□ = K1 on RS or P1 on WS
– = P1 on RS or K1 on WS
O = 1 yo
⋋ = 1 SKP
■ = st which does not exist
Rep from * to *

*(Continued from page 43)*

# cachemire rayé

**Neck shaping:** Bind off center 10 sts and working both sides at same time, bind off from each neck edge, 3 sts twice, 2 sts twice, dec 1 st every 2nd row 4 times, every 4th row twice.

When piece measures 53 (55/57/59) cm or 20⅞ (21⅝/22⅝/23¼)" from beg, shape shoulders as for back.

### SLEEVES

With smaller needles and Fauve, cast on 94 (102/106/114) sts and work 8 rows in striped K2/P2 rib, beg with P1 (K2/K2/K2) and cont in striped st st no. 1, dec 22 (24/22/24) sts evenly spaced across 1st row = 72 (78/84/90) sts. Cont to inc 1 st each side every 2nd row 3 (4/5/6) times = 78 (86/94/102) sts. Work even until piece measures 4 cm or 1½" from beg.

**Cap shaping:** Bind off 3 sts at beg of next 2 (4/4/4) rows, 2 sts at beg of next 2 (6/4/2) rows, dec 1 st each side every 2nd row 13 (10/11/19) times, alternately every 4th and 2nd row 10 (10/5/3) times, bind off 3 sts at beg of next 2 rows, 2 sts at beg of next 0 (0/10/10) rows. Bind off rem 16 sts.

### TO MAKE UP/FINISHING

See tips on page 157.

Join one shoulder seam.

**Neckband:** With smaller needles and Fauve, pick up 178 sts around neck (121 sts along front, 57 sts along back), and P 1 row RS, then cont in K1/P1 rib as foll: *1 row Naturel, 1 row Fauve*. At 3 cm or 1⅛" from beg, bind off all sts.

Sew 2nd shoulder and neckband.

Set in sleeves. Sew side and sleeve seams.

### CARDIGAN

### BACK

With larger needles and Fauve, cast on 164 (166/168/170) sts and work in striped st st no. 2, beg at Row 3 (7/11/3) of chart and inc 1 st at LH side for left shoulder every 8th (10th/12th/14th) row 4 times = 168 (170/172/174) sts. Work 14 rows even, then dec 1 st at LH side for neck on next row, then every 2nd row 3 times, every 4th row 3 times, every 6th row once = 160 (162/164/166) sts. Work 18 rows even, then inc 1 st at LH side for neck on next row, then every 6th row once, every 4th row 3 times, every 2nd row 3 times = 168 (170/172/174) sts. Work 14 rows even, then dec 1 st at LH side for right shoulder on next row, then every 8th (10th/12th/14th) row 3 times = 164 (166/168/170) sts. Work 8 (10/12/14) rows even and bind off.

### RIGHT FRONT

With larger needles and Fauve, cast on 66 (68/70/72) sts and work in striped st st no. 2, inc at RH side for neck as foll: cast on 2 sts 12 times, 3 sts 26 times = 168 (170/172/174) sts. Cont to dec 1 st at RH side for right shoulder, every 14th row 1(1/1/4) times, every 8th (10th/12th/0) row 3 (3/3/0) time = 164(166/168/170) sts. Work 8 (10/12/14) rows and bind off.

### LEFT FRONT

Work to correspond to right front, reversing shaping.

### SLEEVES

With larger needles and Fauve, cast on 10 sts and work in striped st st no. 2, beg at 1st (9th, 3rd, 9th) row of chart and inc at RH side as foll: cast on 10 sts 3 (5/3/1) times, 8 sts 4 (1/4/6) times, 6 sts 0 (1/1/2) times = 72 (74/78/80) sts. Work 110 (114/118/122) rows even then dec at RH side as foll: bind off 6 sts 0 (1/1/2) times, 8 sts 4 (1/4/6) times, 10 sts 4 (6/4/2) times.

### BELT

With smaller needles and Naturel, cast on 22 sts and work in K2/P2 rib for 118 cm or 46½". Bind off.

### MAKE UP/FINISHING

See tips on page 157.

With smaller needles and Naturel, pick up 98 (106/114/122) sts along lower sleeve edges and work 16 cm or 6¼" in K2/P2 rib. Bind off.

With smaller needles and Naturel pick up 166 (180/186/212) sts along back lower edge and work in K2/P2 rib for 3 cm or 1⅛". Bind off.

With smaller needles and Naturel pick up 130 (138/144/152) sts along each front edge and work in K2/P2 rib for 3 cm or 1⅛". Bind off.

For neckline edging with smaller needles and Naturel, cast on 12 sts and work in K1/P1 rib for 170 (172/174/176) cm or 66⅞ (67¾/68½/69¼)". Bind off.

Sew shoulder seams. Set in sleeves. Sew side and sleeve seams.

Slip stitch neckline edging to each front and back neckline. Make 2 twisted cords with 3 strands Naturel 57 cm or 22⅜" long, twisted and folded in half, to measure 27 cm or 10½". Tack first cord at A (see schematics), inside back, 2nd one at beg of right front neckline. With crochet hook work a buttonhole loop (ch 8) at beg of left front neckline. Sew button at B.

*(Continued on page 116)*

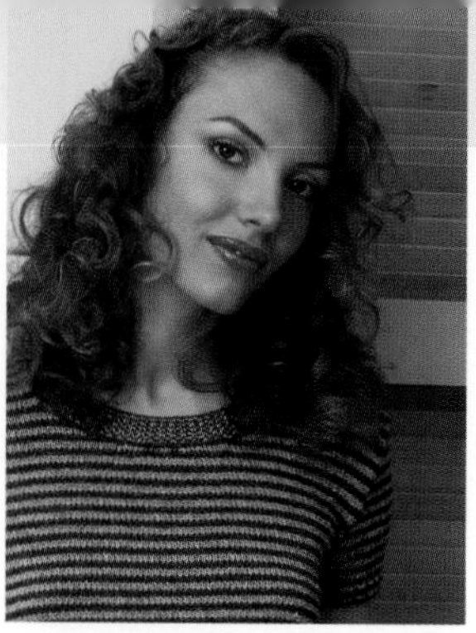

(Continued from page 115)

# cachemire rayé

**Top**

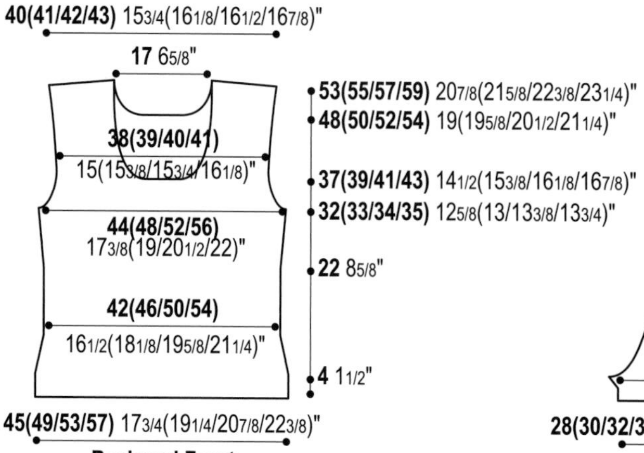
40(41/42/43) 15 3/4(16 1/8/16 1/2/16 7/8)"
17 6 5/8"
53(55/57/59) 20 7/8(21 5/8/22 3/8/23 1/4)"
48(50/52/54) 19(19 5/8/20 1/2/21 1/4)"
38(39/40/41)
15(15 3/8/15 3/4/16 1/8)"
37(39/41/43) 14 1/2(15 3/8/16 1/8/16 7/8)"
32(33/34/35) 12 5/8(13/13 3/8/13 3/4)"
44(48/52/56)
17 3/8(19/20 1/2/22)"
22 8 5/8"
42(46/50/54)
16 1/2(18 1/8/19 5/8/21 1/4)"
4 1 1/2"
45(49/53/57) 17 3/4(19 1/4/20 7/8/22 3/8)"

**Back and Front**

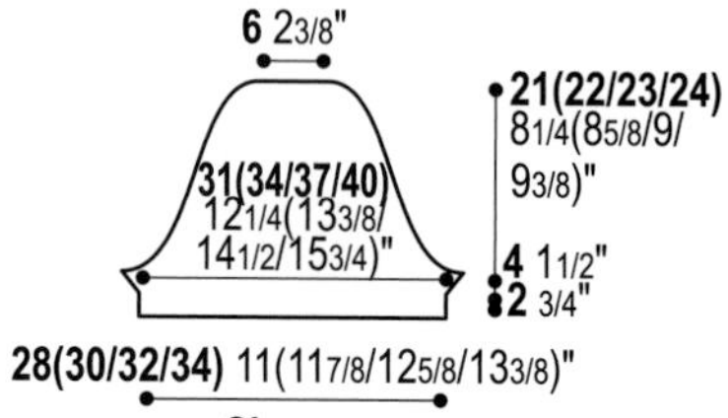
6 2 3/8"
21(22/23/24)
8 1/4(8 5/8/9/
9 3/8)"
31(34/37/40)
12 1/4(13 3/8/
14 1/2/15 3/4)"
4 1 1/2"
2 3/4"
28(30/32/34) 11(11 7/8/12 5/8/13 3/8)"

**Sleeves**

**Cardigan**

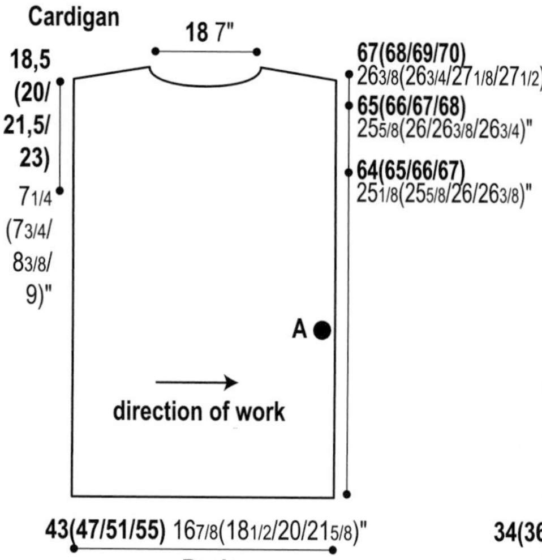
18 7"
18,5
(20/
21,5/
23)
7 1/4
(7 3/4/
8 3/8/
9)"
67(68/69/70)
26 3/8(26 3/4/27 1/8/27 1/2)"
65(66/67/68)
25 5/8(26/26 3/8/26 3/4)"
64(65/66/67)
25 1/8(25 5/8/26/26 3/8)"
A
direction of work
43(47/51/55) 16 7/8(18 1/2/20/21 5/8)"

**Back**

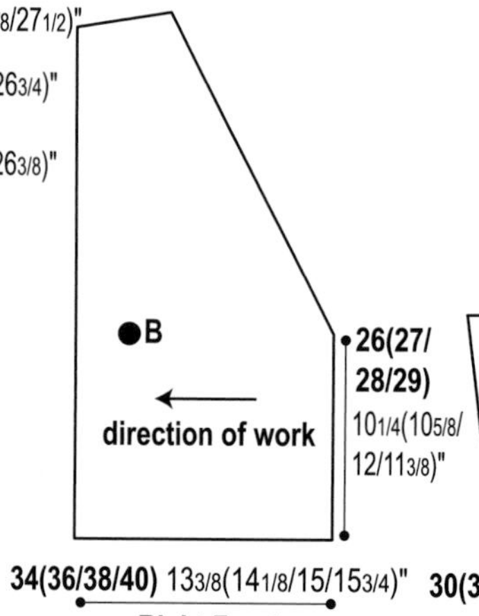
B
direction of work
26(27/
28/29)
10 1/4(10 5/8/
12/11 3/8)"
34(36/38/40) 13 3/8(14 1/8/15/15 3/4)"

**Right Front**

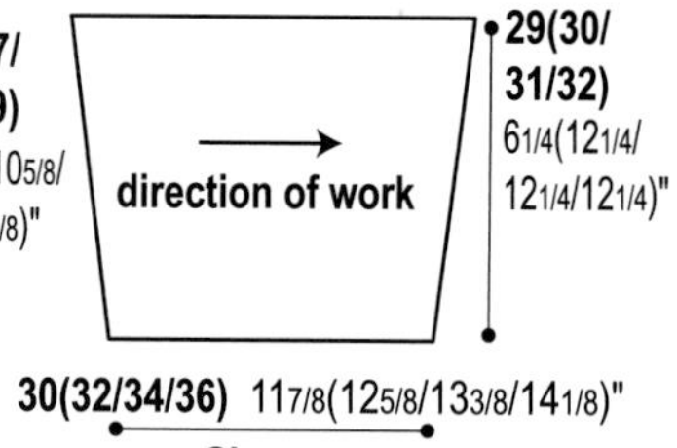
direction of work
29(30/
31/32)
6 1/4(12 1/4/
12 1/4/12 1/4)"
30(32/34/36) 11 7/8(12 5/8/13 3/8/14 1/8)"

**Sleeves**

**Striped stock st n. 2**

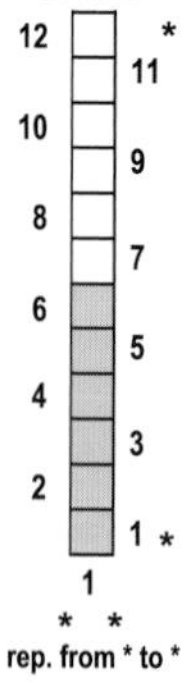
12
11
10
9
8
7
6
5
4
3
2
1
1
* *
rep. from * to *

**Key:**

☐ = Naturel
■ = Fauve

*(Continued from page 44)*

# calybe

Cont to dec 1 st each side at 1 st from edge (1 SKP at RHS, K2tog at LHS): every 8th row once, every 6th row twice = 35 (37/39/41) sts. Work 8 rows even, then inc 1 st (working M1) at 3 sts from each edge, every 4th row 14 times = 63(65/67/69) sts.

**Cap shaping:** Bind off 3 sts at beg of next 2 rows, then dec 1 st each side at 4 sts from edge every 2nd row (K2tog at RHS and at LHS) 8 times, bind off 2 sts at beg of next 2 rows, 3 sts at beg of next 2 rows, 5 sts at beg of next 2 rows. Bind off rem 21 (23/25/27) sts.

### HOOD

Worked in 2 parts.

**Left part:** With Mérinos double strand, cast on 4 sts and work in st st foll chart, inc sts at RHS as foll: 19 sts by alternating *1 st once, 2 sts once* (to inc 1 st, work 1 yo at RHS of center 2 sts. To inc 2 sts, work 1 yo after the first st and 1 yo at RHS of the center 2 sts) at LHS: every 2nd row: 7 sts by alternating *1 st once, 2 sts once* and 2 sts 9 times (to inc 1 st work 1 yo at LHS of center 2 sts, to inc 2 sts work 1 yo after the first st and 1 yo at LHS of

center 2 sts) = 48 sts. Cont to dec 2 sts (K3tog) at LHS at 1 st from edge: every 2nd row 3 times, at RHS work 20 rows even, then work M1 inc 4 times every 2nd row at 5 sts from edge = 46 sts.

At the 71st row of chart bind off at RHS: 3 sts twice, 5 sts once, bind off rem 35 sts.

**Right part:** Work to correspond to left part, reversing shaping, and work SKP instead of K2tog.

### TO MAKE UP/FINISHING

See tips on page 157.

Sew shoulder seams. Set in sleeves. Sew side and sleeve seams. Sew the 2 parts of hood tog for back seam and the top C to D (see schematics). Sew hood around neck (see photo).

Pick up 93 sts all around hood and along front neck (80 sts around hood, 13 sts along front neck), and K 1 row, then bind off sts knitwise.

Pick up 77 (82/88/98) sts at lower edge of pullover from A to B, and K 1 row on WS, then bind off knitwise.

Work in same way at lower edge of sleeves, picking up 41 (43/45/47) sts from A to B.

*(Continued on page 118)*

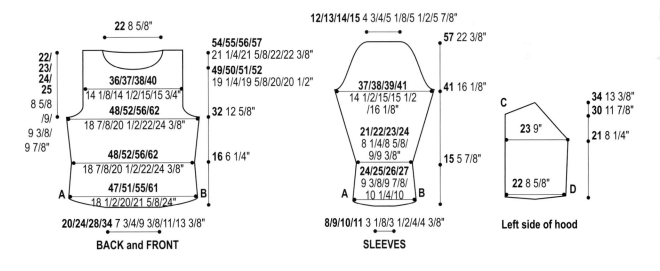

BACK and FRONT

SLEEVES

Left side of hood

(Continued from page 117)

# calybe

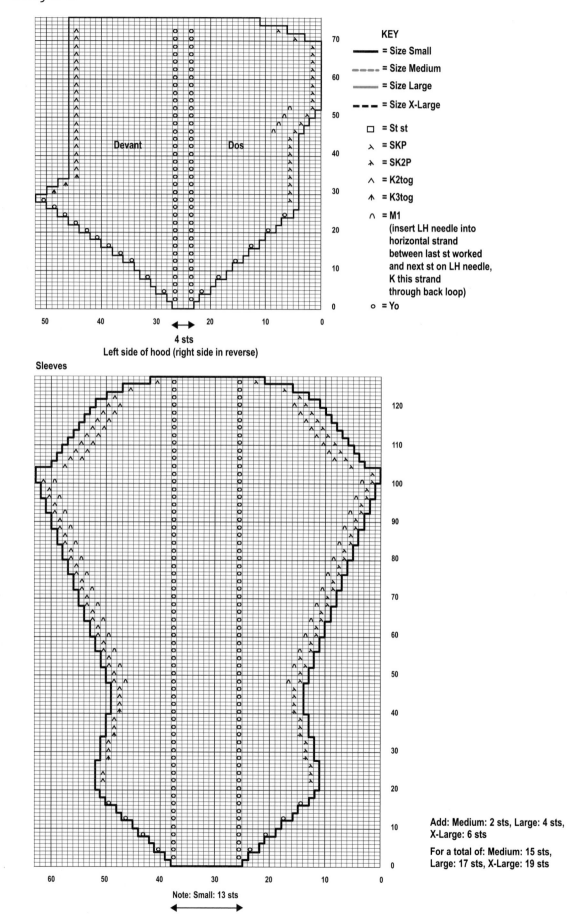

**KEY**

— = Size Small

---- = Size Medium

— = Size Large

- - - = Size X-Large

☐ = St st

⅄ = SKP

⅄ = SK2P

∧ = K2tog

⋏ = K3tog

∩ = M1
(insert LH needle into
horizontal strand
between last st worked
and next st on LH needle,
K this strand
through back loop)

o = Yo

Devant      Dos

4 sts

Left side of hood (right side in reverse)

Sleeves

70
60
50
40
30
20
10
0

50   40   30   20   10   0

120
110
100
90
80
70
60
50
40
30
20
10
0

60   50   40   30   20   10   0

**Add:** Medium: 2 sts, Large: 4 sts,
X-Large: 6 sts

**For a total of:** Medium: 15 sts,
Large: 17 sts, X-Large: 19 sts

Note: Small: 13 sts

Top of Front

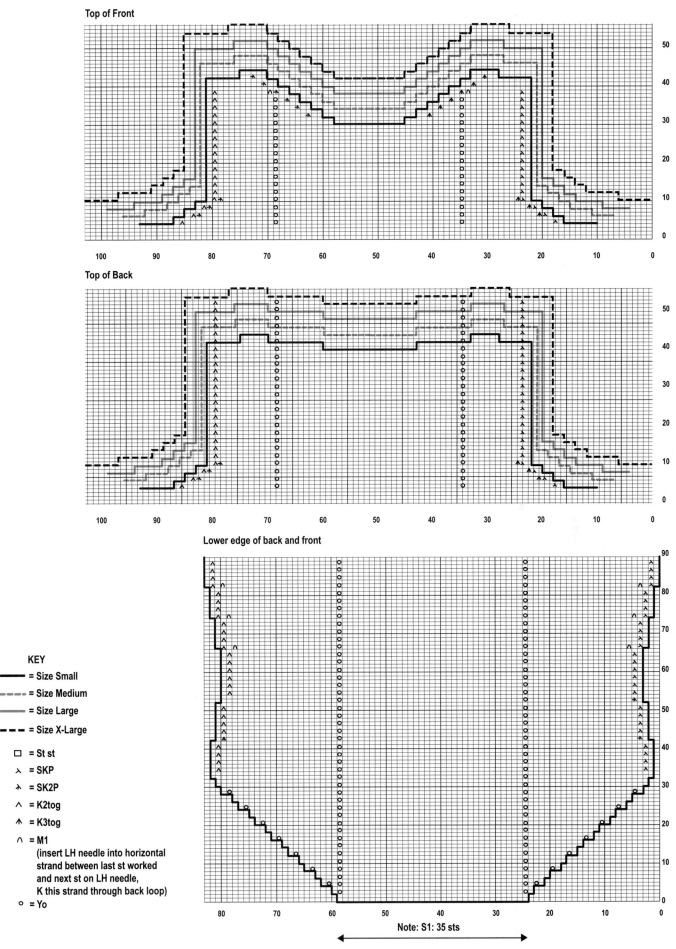

Top of Back

Lower edge of back and front

KEY

━━━ = Size Small

- - - - = Size Medium

━━━ = Size Large

- - - = Size X-Large

□ = St st

⋋ = SKP

⋌ = SK2P

∧ = K2tog

⋏ = K3tog

∩ = M1
(insert LH needle into horizontal
strand between last st worked
and next st on LH needle,
K this strand through back loop)

○ = Yo

Note: S1: 35 sts

Add: Medium: 6 sts, Large: 12 sts, X-Large: 22 sts

For a total of: Medium: 41 sts, Large: 47 sts, X-Large: 57 sts

*(Continued from page 47)*

# nathalie

### RIGHT SLEEVE

With Lichen, cast on 55 (57/59/61) sts and work 1 row on WS same as body beg with P1 (K1/P1/K1), then cont in rib pat, beg with P 2 (1/2/1), then the sl st. When piece measures 6 cm or 2½" from beg, dec 6 sts and reverse the rib pat for end of hem = 49 (51/53/55) sts. Inc 1 st each side at 1 st from edge (work inc sts into pat) every 6th row 21 (19/17/15) times, every 4th row 2 (5/8/11) times = 95 (99/103/107) sts. Work even until piece measures 45 cm or 17¾" from beg.

**Raglan shaping:** Bind off 3 sts at beg of next 2 rows, then work dec, at 3 sts from edge, on WS rows same as body: at RHS: 1 st 34 (36/38/40) times, at LHS: 1 st

39 (41/43/45) times = 16 sts, then cont to bind off from RHS on RS rows 3 sts 3 times, 2 sts twice, 3 sts once.

### LEFT SLEEVE

Work to correspond to right sleeve, reversing raglan shaping.

### TO MAKE UP/FINISHING

See tips on page 157.

Sew raglan sleeve caps to raglan armholes. Fold 6 cm or 2⅜" hems to WS and sew in place.

With 4½ mm crochet hook and Huskye, work around neck as foll: 1 row dc (along front neck, work approx 1 dc for every 2nd row, at center point work 3 dc in 1 st, along back work 1 dc in each st), turn, ch 1, then work 2 rows fur st, end with a 3rd row fur st but with 4 mm crochet hook.

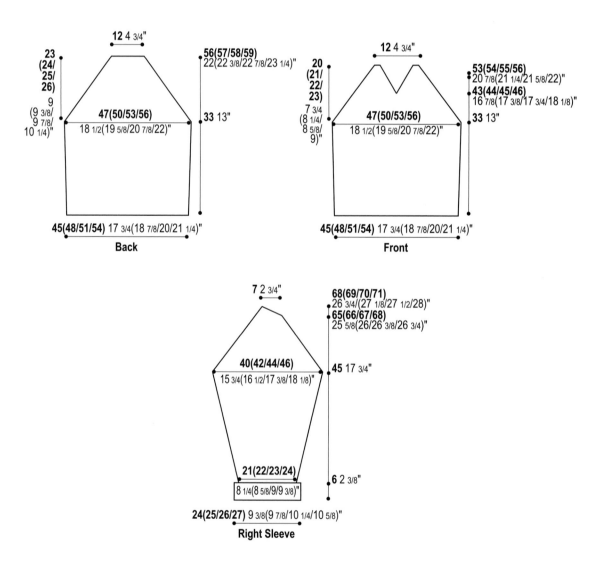

Back

Front

Right Sleeve

*(Continued from page 49)*

# corneille

Work even until piece measures 39 cm or 15⅜" from beg.

**Cap shaping:** Bind off 3 sts at beg of next 2 rows. Dec sts each side every 2nd row as foll: **Small:** Dec 16 sts by alternating *2 sts once, 1 st twice*, then dec 2 sts once, 1 st once, 2 sts once. **Medium:** Dec 16 sts by alternating *2 sts once, 1 st twice*, then 2 sts once, 1 st once, bind off 3 sts at beg of next 2 rows. **Large:** Dec 16 sts by alternating *2 sts once, 1 st twice*, then 2 sts once, 1 st once, 2 sts twice. **X-Large:** Dec 16 sts by alternating *2 sts once, 1 st twice*, 2 sts once, 1 st once, 2 sts once, bind off 3 sts at beg of next 2 rows. Bind off rem 12 sts.

**Crochet border:** With crochet hook, at lower edge of sleeves, with Chimère and Tweed'Anny held tog, work 39 dc, then 3 rows openwork blocks. Fasten off.

TO MAKE UP/FINISHING

See tips on page 157.

Sew one shoulder seam.

**Collar:** Pick up 65 sts around neck (43 sts along front, 22 sts along back), and K 1 row on WS, then cont in K5/P2 rib, beg and end with 1 selvage st. When collar measures 8 cm or 3⅛" from beg, bind off.

Sew 2nd shoulder and collar seam. Set in sleeves. Sew side and sleeve seams. Sew in shoulder pads.

SCARF

With crochet hook and Chimère and Tweed'Anny held tog, ch 23 and work in openwork blocks foll diagram.

On the 4th and 5th rows and 73rd and 74th rows, work with Flamenco Tomette.

On the 77th row, fasten off.

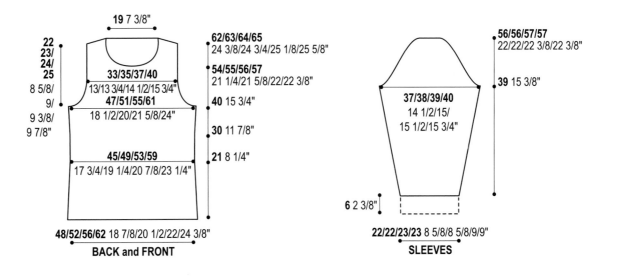

**BACK and FRONT**

**SLEEVES**

**Diamond**

Only the odd-numbered (RS) rows appear on the chart.
Work the even-numbered (WS) rows as K the knit sts and P the purl sts.

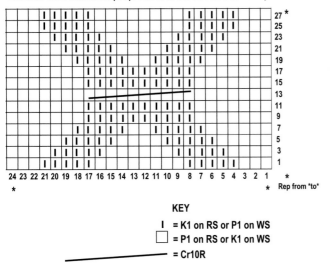

**KEY**

I = K1 on RS or P1 on WS
☐ = P1 on RS or K1 on WS
╱ = Cr10R

**Openwork blocks**

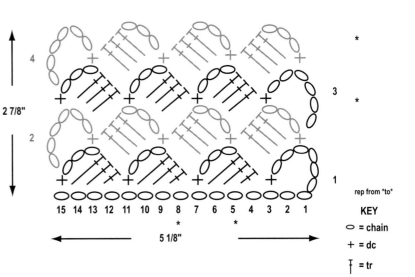

**KEY**

○ = chain
+ = dc
⊤ = tr

*(Continued from page 51)*

# les ecrins

**X-Large:** Bind off 5 sts, K1, K2tog, P1, K3, P1, K3, P1, K2, K2tog, °°P1, K3°°, rep from °°to°° 3 times more, P1, K2tog, K2, P1, K3, P1, K2, K2tog, P1, K3, P1, K3, P1, K2, K2tog, °°P1, K3°°, rep from °°to°° twice more, P1, K2, K2tog, °°P1, K3°°, rep from °°to°° twice more, P1, K2tog, K1, bind off last 5 sts = 85 sts. Cut yarn, cont in K3/P1 rib on WS.

Work even until piece measures 73 (74/75/76) cm or 28¾ (29⅛/29½/29⅞)" from beg.

**Neck shaping:** Bind off center 17 sts for neck and working both sides at once, bind off from each neck edge 4 sts once, 3 sts once. When piece measures 76 (77/78/79) cm or 29 ⅞ (30¼/30¾/31⅛)" from beg, bind off rem 21 (23/25/27) sts each side for shoulders.

### RIGHT FRONT

With 2 strands Domino and 5½mm needles, cast on 41 (41/45/49) sts and work in K3/P1 rib, beg with 1 selvage st, *K3, P1*, rep from *to*, end with K2, P1, 1 selvage st, until piece measures 3 cm or 1⅛" from beg. On next WS row, inc 3 (5/3/2) sts using M1 purlwise as foll:

**Small:** 1 selvage st, K1, P14 inc 2 sts, K1, P15 inc 1 st, K1, P7, 1 selvage st = 44 sts.

**Medium:** 1 selvage st, K1, P14 inc 3 sts, K1, P15 inc 2 sts, K1, P7, 1 selvage st = 46 sts.

**Large:** 1 selvage st, K1, P18, K1, P15 inc 3 sts, K1, P7, 1 selvage st = 48 sts.

**X-Large:** 1 selvage st, K1, P6, K1, *P15 inc 1 st, K1*, rep *to* once more, P7, 1 selvage st = 51 sts.

**Note:** On the 33rd row of diamond motif, in order to work a pocket opening, work the first 35 (37/39/42) sts and the last 9 sts sts separately for 30 rows. Then work again on all 44 (46/48/51) sts until piece measures 54 cm or 21¼" from beg, after 5 diamond motifs have been worked, cont on RS in K3/P1 rib, bind off 4 (4/3/5) sts at RHS for armhole and dec 2 (2/3/2) sts in the 1st row as foll:

**Small:** 1 selvage st, K3, P1, K3, P1, K3, P2tog,°°K3, P1°°, rep from °°to°° twice more, K3, P2tog, K3, P1, K3, P1, K1, bind off last 4 sts = 38 sts. Cut yarn and work K3/P1 rib on WS.

**Medium:** 1 selvage st, °°K3, P1°°, rep from °°to°° twice more, K2, K2tog, P1, K2tog, K2, °°P1, K3°°, rep from °°to°° 4 times more, bind off last 4 sts = 40 sts. Cut yarn and work K3/P1 rib on WS.

**Large:** 1 selvage st, K3, P1, K3, P1,°°K3, P2tog°°, rep from °°to°° twice more, °°K3, P1°°, rep from °°to°° 4 times more, K1, bind off 3 sts = 42 sts. Cut yarn and work K3/P1 rib on WS.

**X-Large:** 1 selvage st, °°K3, P1°°, rep from °°to°° 3 times more, K2tog, K2,°°P1, K3°°, rep from °°to°° 3 times more, P1, K2tog, K2, P1, K3, bind off last 5 sts = 44 sts. Cut yarn and work K3/P1 rib on WS.

Work even until piece measures 67 (68/69/70) cm or 26⅜ (26¾/27⅛/27½)" from beg.

**Neck shaping:** Bind off from LHS for neck 6 sts once, 3 sts twice, 2 sts twice, then dec 1 st every 4th row once. When piece measures 76 (77/78/79) cm or 29⅞ (30¼/30¾/31⅛)" from beg, bind off rem 21 (23/25/27) sts for shoulder.

### LEFT FRONT

Work to correspond to right front, reversing shaping.

### SLEEVES

With 2 strands Domino and 5mm needles, cast on 42 sts and work in K3/P1 rib on WS for turnback cuff as foll: 1 selvage st, P2, *K1, P3*, rep from *to*, end with P2, 1 selvage st. When piece measures 11 cm or 4⅜" from beg, mark for the end of turnback with 1 row garter st. Cont in K3/P1 rib, reversing the sts, and inc 1 st each side every 6th row 13 (13/12/12) times, every 4th row 0 (0/2/2) times = 68 (68/70/70) sts. Work even until piece measures 56 (56/57/57) cm or 22 (22/22⅜/22⅜)" from beg. Bind off all sts.

### TO MAKE UP/FINISHING

See tips on page 157.

Sew shoulder seams. Set in sleeves. Sew side and sleeve seams.

**Pocket Lining:** With WS facing, pick up 32 sts along each pocket opening with single strand Domino and 4 mm needles and work in rev st st for 17 cm or 6⅝". Sew pocket lining in place to WS.

**Pocket Border:** With RS facing, 2 strands Domino and 5mm needles, pick up 25 sts along each pocket edge and work in K3/P1 rib, beg and end with K4, for 3 cm or 1⅛". Bind off all sts.

**Collar:** With 2 strands Domino and 5mm needles, pick up 21 sts along each front, 39 sts along back = 81 sts, and work in K3/P1 rib, beg and end with K4, for 11 cm or 4⅜". Mark the last row for turnback with 1 row garter st then cont K3/P1 rib on WS, reversing the sts.

## Diamond Chart: Sizes Small and X-Large

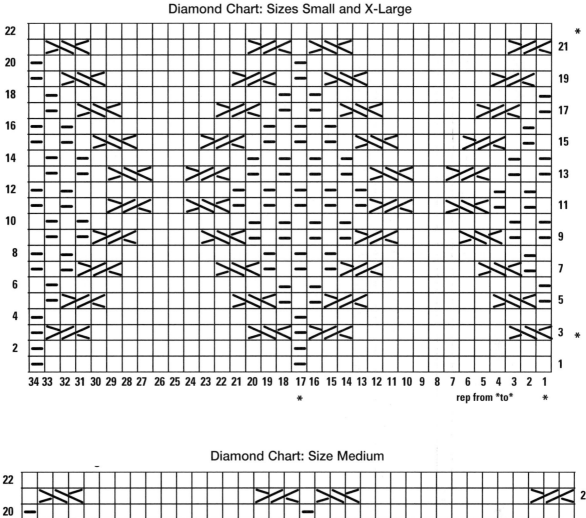

## Diamond Chart: Size Medium

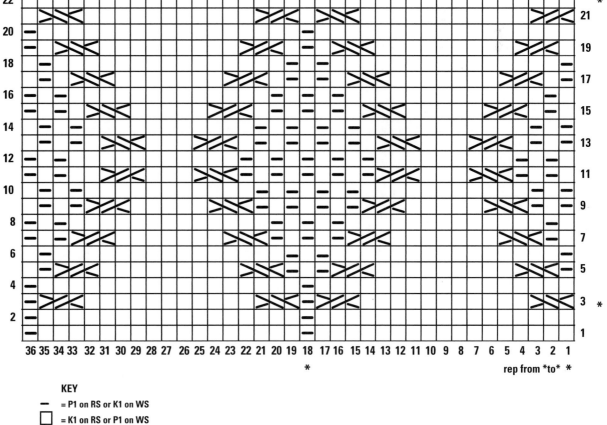

**KEY**

— = P1 on RS or K1 on WS

☐ = K1 on RS or P1 on WS

⟩⟨ = CrK2/1R

⟩⟨ = CrK1/2L

*(Continued on page 124)*

(Continued from page 123)

# les ecrins

**Left front border:** With 2 strands Domino and 5mm needles, beg at garter st row of collar, pick up and K 121 (123/125/127) sts and work in K3/P1 rib, beg with 1 selvage st, P 0 (1/0/1), K3, for 3 cm or 1⅛". Bind off all sts in rib.

**Right front border:** Work same as left front border, but work 6 buttonholes in center of band (bind off 3 sts for each buttonhole, then cast on 3 sts on foll row), with the first one at 11 cm or 4⅜" from lower edge, the last one at 0.5 cm or ¼" below garter row on collar, and the 4 other spaced evenly between.

**Embroidery:** With col. Etain and 4mm crochet hook, make a chain st in center of each of the K2 sts along border of each diamond (see photo).

**Ties:** After laying collar flat to fronts, weave 2 strands Etain at 16 cm or 6¼" from top of points of collar, passing them across 1 st of front, then knot (see photo).

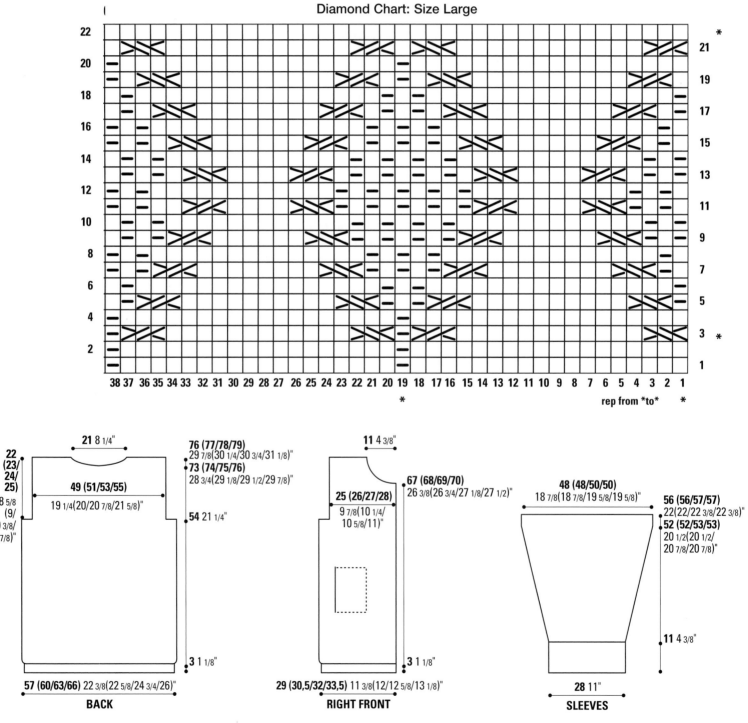

**Diamond Chart: Size Large**

BACK — 21 8¼" · 22 (23/24/25) · 8 5/8 (9/9 3/8/9 7/8)" · 49 (51/53/55) 19¼(20/20 7/8/21 5/8)" · 76 (77/78/79) 29 7/8(30 1/4/30 3/4/31 1/8)" · 73 (74/75/76) 28 3/4(29 1/8/29 1/2/29 7/8)" · 54 21¼" · 3 1 1/8" · 57 (60/63/66) 22 3/8(22 5/8/24 3/4/26)"

RIGHT FRONT — 11 4 3/8" · 25 (26/27/28) 9 7/8(10 1/4/10 5/8/11)" · 67 (68/69/70) 26 3/8(26 3/4/27 1/8/27 1/2)" · 3 1 1/8" · 29 (30,5/32/33,5) 11 3/8(12/12 5/8/13 1/8)"

SLEEVES — 48 (48/50/50) 18 7/8(18 7/8/19 5/8/19 5/8)" · 56 (56/57/57) 22(22/22 3/8/22 3/8)" · 52 (52/53/53) 20 1/2(20 1/2/20 7/8/20 7/8)" · 11 4 3/8" · 28 11"

*(Continued from page 52)*

# carouge

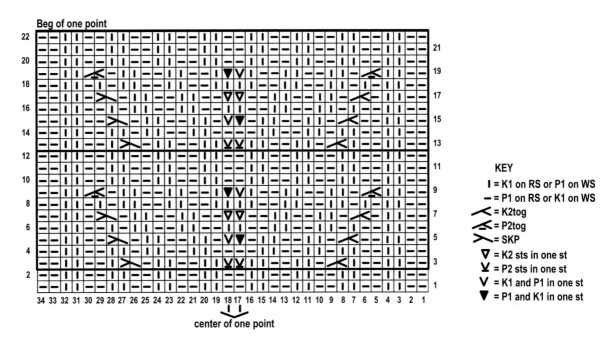

**Beg of one point**

center of one point

**KEY**

**I** = K1 on RS or P1 on WS
**—** = P1 on RS or K1 on WS
= K2tog
= P2tog
= SKP
▽ = K2 sts in one st
= P2 sts in one st
V = K1 and P1 in one st
▼ = P1 and K1 in one st

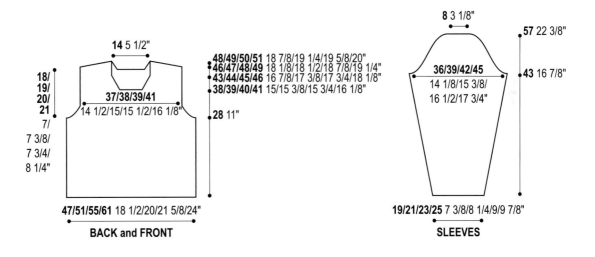

**14** 5 1/2"

**18/ 19/ 20/ 21**
7/ 7 3/8/ 7 3/4/ 8 1/4"

**37/38/39/41**
14 1/2/15/15 1/2/16 1/8"

**48/49/50/51** 18 7/8/19 1/4/19 5/8/20"
**46/47/48/49** 18 1/8/18 1/2/18 7/8/19 1/4"
**43/44/45/46** 16 7/8/17 3/8/17 3/4/18 1/8"
**38/39/40/41** 15/15 3/8/15 3/4/16 1/8"

**28** 11"

**47/51/55/61** 18 1/2/20/21 5/8/24"

**BACK and FRONT**

**8** 3 1/8"

**57** 22 3/8"

**43** 16 7/8"

**36/39/42/45**
14 1/8/15 3/8/
16 1/2/17 3/4"

**19/21/23/25** 7 3/8/8 1/4/9/9 7/8"

**SLEEVES**

*(Continued from page 54)*

# bellecote

**Collar:** With 3½ mm needles, pick up and K 54 along front neck and 40 sts along back neck = 94 sts. Work in K1/P1 rib for 24 cm or 9⅜". Bind off all sts in rib. Sew 2nd shoulder and collar seam, reversing collar seam half way up for turnback. Set in sleeves. Sew side and sleeve seams.

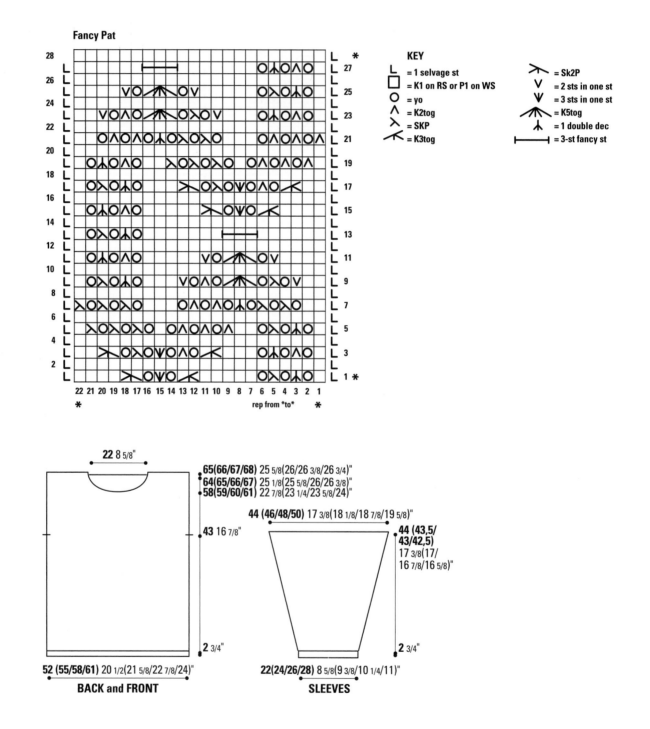

**Fancy Pat**

**KEY**

| | | | |
|---|---|---|---|
| L | = 1 selvage st | ⋋ | = Sk2P |
| □ | = K1 on RS or P1 on WS | V | = 2 sts in one st |
| ○ | = yo | V | = 3 sts in one st |
| ⋋ | = K2tog | ⋀ | = K5tog |
| ⋋ | = SKP | ⋀ | = 1 double dec |
| ⋋ | = K3tog | ⊢⊣ | = 3-st fancy st |

**22** 8 5/8"

**65(66/67/68)** 25 5/8(26/26 3/8/26 3/4)"
**64(65/66/67)** 25 1/8(25 5/8/26/26 3/8)"
**58(59/60/61)** 22 7/8(23 1/4/23 5/8/24)"

**43** 16 7/8"

**44 (46/48/50)** 17 3/8(18 1/8/18 7/8/19 5/8)"

**44 (43,5/ 43/42,5)** 17 3/8(17/ 16 7/8/16 5/8)"

2 3/4"

2 3/4"

**52 (55/58/61)** 20 1/2(21 5/8/22 7/8/24)"
**BACK and FRONT**

**22(24/26/28)** 8 5/8(9 3/8/10 1/4/11)"
**SLEEVES**

*(Continued from page 56)*

# anatolie

**Cap shaping:** Bind off 3 sts at beg of next 2 rows, 2 sts at beg of next 4 rows, dec 1 st each side every other row 14 (14/15/16) times, bind off 2 sts at beg of next 24 (28/30/32) rows, 3 sts at beg of next 2 rows. Bind off rem 25 sts.

TO MAKE UP/FINISHING

See tips on page 157.

**Cuffs:** With Huskye, cast on 25 (25/27/27) sts and work 6 cm or 2⅜" in st st, then bind off.

Sew cuff at lower edge of sleeves, then fold in half to WS and sew in place.

**Collar:** With Huskye, cast on 64 sts and work 10 cm or 4" in st st, then bind off all sts.

Fold collar in half, then sew it edge to edge around neck.

Pick up and K 118 (124/132/142) sts along each front, and work 6 rows garter st, working 10 buttonholes along right front on the 3rd row (bind off 2 sts for each button-hole, then cast on 2 sts on foll row), with the 1st one at 6 sts from right edge, the last one at 2 sts from left edge and the other 8 spaced 10 sts apart.

Sew shoulder seams. Set in sleeves. Sew side and sleeve seams.

Sew on buttons.

**Fancy pat**
**Only the odd-numbered (RS) rows are shown on chart.**
**Work the even-numbered (WS) rows as K the knit sts and P the purl sts.**

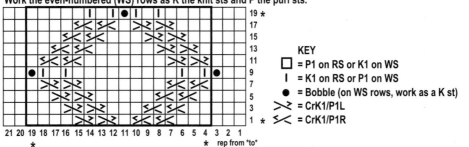

**KEY**

□ = P1 on RS or K1 on WS
I = K1 on RS or P1 on WS
● = Bobble (on WS rows, work as a K st)
⟩⟨ = CrK1/P1L
⟨⟩ = CrK1/P1R

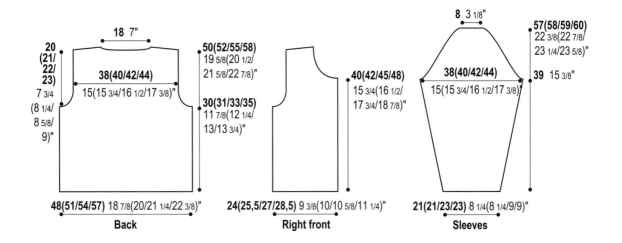

**Back** — 20 (21/22/23) 7 3/4 (8 1/4/8 5/8/9)" — 18 7" — 38(40/42/44) 15(15 3/4/16 1/2/17 3/8)" — 50(52/55/58) 19 5/8(20 1/2/21 5/8/22 7/8)" — 48(51/54/57) 18 7/8(20/21 1/4/22 3/8)"

**Right front** — 30(31/33/35) 11 7/8(12 1/4/13/13 3/4)" — 40(42/45/48) 15 3/4(16 1/2/17 3/4/18 7/8)" — 24(25,5/27/28,5) 9 3/8(10/10 5/8/11 1/4)"

**Sleeves** — 8 3 1/8" — 57(58/59/60) 22 3/8(22 7/8/23 1/4/23 5/8)" — 38(40/42/44) 15(15 3/4/16 1/2/17 3/8)" — 39 15 3/8" — 21(21/23/23) 8 1/4(8 1/4/9/9)"

*(Continued from page 60)*

# calcite

Work even until piece measures 119 (120/121/122) cm or 46⅞ (47¼/47⅝/48)" from beg. Inc 1 st each side at 3 sts from edge every 6th row twice, every 4th row twice = 74 (76/78/82) sts.

Work even until piece measures 129 (130/131/132) cm or 50⅞ (51¼/51⅝/52)" from beg. Place center 22 sts on a holder for neck and working both sides at once, place sts on a holder every 2nd row at each side of neck as foll: 4 sts twice, 1 st once, AT THE SAME TIME, when piece measures 131 (132/133/134) cm or 51⅝ (52/52½/52¾)" from beg, bind off from each shoulder edge: 6 (6/6/7) 2 (3/2/3) times, 5 (0/7/0) sts once.

### BACK

With Fine Kid single strand and 7 mm needles, cast on 170 (177/184/191) and work the first 68 rows same as front = 76 (84/92/104) sts.

Cont with 3 strands of Fine Kid held tog and 5½ mm needles and foll chart no. 1.

Inc 1 st each side at 2 sts from edge (working M1 for inc) every 20th row 4 times = 84 (92/100/104) sts.

Cont foll chart no. 2 of front (do not work the center 2 incs as on front).

Work the same decs and incs each side and same dec and inc in the 4 groups of P2.

Work even until piece measures 113 cm or 44½" from beg, there are 84 (92/100/112) sts. Dec each side for armholes same as front = 64 (66/68/72) sts.

Work even until piece measures 119 (120/121/122) cm or 46⅞ (47¼/47⅝/48)" from beg. Work inc each side at 3 sts from edge same as front = 72 (74/76/80) sts.

Work even until piece measures 129 (130/131/132) cm or 50⅞ (51¼/51⅝/52)" from beg. Place center 32 sts sts on a holder and working both sides at once, place sts on a holder every 2nd row at each side of neck as foll: 1 st 3 times, AT THE SAME TIME, when piece measures 131 (132/133/134)cm or 51⅝ (52/52½/52¾)" from beg, shape shoulders same as front.

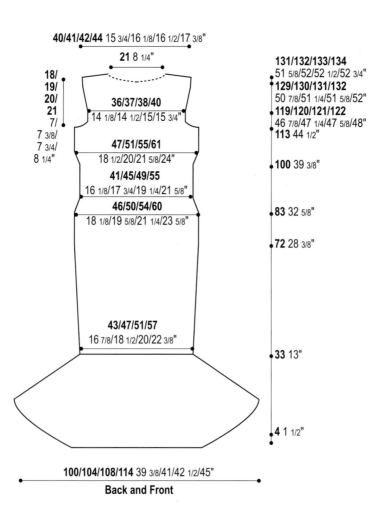

**40/41/42/44** 15 3/4/16 1/8/16 1/2/17 3/8"

**21** 8 1/4"

**18/
19/
20/
21
7/**
7 3/8/
7 3/4/
8 1/4"

**36/37/38/40**
14 1/8/14 1/2/15/15 3/4"

**47/51/55/61**
18 1/2/20/21 5/8/24"

**41/45/49/55**
16 1/8/17 3/4/19 1/4/21 5/8"

**46/50/54/60**
18 1/8/19 5/8/21 1/4/23 5/8"

**43/47/51/57**
16 7/8/18 1/2/20/22 3/8"

**131/132/133/134**
51 5/8/52/52 1/2/52 3/4"
**129/130/131/132**
50 7/8/51 1/4/51 5/8/52"
**119/120/121/122**
46 7/8/47 1/4/47 5/8/48"
**113** 44 1/2"

**100** 39 3/8"

**83** 32 5/8"

**72** 28 3/8"

**33** 13"

**4** 1 1/2"

**100/104/108/114** 39 3/8/41/42 1/2/45"
**Back and Front**

## TO MAKE UP/FINISHING

See tips on page 157.

Sew one shoulder seam. With 5½ mm needles work the
78 sts from holder on back and front neck and cont the
points for 6 rows with Fine Kid triple strand, then 4 rows
Muguet double strand and bind off all sts.

Sew 2nd shoulder and neckband seam.

Sew side seams.

*(Continued on page 130)*

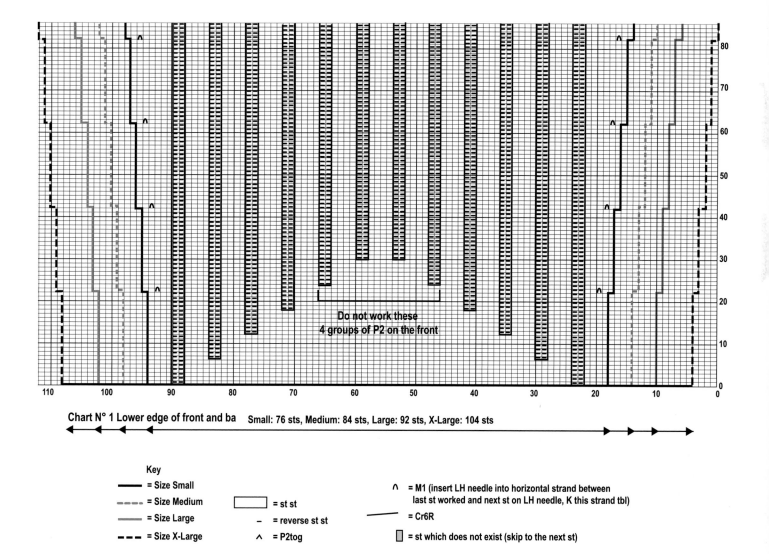

**Chart N° 1 Lower edge of front and ba**   Small: 76 sts, Medium: 84 sts, Large: 92 sts, X-Large: 104 sts

Do not work these
4 groups of P2 on the front

**Key**

— = Size Small

---- = Size Medium

— = Size Large

--- = Size X-Large

☐ = st st

− = reverse st st

∧ = P2tog

∧ = M1 (insert LH needle into horizontal strand between last st worked and next st on LH needle, K this strand tbl)

╱ = Cr6R

▯ = st which does not exist (skip to the next st)

*(Continued from page 129)*

# calcite

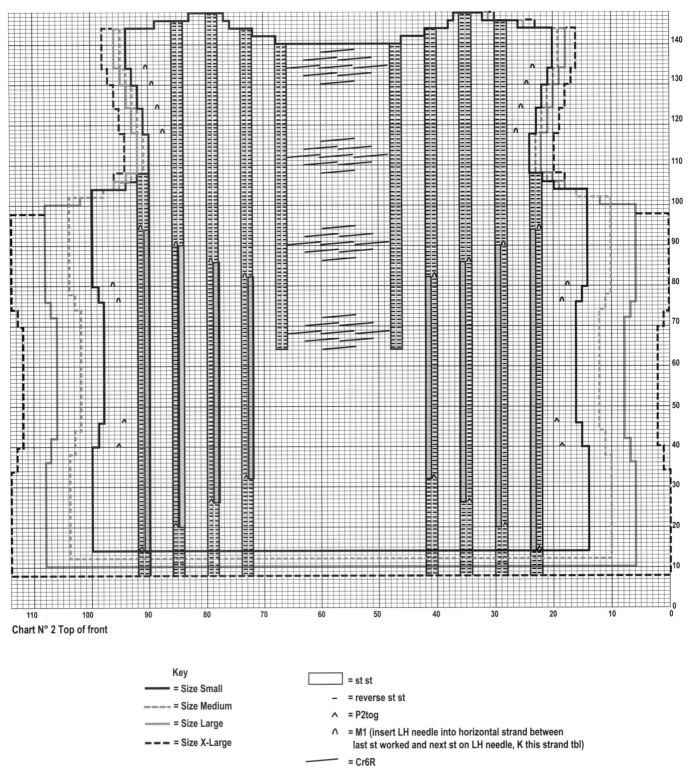

**Chart N° 2 Top of front**

**Key**

—— = Size Small

- - - - = Size Medium

—— = Size Large

- - - = Size X-Large

☐ = st st

– = reverse st st

∧ = P2tog

∧ = M1 (insert LH needle into horizontal strand between last st worked and next st on LH needle, K this strand tbl)

—— = Cr6R

▨ = st which does not exist (skip to the next st)

*(Continued from page 62)*

# roche

**2nd part:** With Angora Super and 4 mm needles, cast on 60 (60/66/66) sts and work in entrelac, foll chart for yarns, for 7 rows of rectangles, then bind off all sts.

### RIGHT FRONT

With Victoria col. Noir and 3½ mm needles, cast on 50 (54/59/65) sts and work in garter st for 1 cm or ⅜".

Cont in st st with Angora Super and 4 mm needles, working decs, incs and armhole decs at LHS same as back = 42 (42/45/45) sts. Work even until piece measures 40 (41/42/43) cm or 15¾ (16⅛/16½/16⅞)" from beg.

**Neck shaping:** Bind off at RHS 8 sts once, 6 sts once, 2 sts twice and 1 st twice.

Work even until piece measures 50 (51/52/53) cm or 19⅝ (20/20½/20⅞)" from beg. Bind off rem 22 (22/25/25) sts for shoulder.

### LEFT FRONT

Work to correspond to right front, reversing shaping.

### SLEEVES

Worked in 2 parts.

**1st part:** With Angora Super and 4 mm needles, cast on 48 (48/54/54) sts and work in st st, inc 1 st each side at 3 sts from edges, every 6th (6th/6th/4th) rows 4 (14/14/10) times, every 8th (0/0/6th) row 7 (0/0/7) times = 70 (76/82/88) sts. Work even until piece measures 29 cm or 11⅜" from beg.

**Cap shaping:** Bind off 3 sts at beg of next 2 rows, 0 (2/2/2) sts at beg of next 0 (4/6/10) rows, dec 1 st each side every other row 20 (17/14/11) times, bind off 3 (2/2/2) sts at beg of next 2 (2/6/8) rows, bind off 0 (3/3/3) sts at beg of next 0 (2/2/2) rows.

Bind off rem 18 sts.

**2nd part:** With Angora Super and 4 mm needles, cast on 36 (36/42/42) sts and work in entrelac, foll chart for yarns, for 5 rows of rectangles, then bind off all sts.

*(Continued on page 132)*

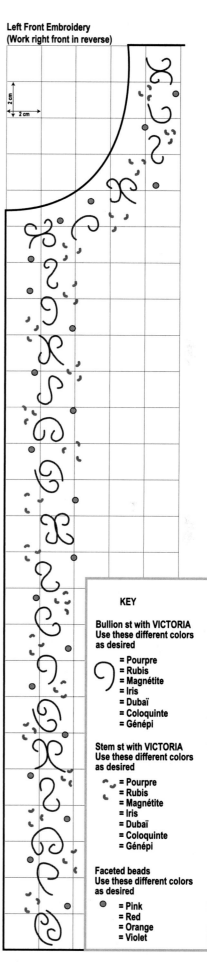

**Left Front Embroidery**
**(Work right front in reverse)**

2 cm

2 cm

**KEY**

**Bullion st with VICTORIA**
**Use these different colors as desired**

= Pourpre
= Rubis
= Magnétite
= Iris
= Dubaï
= Coloquinte
= Génépi

**Stem st with VICTORIA**
**Use these different colors as desired**

= Pourpre
= Rubis
= Magnétite
= Iris
= Dubaï
= Coloquinte
= Génépi

**Faceted beads**
**Use these different colors as desired**

= Pink
= Red
= Orange
= Violet

*(Continued from page 131)*

# roche

### TO MAKE UP/FINISHING

See tips on page 157.

Embroider and attach beads foll diagram.

At top of 1st part of back and on lower edge of 1st part of sleeves, crochet 1 row dc with Gyps.

Join the 2 parts of back and sleeves with 1 black bead (but not along the width of the border).

Sew shoulder seams. Set in sleeves. Sew side and sleeve seams.

Around neck, with Victoria col. Noir and 3½ mm needles, pick up 94 sts (32 along each front and 30 along back), and work in garter st for 1 cm or ⅜" and bind off.

Along each front, work in same way, but pick up 90 (93/96/99) sts.

Embroider a tr button loop with Victoria col. Noir at angle of right front neck and attach button on other side.

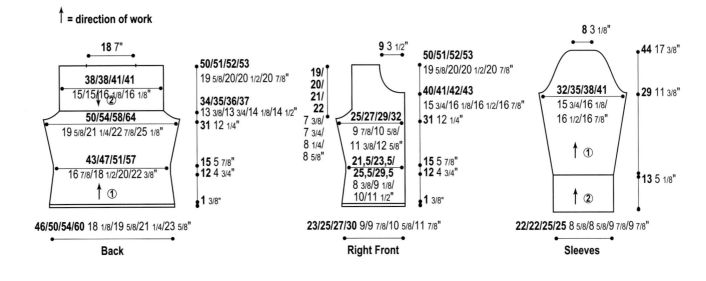

↑ = direction of work

**Back**

18 7"
38/38/41/41
15/15/16 1/8/16 1/8" ②
50/54/58/64
19 5/8/21 1/4/22 7/8/25 1/8"
43/47/51/57
16 7/8/18 1/2/20/22 3/8"
↑ ①
46/50/54/60 18 1/8/19 5/8/21 1/4/23 5/8"

50/51/52/53
19 5/8/20/20 1/2/20 7/8"
34/35/36/37
13 3/8/13 3/4/14 1/8/14 1/2"
31 12 1/4"
15 5 7/8"
12 4 3/4"
1 3/8"

**Right Front**

9 3 1/2"
19/
20/
21/
22
7 3/8/
7 3/4/
8 1/4/
8 5/8"
25/27/29/32
9 7/8/10 5/8"
11 3/8/12 5/8"
21,5/23,5/
25,5/29,5
8 3/8/9 1/8/
10/11 1/2"
23/25/27/30 9/9 7/8/10 5/8/11 7/8"

50/51/52/53
19 5/8/20/20 1/2/20 7/8"
40/41/42/43
15 3/4/16 1/8/16 1/2/16 7/8"
31 12 1/4"
15 5 7/8"
12 4 3/4"
1 3/8"

**Sleeves**

8 3 1/8"
44 17 3/8"
32/35/38/41
15 3/4/16 1/8/
16 1/2/16 7/8"
29 11 3/8"
↑ ①
13 5 1/8"
↑ ②
22/22/25/25 8 5/8/8 5/8/9 7/8/9 7/8"

2nd part of back

1st and 2nd size

3rd and 4th size

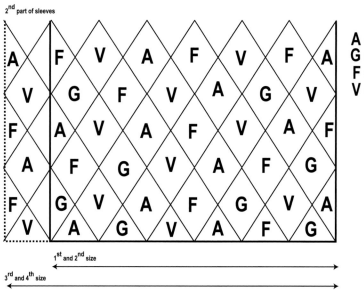

2nd part of sleeves

1st and 2nd size

3rd and 4th size

KEY

**A** = ANGORA SUPER  Noir + 1 strand PAILL
**G** = GYPS Noir  (double strand)
**F** = FÉLINE Noir
**V** = VICTORIA Noir

*(Continued from page 65)*

# anemone

### TO MAKE UP/FINISHING

See tips on page 157.

With Kanpur, embroider chain st on front foll diagram. With Kanpur and 3½ mm crochet hook, work 1 row along top of back front and sleeves as foll: *1 dc, ch 3, sk 3 sts*, rep from *to*. Sew side and sleeve seams. Set in sleeves. For shoulders seams, place the front and back.

KEY
Embroidery
in chain st
= KANPUR, col. Prune

2 cm or ¾"

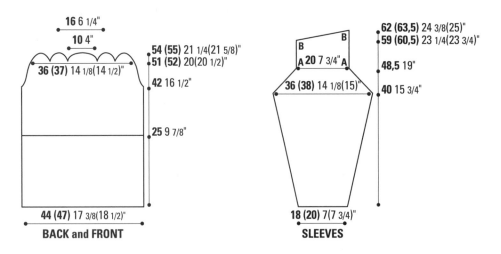

**16** 6 1/4"
**10** 4"
**54 (55)** 21 1/4(21 5/8)"
**51 (52)** 20(20 1/2)"
**36 (37)** 14 1/8(14 1/2)"
**42** 16 1/2"
**25** 9 7/8"
**44 (47)** 17 3/8(18 1/2)"

**BACK and FRONT**

**62 (63,5)** 24 3/8(25)"
**59 (60,5)** 23 1/4(23 3/4)"
B        B
A **20** 7 3/4" A
**48,5** 19"
**36 (38)** 14 1/8(15)"
**40** 15 3/4"
**18 (20)** 7(7 3/4)"

**SLEEVES**

*(Continued from page 66)*

# semones

**Armhole shaping:** Bind off 4 sts at beg of next 2 rows, 3 sts at beg of next 2 (2/4/4) rows, 2 sts at beg of next 4 (6/6/8) rows, dec 1 st each side every other row 2 (3/2/3) times = 95 (97/99/101) sts. Work even until piece measures 42 (43/44/45) cm or 16½ (16⅞/17⅜/17¾)" above garter st.

**Neck shaping:** Bind off center 15 sts and working both sides at once, bind off from each neck edge 4 sts once, 3 sts once, 2 sts 3 times, 1 st 3 times. Work even until piece measures 48 (49/50/51) cm or 18⅞ (19¼/19⅝/20)" above garter st.

**Shoulder shaping:** Bind off 12 (12/13/13) sts at beg of next 2 rows (at outside edges), 12 (13/13/14) sts at beg of next 2 rows.

### FRONT

Work as for back until piece measures 36 (37/38/39) cm or 14⅛ (14½/15/15⅜)" above garter st.

**Neck shaping:** Bind off center 7 sts and working both sides at once, bind off from each neck edge 2 sts 10 times. Work even until piece measures 48 (49/50/51) cm or 18⅞ (19¼/19⅝/20)" above garter st. Shape shoulders as for back.

### TO MAKE UP/FINISHING

See tips on page 157.

Sew one shoulder seam. With 4 mm needles, pick up and K148 sts evenly around neck edge: 60 sts along back neck and 88 sts along front neck. K 1 row on WS, then bind off all sts. Sew rem shoulder seam. With 4 mm needles, pick up and K102 (106/110/114) sts evenly around

each armhole edge. Work same as for neck edge. Sew side seams. With crochet hook, work 1 row dc and 1 row picot around neck and armhole edges.

### CARDIGAN

With 4 mm needles, cast on 117 (125/131/137) sts. Work in garter st for 2 cm or ¾", then K 1 row on WS, inc 12 sts evenly across = 129 (137/143/149) sts. Work as foll: 1 selvage st, 1 st rev st st, 2 sts Fancy Cable pat, 4 (8/11/14) sts rev st st, *11 sts Lozenge pat, 6 sts rev st st*, rep from *to* 5 times more, work 11 sts Lozenge pat, 4 (8/11/14) sts rev st st, 2 sts Fancy Cable pat, 1 st rev st st, 1 selvage st. Cont in pat as established, dec 1 st each side (4 sts in from each edge) every 4th row 7 times, every other row 3 times = 109 (117/123/129) sts, AT THE SAME TIME, on 23rd row above garter st, replace the 1st, 3rd, 5th and 7th Lozenge pats with rev st st. Work even until piece measures 14 cm or 5½" above garter st. Inc 1 st each side (4 sts in from each edge) on next row, then every 6th row 6 times more, every 4th row 3 times = 129 (137/143/149) sts. Work even until piece measures 31 cm or 12¼" above garter st.

**Armhole shaping:** Bind off 4 sts at beg of next 2 rows, 3 sts at beg of next 2 (4/4/4) rows, 2 sts at beg of next 6 (6/8/8) rows, dec 1 st each side every other row 2 (2/2/4) times = 99 (101/103/105) sts. Work even until piece measures 51 (52/53/54) cm or 20 (20½/20⅞/21¼)" above garter st.

**Shoulders and neck shaping:** Bind off 13 (13/14/14) sts at beg of next 2 rows, 13 (14/14/15) sts at beg of next 2 rows, AT THE SAME TIME, bind off center 47 sts for neck and, working both sides at once, work even.

*(Continued on page 136)*

**Cardigan**

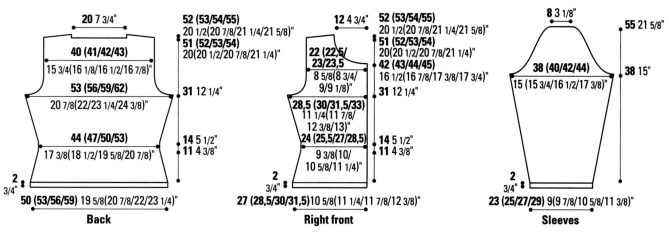

Back

Right front

Sleeves

(Continued from page 135)

# semones

### RIGHT FRONT

With 4 mm needles, cast on 64 (68/71/74) sts. Work in garter st for 2 cm or ¾", then K 1 row on WS, inc 7 sts evenly across = 71 (75/78/81) sts. Work as foll: 1 selvage st, *11 sts of Lozenge pat, 6 sts rev st st*, rep from *to* twice more, work 11 sts of Lozenge pat, 4 (8/11/14) sts rev st st, 2 sts Fancy Cable pat, 1 st rev st st, 1 selvage st. Cont in pat as established, working same decs, incs and armhole shaping at LHS as for back, AT THE SAME TIME, on 23rd row above garter st, replace 2nd and 4th Lozenge pat with rev st st. Work even until piece measures 42 (43/44/45) cm or 16½ (16⅞/17⅜/17¾)" above garter st.

**Neck shaping:** Bind off 5 sts at RHS of next row, then cont to bind off at same edge every other row: 4 sts once, 3 sts 3 times, 2 sts 4 times, 1 st 4 times. Work even until piece measures 51 (52/53/54) cm or 20 (20½/20⅞/21¼)" above garter st. Shape shoulder at LHS as for back.

### LEFT FRONT

Work as for right front, but in reverse.

### SLEEVES

With 4 mm needles, cast on 55 (59/63/69) sts. Work in garter st for 2 cm or ¾", then K 1 row on WS, inc 6 sts evenly across = 61 (65/69/75) sts. Work as foll: 1 selvage st, 1 st rev st st, 2 sts Fancy Cable pat, 0 (1/3/6) sts rev st st, 10 (11/11/11) sts of Lozenge pat beg with st 2 (1/1/1) of chart, 11 sts rev st st, 11 sts of Lozenge pat, 11 sts rev st st, 10 (11/11/11) sts of Lozenge pat beg with st 1 of chart, 0 (1/3/6) sts rev st st, 2 sts Fancy Cable pat, 1 st rev st st, 1 selvage st. Cont in pat as established, inc 1 st each side (4 sts in from each edge, and working inc sts into rev st st) every 8th row 9 times, every 6th row 6 times = 91 (95/99/105) sts, AT THE SAME TIME, on 23rd row above garter st, replace 1st and 3rd Lozenge pat with rev st st. Work even until piece measures 38 cm or 15" above garter st.

**Cap shaping:** Bind off 3 sts at beg of next 2 rows, 2 sts at beg of next 8 (12/16/22) rows, dec 1 st each side every other row 19 (17/15/12) times, bind off 2 sts at beg of next 2 rows, bind off 3 sts at beg of next 2 rows. Bind off rem 21 sts.

### TO MAKE UP/FINISHING

See tips on page 157.

Sew shoulder seams. With 4 mm needles, pick up and k165 (167/169/171) sts evenly along right side: 102 (104/106/108) sts along right front edge, 29 sts along front neck and 24 sts along half of back neck. K 1 row on WS, then bind off all sts. Work in same way on left side. Sew side seams. Sew sleeve seams. Sew sleeves into armholes. With crochet hook, work 1 row dc and 1 row crab st along front and neck edges. Note: Work 5 pairs of buttonholes (by ch 2, sk 2 sts for each buttonhole) on dc row of right front. Sew on buttons.

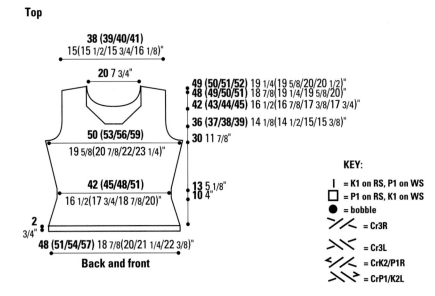

**Top**

38 (39/40/41)
15 (15 1/2/15 3/4/16 1/8)"

20 7 3/4"

49 (50/51/52) 19 1/4 (19 5/8/20/20 1/2)"
48 (49/50/51) 18 7/8 (19 1/4/19 5/8/20)"
42 (43/44/45) 16 1/2 (16 7/8/17 3/8/17 3/4)"
36 (37/38/39) 14 1/8 (14 1/2/15/15 3/8)"
30 11 7/8"

50 (53/56/59)
19 5/8 (20 7/8/22/23 1/4)"

42 (45/48/51)
16 1/2 (17 3/4/18 7/8/20)"

13 5 1/8"
10 4"

2 3/4"

48 (51/54/57) 18 7/8 (20/21 1/4/22 3/8)"

**Back and front**

**KEY:**

| = K1 on RS, P1 on WS
□ = P1 on RS, K1 on WS
● = bobble
╱╳ = Cr3R
╲╳ = Cr3L
╱╳ = CrK2/P1R
╲╳ = CrP1/K2L

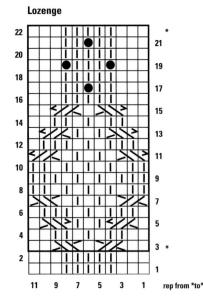

**Lozenge**

rep from *to*

*(Continued from page 69)*

# chili

### SLEEVES

With Louxor and 3½ mm needles, cast on 64 (70/74/80) sts and work 12 rows border, then work in woven st, inc 1 st each side every 8th row 7 (6/5/3) times, every 6th row 18 (19/20/22) times = 114 (120/124/130) sts. Work even until piece measures 38.5 (38/37.5/37) cm or 15⅛ (15/14⅝/14½)" above border. Bind off all sts.

### COLLAR

Beg at top edge. With Louxor and 3½ mm needles, cast on 90 sts and work in woven st, inc 1 st each side, alternately every 4th and 2nd row 4 times = 98 sts. Work even until piece measures 3 cm or 1⅛" from beg. Dec 1 st each side of next row, then every other row 8 times, AT THE SAME TIME, when piece measures 5 cm or 2" from beg, bind off center 48 sts for neck and working both sides at once, bind off from each neck edge 4 sts once, 3 sts 3 times. Bind off rem 3 sts each side.

### TO MAKE UP/FINISHING

See tips on page 157.

Embroider woven st diagonally on back, fronts, sleeves and collar and attach paillettes foll diagrams. Sew shoulder seams. Sew in sleeves so that bound-off row shows. Sew side and sleeve seams. Fold borders in half to WS at turning ridge and sew in place. Along each front, with Louxor and 3½ mm needles, pick up and K 128 (130/132/134) sts 110 (112/114/116) sts from A to B (see schematic), 18 sts from B to C) and work 12 rows border, inc 1 st at point B every other row twice, then dec 1 st at point B every other row twice. Bind off all sts. Fold in half to WS and sew in place. Around collar, with Louxor and 3⅛ mm needles, pick up and K 142 sts (12 from D to E, 17 from E to F, 84 from F to G, 17 form G to H and 12 from H to J) and work 12 rows border. Bind off. Sew on collar (on WS of body), matching points FC and EO on left front then GC and HO on right front. Sew on buttons.

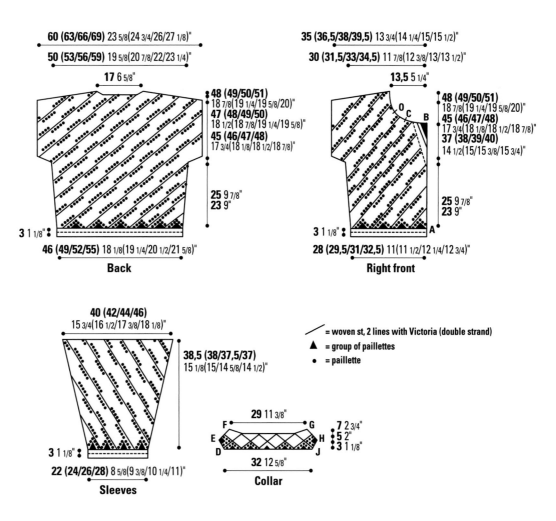

**60 (63/66/69)** 23 5/8(24 3/4/26/27 1/8)"
**50 (53/56/59)** 19 5/8(20 7/8/22/23 1/4)"
**17** 6 5/8"
**48 (49/50/51)** 18 7/8(19 1/4/19 5/8/20)"
**47 (48/49/50)** 18 1/2(18 7/8/19 1/4/19 5/8)"
**45 (46/47/48)** 17 3/4(18 1/8/18 1/2/18 7/8)"
**25** 9 7/8"
**23** 9"
**3** 1 1/8"
**46 (49/52/55)** 18 1/8(19 1/4/20 1/2/21 5/8)"
**Back**

**35 (36,5/38/39,5)** 13 3/4(14 1/4/15/15 1/2)"
**30 (31,5/33/34,5)** 11 7/8(12 3/8/13/13 1/2)"
**13,5** 5 1/4"
**48 (49/50/51)** 18 7/8(19 1/4/19 5/8/20)"
**45 (46/47/48)** 17 3/4(18 1/8/18 1/2/18 7/8)"
**37 (38/39/40)** 14 1/2(15/15 3/8/15 3/4)"
**25** 9 7/8"
**23** 9"
**3** 1 1/8"
**28 (29,5/31/32,5)** 11(11 1/2/12 1/4/12 3/4)"
**Right front**

**40 (42/44/46)** 15 3/4(16 1/2/17 3/8/18 1/8)"
**38,5 (38/37,5/37)** 15 1/8(15/14 5/8/14 1/2)"
**3** 1 1/8"
**22 (24/26/28)** 8 5/8(9 3/8/10 1/4/11)"
**Sleeves**

/ = woven st, 2 lines with Victoria (double strand)
▲ = group of paillettes
• = paillette

**29** 11 3/8"
**7** 2 3/4"
**5** 2"
**3** 1 1/8"
**32** 12 5/8"
**Collar**

*(Continued from page 71)*

# malachite

TO MAKE UP/FINISHING

See tips on page 157.

Sew shoulder seams. Set in sleeves. Sew side and sleeve seams.

Work 56 sts from holder (14 sts at each front, 28 sts at back), and work 10 cm or 4" in fancy pat, then bind off all sts.

Fold collar in half to WS and sew in place. Work 1 row dc along lower edge of body.

Pick up along each front 92 (94/96/98) sts with Noir and work 2 rows st st, then bind off all sts.

Sew in zipper.

Make a 5 cm or 2" hem at lower edge of sleeves.

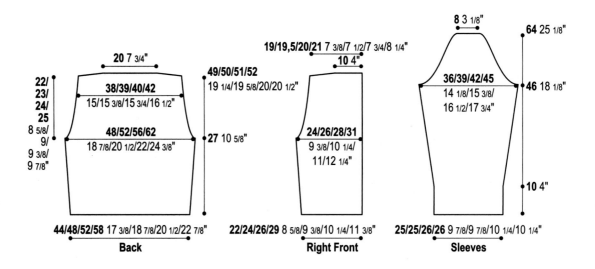

*(Continued from page 72)*

# léto

**KEY**

━━━ = Size Small
┅┅┅ = Size Medium
─── = Size Large
╌╌╌ = Size X-Large

☐ = st st
▨ = rev st st

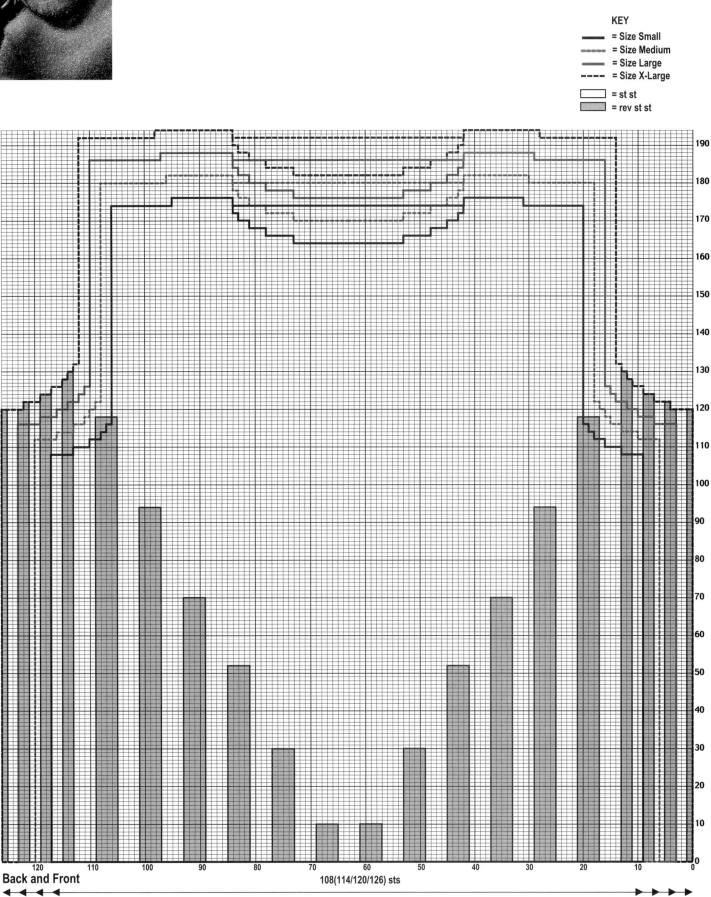

**Back and Front**

108(114/120/126) sts

*(Continued from page 139)*

# léto

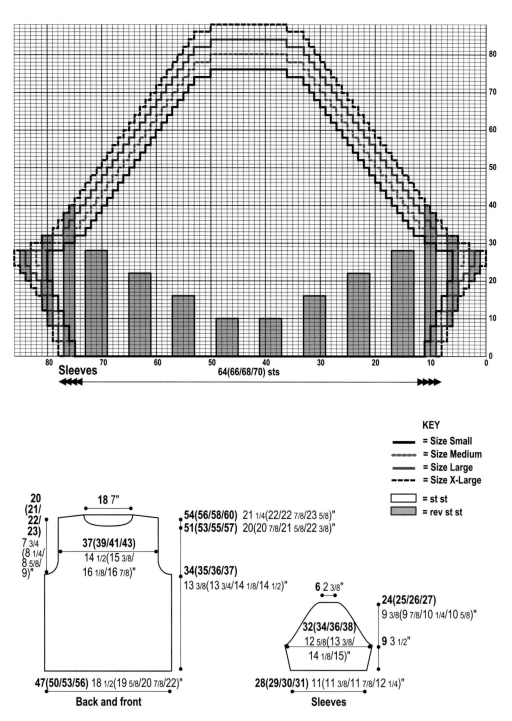

**Sleeves** 64(66/68/70) sts

**KEY**

—— = Size Small

- - - - - = Size Medium

—— = Size Large

- - - - = Size X-Large

□ = st st

▨ = rev st st

**20
(21/
22/
23)**
7 3/4
(8 1/4/
8 5/8/
9)"

**18** 7"

**37(39/41/43)**
14 1/2(15 3/8/
16 1/8/16 7/8)"

**54(56/58/60)** 21 1/4(22/22 7/8/23 5/8)"
**51(53/55/57)** 20(20 7/8/21 5/8/22 3/8)"

**34(35/36/37)**
13 3/8(13 3/4/14 1/8/14 1/2)"

**47(50/53/56)** 18 1/2(19 5/8/20 7/8/22)"
**Back and front**

**6** 2 3/8"

**32(34/36/38)**
12 5/8(13 3/8/
14 1/8/15)"

**24(25/26/27)**
9 3/8(9 7/8/10 1/4/10 5/8)"

**9** 3 1/2"

**28(29/30/31)** 11(11 3/8/11 7/8/12 1/4)"
**Sleeves**

*(Continued from page 75)*

# sayoun

### TO MAKE UP/FINISHING

See tips on page 157.

Sew on paillettes, beads (on top of paillettes) and the crystals (see charts). Sew shoulder seams. Set in sleeves. Sew side and sleeve seams. With Louxor and crochet hook, work 1 row dc around neck, and at lower edges of body and sleeves. Then work 1 row as foll: *1 dc, ch 2, sk 1 st*, rep from *to*.

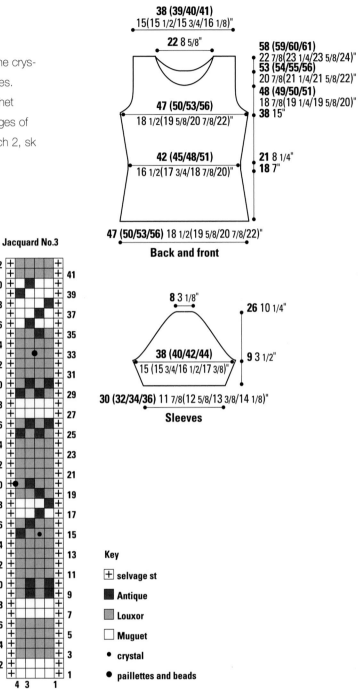

**Back and front**

**Sleeves**

**Jacquard No.1**

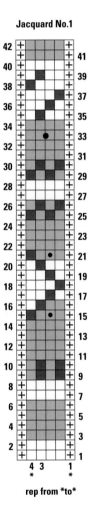

rep from *to*

**Jacquard No.2**

**Jacquard No.3**

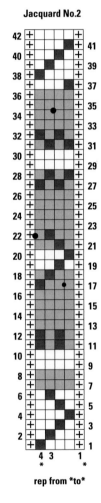

rep from *to*

**Key**

⊞ selvage st

■ Antique

▨ Louxor

☐ Muguet

• crystal

⬤ paillettes and beads

*(Continued from page 77)*

# blanc neige

### BACK

**Note:** The number of sts after the decs and incs is not always a multiple of 14 for fancy pat no. 1 or a multiple of 6 for fancy pat no. 2.

With Louxor and 3 mm needles, cast on 191 (201/213/223) sts and work in garter st for 1 cm or ⅜".

Change to 3½ mm needles and work in Fancy pat as foll: 13 (18/24/15) sts fancy pat no. 2, beg with 1 selvage st and st 4 (5/1/2) of chart, 5 sts cord st, 155 (155/155/183) sts fancy pat no. 1, beg with st 1 of chart, 5 sts cord st, 13 (18/24/15) sts fancy pat no. 2, beg with st 3 of chart. Cont as established, dec 1 st each side every 6th row 5 times, every 4th row 4 times = 173 (183/195/205) sts. Work even until piece measures 17 cm or 6⅝" above garter st. Inc 1 st each side of next row, then every 6th row 7 times, every 4th row 5 times = 199 (209/221/231) sts. Work even until piece measures 34 cm or 13⅜" above garter st.

**Armhole shaping:** Bind off 6 sts at beg of next 2 rows, 5 sts at beg of next 2 rows, 4 sts at beg of next 2 (2/4/4) rows, 3 sts at beg of next 2 (4/4/6) rows, 2 sts at beg of next 4 rows, dec 1 st each side every other row 2 (2/3/3) times = 151 (155/157/161) sts. Work even until piece measures 51 (52/53/54) cm or 20 (20½/20⅞/21¼)" above garter st.

**Neck shaping:** Bind off center 63 sts for back neck and, work both sides at once until piece measures 52 (53/54/55) cm or 20½ (20⅞/21¼/21⅝)" above garter st. Bind off rem 44 (46/47/49) sts each side for shoulders.

### RIGHT FRONT

With Louxor and 3 mm needles, cast on 95 (100/106/111) sts and work in garter st for 1 cm or ⅜". Change to 3½ mm needles and work in Fancy pat as foll: 1 selvage st, 5 sts cord st, 71 (71/71/85) sts fancy pat no. 1, beg with st 1 of chart, 5 sts cord st, 13 (18/24/15) sts fancy pat no. 2, beg with st 3 of chart. Cont as established, work same decs, incs and armhole shaping at LHS as for back. Work even until piece measures 40

(41/42/43) cm or 15¾ (16⅛/16½/16⅞)" above garter st.

**Neck shaping:** Bind off 6 sts at RHS of next row, then cont to bind off at same edge every other row: 5 sts once, 4 sts twice, 3 sts once, 2 sts 3 times, dec 1 st every other row 3 times. When piece measures 52 (53/54/55) cm or 20½ (20⅞/21¼/21⅝)" above garter st, bind off rem 44 (46/47/49) sts for shoulders.

### LEFT FRONT

Work as for right front, reversing shaping. Beg Fancy st no. 2 as for back.

### SLEEVE

With Louxor and 3 mm needles, cast on 99 (105/113/121) sts and work in garter st for 1 cm or ⅜". Change to 3½ mm needles and work in Fancy pat as foll: 16 (19/23/27) sts fancy pat no. 2, beg with 1 selvage st and st 0 (1/0/1) of chart, 5 sts cord st, 57 sts fancy pat no. 1, beg with st 1 of chart, 5 sts cord st, 16 (19/23/27) sts fancy pat no. 2, beg with st 3 of chart. Cont as established, AT SAME TIME, inc 1 st each side (working inc sts into fancy pat no. 2) every 6th row 15 times, every 4th row 3 times = 135 (141/149/157) sts. Work even until piece measures 27 cm or 10⅝" above garter st.

**Cap shaping:** Bind off 3 sts at beg of next 2 rows, 2 sts at beg of next 32 (38/46/54) rows, dec 1 st each side every other row 12 (9/5/1) times, bind off 2 sts at beg of next 2 rows, 3 sts at beg of next 2 rows. Bind off rem 31 sts.

### TO MAKE UP/FINISHING

See tips on page 157.

Sew shoulder seams. With Louxor and 3 mm needles, pick up and K 138 sts evenly around neck edge (45 sts along each front and 48 sts along back). K 1 row, then bind off all sts. Work in same way along each front, but pick up 116 (118/122/124) sts. Set in sleeves. Sew side and sleeve seams. With Louxor and 3 mm crochet hook, work 2 rows dc and 1 row crab st around neck and along each front. **Note:** On the 2nd dc row along right front, work 7 buttonholes (by ch 2, sk 2 sts), with the 1st buttonhole at beg of neck shaping, the other 6 spaced 6 cm or 2⅜" apart. Sew on buttons. Sew in shoulder pads.

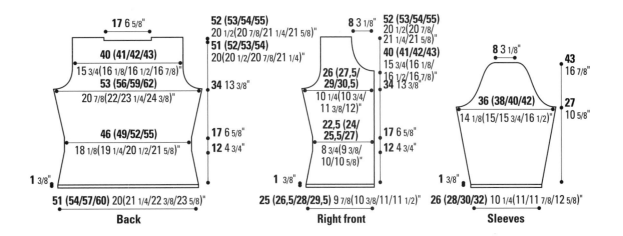

**17** 6 5/8"

**40 (41/42/43)**
15 3/4(16 1/8/16 1/2/16 7/8)"

**53 (56/59/62)**
20 7/8(22/23 1/4/24 3/8)"

**46 (49/52/55)**
18 1/8(19 1/4/20 1/2/21 5/8)"

**1** 3/8"

**51 (54/57/60)** 20(21 1/4/22 3/8/23 5/8)"

**Back**

**52 (53/54/55)**
20 1/2(20 7/8/21 1/4/21 5/8)"
**51 (52/53/54)**
20(20 1/2/20 7/8/21 1/4)"

**34** 13 3/8"

**17** 6 5/8"
**12** 4 3/4"

**8** 3 1/8"

**52 (53/54/55)**
20 1/2(20 7/8/
21 1/4/21 5/8)"
**40 (41/42/43)**
15 3/4(16 1/8/
16 1/2/16 7/8)"

**34** 13 3/8"

**26 (27,5/
29/30,5)**
10 1/4(10 3/4/
11 3/8/12)"

**22,5 (24/
25,5/27)**
8 3/4(9 3/8/
10/10 5/8)"

**17** 6 5/8"
**12** 4 3/4"

**1** 3/8"

**25 (26,5/28/29,5)** 9 7/8(10 3/8/11/11 1/2)"

**Right front**

**8** 3 1/8"

**43**
16 7/8"

**36 (38/40/42)**
14 1/8(15/15 3/4/16 1/2)"

**27**
10 5/8"

**1** 3/8"

**26 (28/30/32)** 10 1/4(11/11 7/8/12 5/8)"

**Sleeves**

### Fancy Pat no. 1

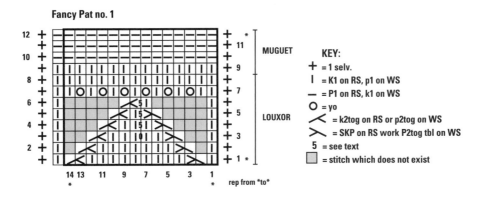

MUGUET

LOUXOR

14 13  11  9  7  5  3  1
*                    *      rep from *to*

**KEY:**

+ = 1 selv.

I = K1 on RS, p1 on WS

− = P1 on RS, k1 on WS

O = yo

⟋ = k2tog on RS or p2tog on WS

⟋ = SKP on RS work P2tog tbl on WS

5 = see text

▨ = stitch which does not exist

### Fancy Pat no. 2

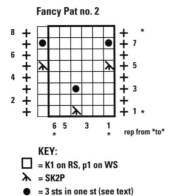

6 5  3  1
*           *   rep from *to*

**KEY:**

☐ = K1 on RS, p1 on WS

⅄ = SK2P

● = 3 sts in one st (see text)

*(Continued from page 81)*

# axis

**X-Small:** 1 single dec every 4th row twice and 1 single dec every 2nd row 33 times.

**Small:** 1 single dec every 4th row twice and 1 single dec every 2nd row 35 times.

**Medium:** 1 single dec every 4th row once and 1 single dec every 2nd row 38 times.

**Large:** 1 single dec every 2nd row 42 times.

**All sizes:** Bind off at RHS: 4 sts 3 times and 3 sts 3 times and at LHS: work 1 single dec every 2nd row 5 times.

## LEFT SLEEVE

Work as for right sleeve, reversing raglan shaping. The shorter side corresponds to the front raglan.

## TO MAKE UP/FINISHING

See tips on page 157.

Sew raglan sleeve caps to raglan armhole, leaving one back seam open.

Pick up 98 sts with col. Gaïa around neck (28 sts along back, 16 sts along each sleeve and 38 sts along front), and P 1 row on WS, then cont in fancy pat until piece measures 7 cm or 2¾" from beg. Reverse pat as foll: P 1 row on RS. **Row 2:** *P1, K1*, rep from *to*. Rep these 2 rows until piece measures 9 cm or 3½" from beg. Work stripes as foll: 2 rows col. Ultraviolet, 6 rows col. Gaïa, 2 rows col. Améthyste, 6 rows col. Gaïa, 2 rows col. Coloquinte, 6 rows col. Gaïa, 2 rows col. Ultraviolet, 4 rows col. Gaïa, binding off on the 4th row.

Sew last raglan seam and collar seam, reversing collar seam at 10 cm or 4" for turn back. Sew side and sleeve seams.

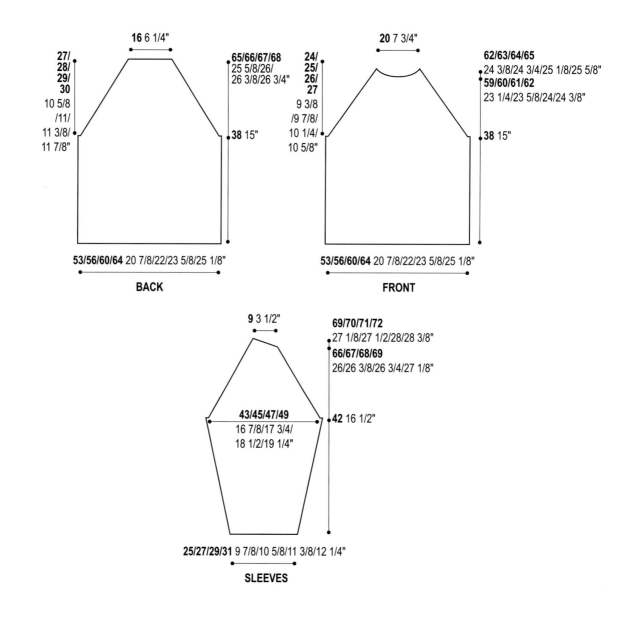

(Continued from page 83)

# cap ferrat/st. tropez

**Note:** The elongated sts correspond to the K sts of K1/P1 rib.

Inc 1 st each side every 6th row 1(1/0) times, every 4th row 12(12/14) times = 59 (59/61) sts. Work even until piece measures 47 cm or 18½" from beg.

**Cap shaping:** Bind off 7 (7/5) sts at beg of next 2 (2/4) rows, 8 (8/7) sts at beg of next 4 rows. Bind off rem 13 sts.

## COLLAR

With 10 mm needles and double strand, cast on 65 sts and work 4 cm or 1½" in K1/P1 rib. Cont 12 rows in reverse st st, working 1 bobble on 3rd row on the 5th st and the foll spaced 7 sts apart. On the 9th row, work bobbles in groups of five, with the 1st on the 9th st, the foll spaced 7 sts apart. After 12 rows have been worked, change to 12 mm needles and work in K1/P1 rib for 13 cm or 5⅛". Bind off all sts.

(Continued on page 146)

**WOMAN'S PULLOVER**

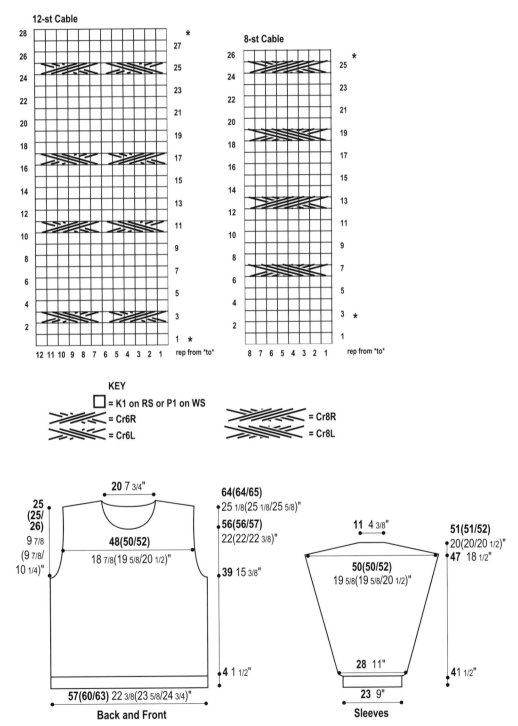

*(Continued from page 145)*

# cap ferrat/st. tropez

### TO MAKE UP/FINISHING

See tips on page 157.

Sew one shoulder seam. Sew collar around neck. Sew 2nd shoulder and collar seam. Set in sleeves. Sew side and sleeve seams.

### MAN'S PULLOVER

### STITCHES USED

**Garter st.**

See explanation of sts on page 157.

**Fancy pat:** Multiple of 10 sts plus 7 (see chart).

### BACK

With 3 mm needles, cast on 159 (171/183) sts and work 2 rows garter st. Change to 3½ mm needles and work in fancy pat, beg with the 10th (9th/8th) st of chart. Inc 1 st each side every 16th row 3 times = 165 (177/189) sts. Work even until piece measures 42 cm or 16½" from beg.

**Armhole shaping:** Bind off 3 sts at beg of next 4 rows, 2 sts at beg of next 2 (4/4) rows, dec 1 st each side every other row 2 (1/2) times = 145 (155/165) sts. Work even until piece measures 65 (66/67) cm or 25⅝ (26/26⅜)" from beg.

**Neck shaping:** Bind off center 43 sts sts for neck, and working both sides at once, bind off from each neck edge 7 sts once. When piece measures 66 (67/68) cm or 26 (26⅜/26¾)" from beg, bind off rem 44 (49/54) sts each side for shoulders.

### FRONT

Work same as back until piece measures 52 (53/54) cm or 20½ (20 ⅞/21¼)" from beg.

**Neck shaping:** Bind off center st for neck, and working both sides at once, dec at each neck edge every other row at 2 sts from edge: alternately *2 sts once, and 1 st once* for a total of 15 decs, then 1 st 13 times (at RHS work K2tog for dec 1, K3tog for dec 2, K1, P1 at LHS work P1, K1, SKP for dec 1, SK2P for dec 2). When piece measures 66 (67/68) cm or 26 (26⅜/26¾)" from beg, bind off rem 44 (49/54) sts each side for shoulders.

### SLEEVES

Cast on 77 (79/81) sts with 3 mm needles, and work 2 rows garter st. Change to 3½ mm needles and cont in fancy pat, beg with the 1st (10th/9th) st of chart. Inc 1 st each side every 6th row 12 (8/4) times, every 4th row 22 (28/34) times = 145 (151/157) sts. Work even until piece measures 53 cm or 20⅞" from beg.

**Cap shaping:** Work decs each side every other row at 2 sts from edge (at RHS work P1, K1, SKP for dec 1, SK2P for dec 2, at LHS work K2tog for dec 1, K3tog for dec 2, K1, P1): dec 2 sts 5 (5/3) times, dec 1 st 2 (2/6) times. Bind off rem 121 (127/133) sts.

### TO MAKE UP/FINISHING

See tips on page 157.

Sew one shoulder seam.

With 3 mm needles, pick up and K 145 sts around neck (44 sts along back, 50 sts along each front edge and 1 center st), work in garter st, working 1 double dec every other row over center 3 sts at center front as foll: sl 2 tog to RH needle, K1 then pass the 2 sts slipped sts over the K st). On the 6th row of garter st, bind off all sts. Sew 2nd shoulder and collar seam. Set in sleeves. Sew side and sleeve seams.

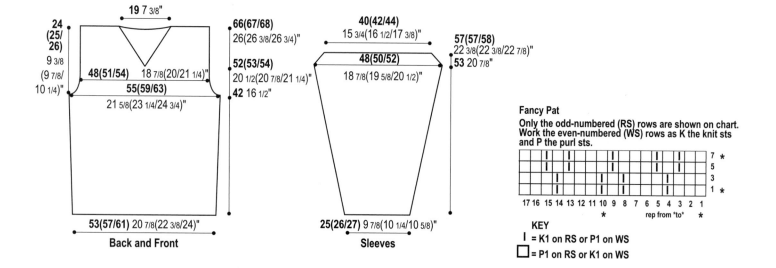

**Fancy Pat**
**Only the odd-numbered (RS) rows are shown on chart. Work the even-numbered (WS) rows as K the knit sts and P the purl sts.**

17 16 15 14 13 12 11 10 9 8 7 6 5 4 3 2 1

rep from *to*

**KEY**
I = K1 on RS or P1 on WS
☐ = P1 on RS or K1 on WS

**Back and Front**

**Sleeves**

*(Continued from page 85)*

# cannes/boulogne

**Note:** On the 4th row with Victoria, make 1 buttonhole (yo, K2tog) at 24 (29/34/41) sts from each edge.

Cont in fancy pat with No. 4 as foll: 8 (13/18/25) sts fancy pat, bind off next 34 sts and work sts of one pocket lining to replace bound-off sts, 43 sts fancy pat, bind off next 34 sts and work sts of 2nd pocket lining to replace bound-off sts, 8 (13/18/25) sts fancy pat. Cont on all sts until piece measures 44 cm or 17⅜" from beg.

**Armhole shaping:** Bind off 4 sts at beg of next 2(2/2/4) rows, 3 sts at beg of next 2 (4/4/4) rows, 2 sts at beg of next 4 (4/8/8) rows and 1 st at beg of next 2 (4/4/4) rows = 103 (105/107/113) sts. Work even until piece measures 47 (48/49/50) cm or 18½ (18⅞/19¼/19⅝)" from beg.

**Placket shaping:** Bind off center st and work both sides at same time until piece measures 57 (58/59/60) cm or 22⅜ (22⅞/23¼/23⅝)" from beg.

**Neck shaping:** Bind off from each neck edge 4 sts once, 3 sts twice, 2 sts 4 times and 1 st 4 times. When piece measures 63 (64/65/66) cm or 24¾ (25⅛/25⅝/26)" from beg, shape shoulders same as back.

## SLEEVES

With No. 4, cast on 71 (77/81/87) sts and work as foll: 2 (3/3/4) sts reverse st st, 10 sts cable no. 1, 2 (3/4/5) sts reverse st st, 10 sts cable no. 1, 2 (3/4/5) sts reverse st st, 19 sts cable no. 2, 2 (3/4/5) sts reverse st st, 10 sts cable no. 1, 2(3/4/5) sts reverse st st, 10 sts cable no. 1, 2 (3/3/4) sts reverse st st. Inc 1 st each side every 8th row 3 times and every 10th row 3 times = 83 (89/93/99) sts. Work even until piece measures 21 cm or 8¼" from beg. Work 2 rows woven st, dec 6 sts on first row = 77

(83/87/93) sts. Work 4 rows woven st with Victoria and 4 rows with Kanpur. Cont in fancy pat with No. 4. Inc 1 st each side every 4th row 2 (5/11/11) times and every 6th row 8 (6/2/2) times = 97 (105/113/119) sts. Work even until piece measures 40 cm or 15¾" from beg.

**Cap shaping:** Bind off 3 sts at beg of next 2 rows, 2 sts at beg of next 6 (10/14/16) rows, dec 1 st each side every other row 22 (18/14/11) times, bind off 2 sts at beg of next 4 (8/12/16) rows and 3 sts at beg of next 2 rows. Bind off rem 21 sts.

## COLLAR

With No. 4, cast on 96 sts and work 2 sts fancy pat, 1 st reverse st st, 10 sts cable no. 1 9 times, 1 st reverse st st and 2 sts fancy pat. Work even until piece measures 5 cm or 2" from beg. Inc 2 sts in the center 4 groups of P-4 sts = 104 sts. When piece measures 10 cm or 4" from beg, bind off all sts.

## TO MAKE UP/FINISHING

See tips on page 157.

Sew pocket linings in place.

Along RHS of placket, pick up and K 22 sts with Kanpur, work 1 row in garter st, then 2 rows with Victoria, working 1 buttonhole (yo, K2tog) on the 2nd row at 2 sts from edge. Bind off with Victoria.

Work in same way along LHS, omitting buttonhole. Sew end of these 2 bands, overlapping them.

With Kanpur, pick up and K 20 sts each side of collar and work as before.

Set in sleeves. Sew side and sleeve seams.

Sew collar around neck.

Sew on buttons (one for each pocket and one at neck).

*(Continued on page 148)*

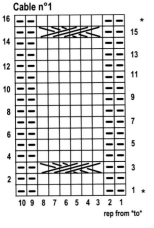

**Cable n°1**

16  15
14  13
12  11
10  9
8   7
6   5
4   3
2   1

10 9 8 7 6 5 4 3 2 1
rep from *to*

**WOMAN'S CHARTS AND SCHEMATICS**

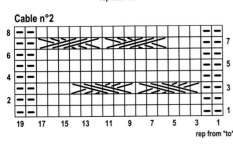

**Cable n°2**

8  7
6  5
4  3
2  1

19  17  15  13  11  9  7  5  3  1
rep from *to*

**KEY**

− = P1 on RS or K1 on WS
□ = K1 on RS or P1 on WS
⤬ = Cr6R
⤬ = Cr6L

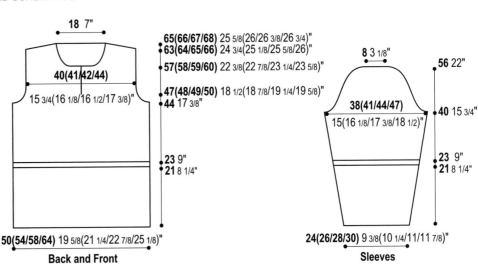

18 7"

65(66/67/68) 25 5/8(26/26 3/8/26 3/4)"
63(64/65/66) 24 3/4(25 1/8/25 5/8/26)"
57(58/59/60) 22 3/8(22 7/8/23 1/4/23 5/8)"
47(48/49/50) 18 1/2(18 7/8/19 1/4/19 5/8)"
44 17 3/8"

40(41/42/44)
15 3/4(16 1/8/16 1/2/17 3/8)"

23 9"
21 8 1/4"

50(54/58/64) 19 5/8(21 1/4/22 7/8/25 1/8)"

**Back and Front**

8 3 1/8"
56 22"

38(41/44/47)
15(16 1/8/17 3/8/18 1/2)"
40 15 3/4"

23 9"
21 8 1/4"

24(26/28/30) 9 3/8(10 1/4/11/11 7/8)"

**Sleeves**

*(Continued from page 147)*

# cannes/boulogne

### MAN'S PULLOVER

### STITCHES USED

K2/P2 rib, st st.

See explanation of sts on page 157.

**Cables no. 1 and no. 2:** See charts.

**CrK4R:** Slip 2 sts to cn and hold to back, K2, K2 from cn.

**CrK4L:** Slip 2 sts to cn and hold to front, K2, K2 from cn.

### FRONT

With 3½ mm needles, cast on 122 (130/138/146) sts and work in K2/P2 rib, beg and end with P2, for 6 cm or 2⅜", then P 1 row on WS, inc 2 (2/2/4) sts = 124 (132/140/150) sts. Change to 4 mm needles and cont in st st and cables, foll chart until piece measures 39 cm or 15⅜" from beg.

**Armhole shaping:** Bind off 4 sts at beg of next 2 rows, 3 sts at beg of next 2 rows, 2 sts at beg of next 2 rows and 1 st at beg of next 4 rows = 102 (110/118/128) sts. Work even until piece measures 59 (60/61/62) cm or 23¼ (23⅝/24/24⅜)" from beg.

**Neck shaping:** Bind off center 20 sts for neck, and working both sides at once, bind off from each neck edge 5 sts once, 3 sts once, 2 sts once and 1 st once. Work even until piece measures 63 (64/65/66) cm or 24¾ (25⅛/25⅝/26)" from beg.

**Shoulder shaping:** Bind off from each shoulder edge 10 (11/12/14) sts 3 (2/1/2) times, 0 (12/13/15) sts 0 (1/2/1) times.

### BACK

Work same as front, but reverse the st st and cables, until piece measures 63 (64/65/66) cm or 24¾ (25⅛/25⅝/26)" from beg.

**Shoulder and neck shaping:** Shape shoulder same as front, AT THE SAME TIME, bind off center 14 sts for neck and working both sides at once, bind off from each neck edge 14 sts once.

### SLEEVES

With 3½ mm needles, cast on 58(62/66/70) sts and work in K2/P2 rib for 6 cm or 2⅜". Change to 4 mm needles and cont in st st and cables, foll chart, inc 1 st each side every 4th row 22 (23/24/27) times and every 6th row 5 (4/3/0) times = 112 (116/120/124) sts. Work even until piece measures 49 (48.5/47.5/45.5) cm or 19¼ (19/18¾/17⅞)" from beg.

**Cap shaping:** Bind off 6 (6/6/7) sts at beg of next 2 rows, 4 sts at beg of next 6 (8/10/10) rows, 3 sts at beg of next 4 (4/4/6) rows and 2 sts at beg of next 6 (4/2/0) rows. Bind off rem 52 sts.

### TO MAKE UP/FINISHING

See tips on page 157.

Sew one shoulder seam.

With 3½ mm needles, pick up and K106 sts around neck (60 along front and 46 along back), and work in K2/P2 rib for 4 cm or 1½", then bind off all sts.

Sew 2nd shoulder and neckband seam. Set in sleeves. Sew side and sleeve seams.

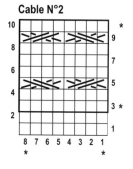

**Cable N°2**

**Cable N°1**

rep from *to*

### KEY

☐ = K1 on RS or P1 on WS

⤬ = CrK4R

⤬ = CrK4L

### MAN'S CHARTS AND SCHEMATICS

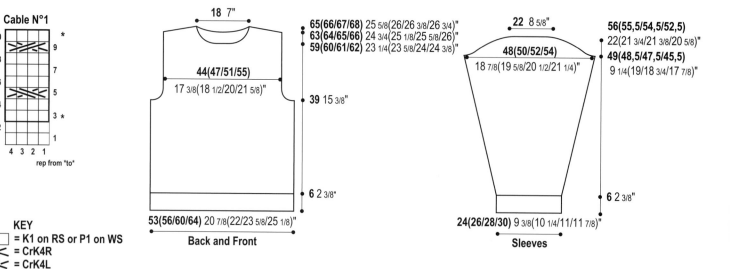

18  7"

65(66/67/68) 25 5/8(26/26 3/8/26 3/4)"
63(64/65/66) 24 3/4(25 1/8/25 5/8/26)"
59(60/61/62) 23 1/4(23 5/8/24/24 3/8)"

44(47/51/55)
17 3/8(18 1/2/20/21 5/8)"

39 15 3/8"

6 2 3/8"

53(56/60/64) 20 7/8(22/23 5/8/25 1/8)"

**Back and Front**

22  8 5/8"

56(55,5/54,5/52,5)
22(21 3/4/21 3/8/20 5/8)"

48(50/52/54)
18 7/8(19 5/8/20 1/2/21 1/4)"

49(48,5/47,5/45,5)
9 1/4(19/18 3/4/17 7/8)"

6 2 3/8"

24(26/28/30) 9 3/8(10 1/4/11/11 7/8)"

**Sleeves**

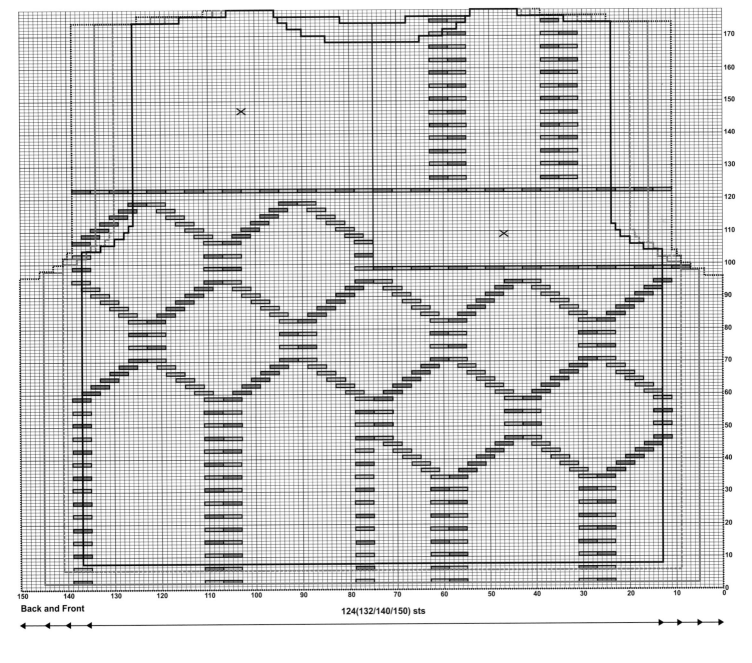

Back and Front

124(132/140/150) sts

**KEY**

—— = Size **X**-Small

------ = Size Small

—— = Size Medium

.......... = Size Large

background in st st

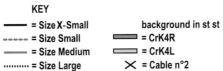 = CrK4R

= CrK4L

X = Cable n°2

*(Continued on page 150)*

*(Continued from page 149)*

# cannes/boulogne

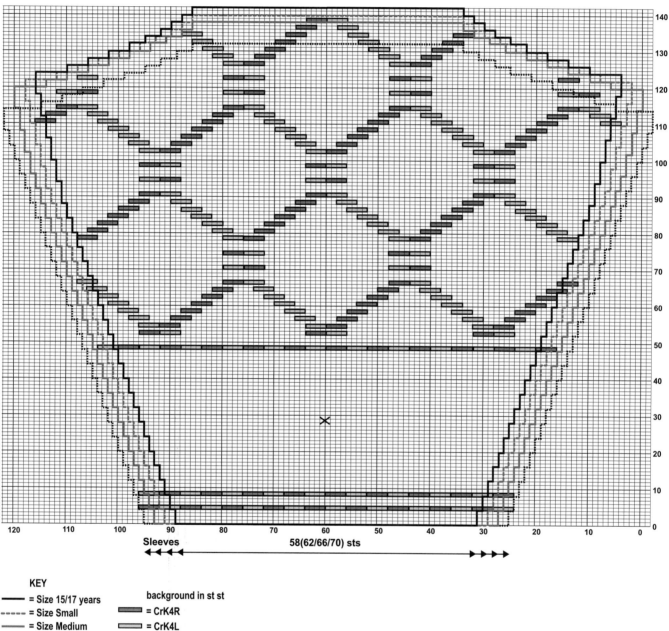

**KEY**

| | |
|---|---|
| ——— = Size 15/17 years | **background in st st** |
| ----- = Size Small | ▬▬▬ = CrK4R |
| ——— = Size Medium | ▬▬▬ = CrK4L |
| ········ = Size Large | ✕ = Cable n°2 |

*(Continued from page 87)*

# antre/atrium

Work even until piece measures 140 (144/148) cm or 55 (56¾/58⅜)" from beg. Bind off all sts.

### WAISTBANDS

Cast on 140 (152/164) sts and work in 6-st cable for 12 (13/14) cm or 4¾ (5⅛/5½)" from beg. Dec 1 P st in each group of P2 = 116 (126/136) sts.

Work even until piece measures 14 (15/16) cm or 5½ (5⅞/6¼)" from beg. Bind off all sts. Work a 2nd band in same way.

### TO MAKE UP/FINISHING

See tips on page 157.

Sew each waistband to lower edge of body.

Sew side and sleeve seams.

### MAN'S SWEATER

### STITCHES USED

**K1/P1 rib.**

See explanation of sts on page 157.

**Fancy pat:** See chart.

**Dec 1 st at 1 st from edge:** at RHS, K2tog, work 1 st. At LHS, work 1 st, 1 SKP.

### BACK

With 2 ½ mm needles and Noir, cast on 135 (143/149) sts and work sts as foll: 46 (50/53) sts K1/P1 rib, 43 sts fancy pat beg with the 6th st, 46 (50/53) sts K1/P1 rib and on the 3rd row, 8th row, 13th row, 18th row and 22nd row of chart, work in short rows as foll: work the first 89 (93/96) sts, turn work, work 43 sts fancy pat, turn work, work the last 89 (93/96) sts = 32 rows in fancy pat and 22 rows in K1/P1 rib.

When piece measures 5 cm or 2" from beg, cont in fancy pat with 3 mm needles, inc 16 sts on first row and work sts as foll:

**Small:** *1 st Noir, 1 st Patine, 7 sts Noir, 1 st Patine*, rep from *to*, then foll chart beg with the 12th st of 6th row = 151 sts.

**Medium:** *3 sts Noir, 1 st Patine, 1 st Noir, 1 st Patine, 4 sts Noir*, rep from *to*, then foll chart beg with the 8th st of 6th row = 159 sts.

**Large:** *6 sts Noir, 1 st Patine, 1 st Noir, 1 st Patine, 1 st Noir*, rep from *to*, then foll chart beg with the 5th st of 6th row = 165 sts.

Work even until piece measures 40 cm or 15¾" from beg.

**Armhole shaping:** Bind off 5 sts at beg of next 2 rows, 3

sts at beg of next 2 rows, 2 sts at beg of next 4 rows, 1 st at beg of next 4 rows = 123 (131/137) sts.

Work even until piece measures 63 (64/65) cm or 24¾ (25⅛/25⅝)" from beg. Bind off rem sts.

### FRONT

Work same as back until piece measures 47 (48/49) cm or 18½ (18⅞/19¼)" from beg.

**Neck shaping:** Bind off center st and working both sides at once, dec 1 st at 1 st from neck edge alternately every 4th and 2nd row a total of 26 times.

Work even until piece measures 63 (64/65) cm or 24¾ (25⅛/25⅝)" from beg. Bind off rem 35 (39/42) sts each side for shoulders.

### SLEEVES

With 2½ mm needles and Noir, cast on 63 (69/75) sts and work sts as foll: 20 (23/26) sts K1/P1 rib, 23 sts fancy pat, 20 23 (26) sts K1/P1 rib, at the 3rd row, 8th row, 13th row, 18th row and 22nd row of chart work in rows as foll: work first 43 (46/49) sts in K1/P1 rib, turn, work 23 sts fancy pat, turn, work last 43 (46/49) in K1/P1 rib = 32 rows in fancy pat and 22 rows in K1/P1 rib.

Work even until piece measures 5 cm or 2" from beg. Cont in fancy pat with 3 mm needles, working Row 1 as foll:

**Small:** *5 sts Noir, 1 st Patine, 1 st Noir, 1 st Patine, 2 sts Noir*, rep from *to*, then foll chart beg with the 12th st of the 6th row, inc 1 st each side every 8th row 28 times = 119 sts.

**Medium:** *1 st Patine, 7 sts Noir, 1 st Patine, 1 st Noir*, rep from *to*, then foll chart beg with the 8th st of the 6th row, inc 1 st each side every 8th row 28 times = 125 sts.

**Large:** *1 st Noir, 1 st Patine, 1 st Noir, 1 st Patine, 6 sts Noir*, rep from *to*, then foll chart beg with the 5th st of the 6th row, inc 1 st each side every 8th row 28 times = 131 sts.

Work even until piece measures 48 cm or 18⅞" from beg.

**Cap shaping:** Bind off 5 (5/4) sts at beg of next 2 rows, 2 sts at beg of next 6 (8/10) rows, 1 st at beg of next 2 (4/8) rows. Bind off rem 95 sts.

### TO MAKE UP/FINISHING

See tips on page 157.

Sew shoulders seams. Set in sleeves. Sew side and sleeve seams.

With 2½ mm needles and Noir, cast on 12 sts and work 55 cm or 21⅝" in K1/P1 rib, then bind off.

Sew band around neck, overlapping left over right and sew to point at center front (see photo)

*(Continued on page 152)*

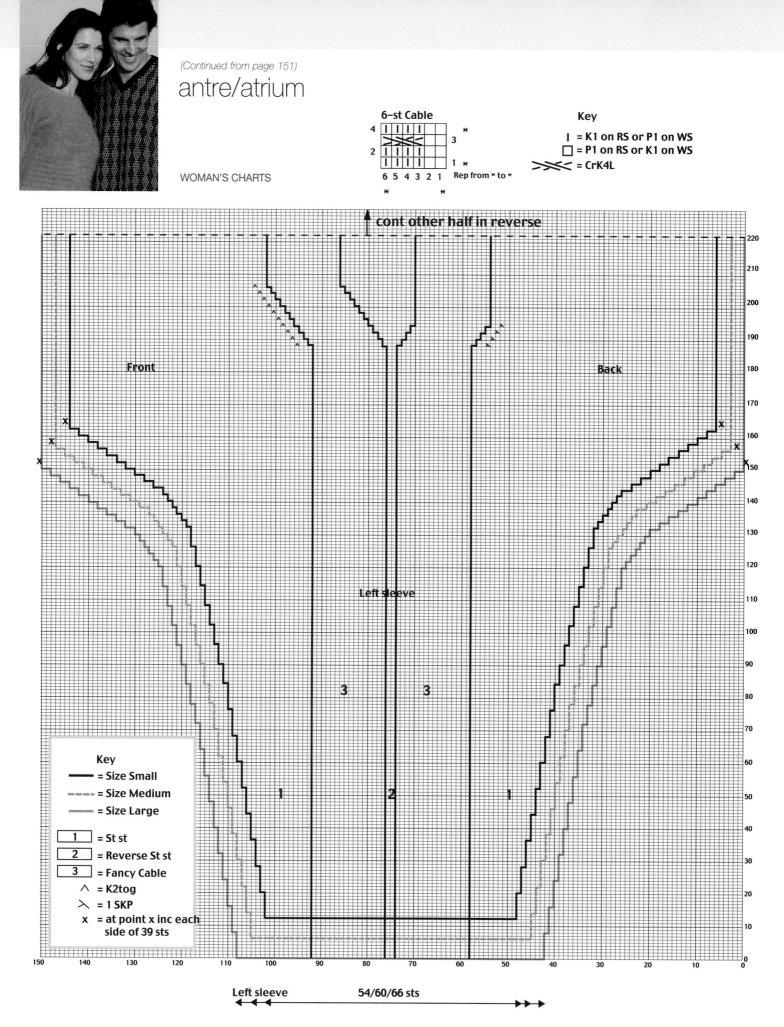

(Continued from page 151)

# antre/atrium

**WOMAN'S CHARTS**

**6-st Cable**

4 | | | | | |
        3 *
2 | | | | | |
        1 *
6 5 4 3 2 1    Rep from * to *

**Key**

| = K1 on RS or P1 on WS

□ = P1 on RS or K1 on WS

✕ = CrK4L

cont other half in reverse

Front

Back

Left sleeve

Left sleeve

**Key**

— = Size Small

--- = Size Medium

— = Size Large

1 = St st

2 = Reverse St st

3 = Fancy Cable

∧ = K2tog

⅄ = 1 SKP

x = at point x inc each side of 39 sts

54/60/66 sts

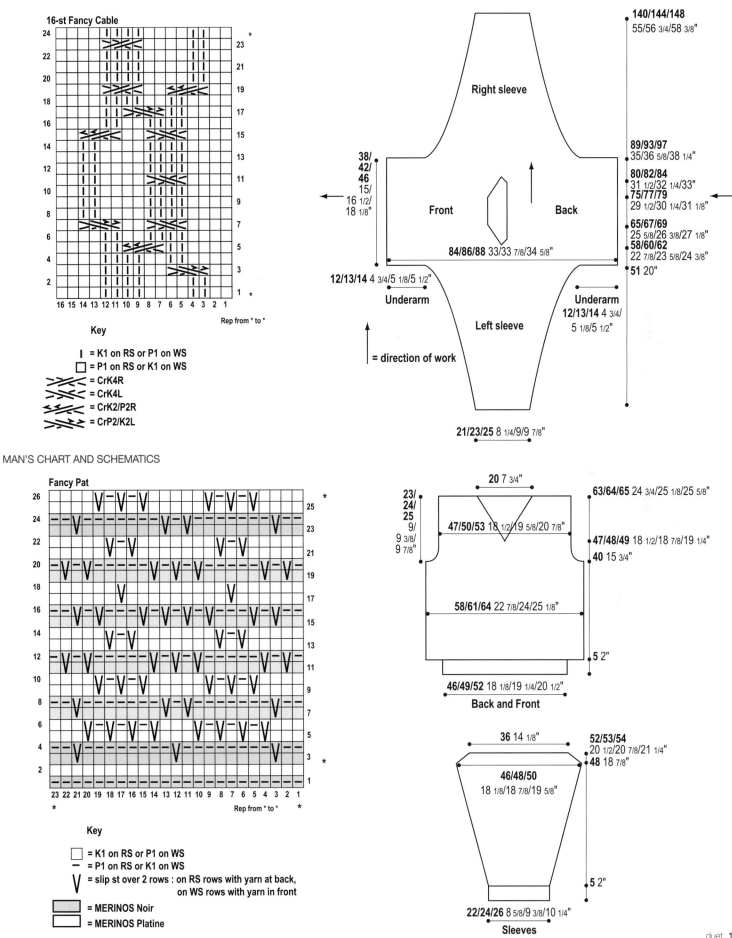

### 16-st Fancy Cable

24 22 20 18 16 14 12 10 8 6 4 2

23 21 19 17 15 13 11 9 7 5 3 1

16 15 14 13 12 11 10 9 8 7 6 5 4 3 2 1

Rep from * to *

### Key

I = K1 on RS or P1 on WS
☐ = P1 on RS or K1 on WS
= CrK4R
= CrK4L
= CrK2/P2R
= CrP2/K2L

### Right sleeve

140/144/148 55/56 3/4/58 3/8"

38/ 42/ 46 15/ 16 1/2/ 18 1/8"

Front        Back

89/93/97 35/36 5/8/38 1/4"
80/82/84 31 1/2/32 1/4/33"
75/77/79 29 1/2/30 1/4/31 1/8"
65/67/69 25 5/8/26 3/8/27 1/8"
58/60/62 22 7/8/23 5/8/24 3/8"
51 20"

84/86/88 33/33 7/8/34 5/8"

12/13/14 4 3/4/5 1/8/5 1/2"

Underarm

Left sleeve

Underarm
12/13/14 4 3/4/ 5 1/8/5 1/2"

= direction of work

21/23/25 8 1/4/9/9 7/8"

## MAN'S CHART AND SCHEMATICS

### Fancy Pat

26 24 22 20 18 16 14 12 10 8 6 4 2

25 23 21 19 17 15 13 11 9 7 5 3 1

23 22 21 20 19 18 17 16 15 14 13 12 11 10 9 8 7 6 5 4 3 2 1

Rep from * to *

### Key

☐ = K1 on RS or P1 on WS
− = P1 on RS or K1 on WS
V = slip st over 2 rows : on RS rows with yarn at back,
    on WS rows with yarn in front
▨ = MERINOS Noir
☐ = MERINOS Platine

20 7 3/4"

23/ 24/ 25 9/ 9 3/8/ 9 7/8"

47/50/53 18 1/2/19 5/8/20 7/8"

63/64/65 24 3/4/25 1/8/25 5/8"
47/48/49 18 1/2/18 7/8/19 1/4"
40 15 3/4"

58/61/64 22 7/8/24/25 1/8"

46/49/52 18 1/8/19 1/4/20 1/2"

### Back and Front

5 2"

36 14 1/8"

46/48/50 18 1/8/18 7/8/19 5/8"

52/53/54 20 1/2/20 7/8/21 1/4"
48 18 7/8"

5 2"

22/24/26 8 5/8/9 3/8/10 1/4"

### Sleeves

*(Continued from page 88)*

# dijon

**TO MAKE UP/FINISHING**

See tips on page 157.

Sew one shoulder seam.

With 3 mm needles and Vert de Gris, pick up and K110 sts evenly around neck (48 sts along back, 62 sts along front), and work in K2/P2 rib, beg with K2, for 7 cm or 2¾".

Change to 3½ mm needles and cont in rib until piece measures 18 cm or 7" from beg. Bind off all sts.

Sew 2nd shoulder and neckband seam.

Set in sleeves. Sew side and sleeve seams.

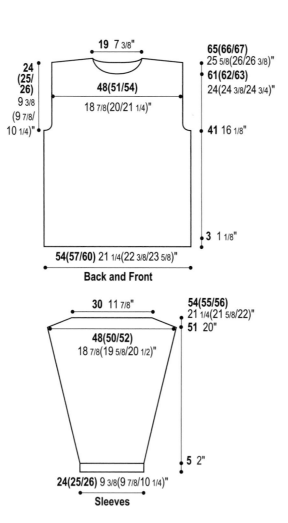

**19**  7 3/8"

**65(66/67)** 25 5/8(26/26 3/8)"

**48(51/54)** **61(62/63)** 24(24 3/8/24 3/4)"

18 7/8(20/21 1/4)"

**24 (25/ 26)** 9 3/8 (9 7/8/ 10 1/4)"

**41** 16 1/8"

**3** 1 1/8"

**54(57/60)** 21 1/4(22 3/8/23 5/8)"

**Back and Front**

**30**  11 7/8"

**54(55/56)** 21 1/4(21 5/8/22)"

**48(50/52)** **51** 20"

18 7/8(19 5/8/20 1/2)"

**5** 2"

**24(25/26)** 9 3/8(9 7/8/10 1/4)"

**Sleeves**

**Jacquard**

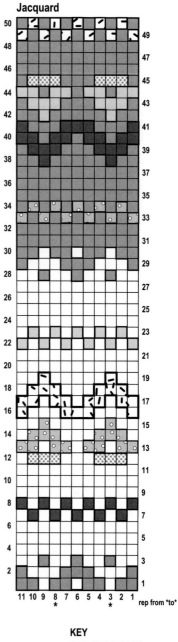

rep from *to*

**KEY**
**CACHEMIR'ANNY**

= Boisé

= Écru

= Miel

= Bronze

= Dubaï

= Vert de gris

= Camel

(Continued from page 91)

# amazone/aucuba

### MAN'S SWEATER

### STITCHES USED

K2/P2 rib.

See explanation of sts on page 157.

**Fancy pat:** See chart

**CrSl1/K1L:** K the 2nd st passing behind the first st, then sl the first st and drop sts from LH needle at same time.

**CrK1/Sl1R:** Sl the 2nd st passing in front of the first st, then K the first st and drop sts from LH needle at same time.

### BACK

Cast on 170 (182/194) sts and work in fancy pat beg with the 24th (18th/12th) st of chart.

Inc 1 st each side every 28th (30th/26th) row 4 (2/6) times, every 26th (28th/24th) row 2 (4/1) times = 182 (194/208) sts.

Work even until piece measures 42 (44/46) cm or 16½ (17⅜/18⅛)" from beg.

**Armhole shaping:** Bind off 2 sts at beg of next 2 rows, dec 1 st each side every other row 12 (13/16) times = 154 (164/172) sts.

Work even until piece measures 65 (68/71) cm or 25⅝ (26¾/28)" from beg.

**Shoulder shaping:** Bind off 20 (23/25) sts at beg of next 4 (2/2) rows, 0 (22/24) sts at beg of next 0 (2/2) rows. Place rem 74 sts on a holder for back neck.

### FRONT

Work same as back until piece measures 61 (64/67) cm or 24 (25⅛/26⅜)" from beg.

**Neck shaping:** Place center 36 sts on a holder for neck,

and working both sides at once, bind off from each neck edge 5 sts once, 4 sts once, 3 sts once, 2 sts twice, 1 st 3 times.

Work even until piece measures 65 (68/71) cm or 25⅝ (26¾/28)" from beg. Shape shoulder same as back.

### SLEEVES

Cast on 70 (76/82) sts and work in fancy pat, beg with the 20th (17th/14th) st of chart.

Inc 1 st each side every 6th row 23 times, every 4th row 16 times = 148 (154/160) sts.

Work even until piece measures 51 cm or 20" from beg.

**Cap shaping:** Bind off 2 sts at beg of next 6 rows, dec 1 st each side every 2nd row 7 times. Bind off rem 122 (128/134) sts.

### TO MAKE UP/FINISHING

See tips on page 157.

Sew left shoulder seam.

Pick up and K 26 sts along side of front neck, work 36 sts from holder, pick up and K 26 sts along other side of front neck, work 74 sts from back neck holder, and work as foll: 1 selvage st, K1, *P2, K2*, rep from *to* 2 times, 68 sts in fancy pat, 18 sts K2/P2 rib beg with K2, 56 sts fancy pat, 9 sts K2/P2 rib beg with K2, 1 selvage st.

Cont as established until piece measures 11 cm or 4⅜" from beg. Work as foll: 1 selvage st, K1, *P2, K2*, rep from *to* 2 times, °K2tog°, rep from °to° 34 times, 18 sts K2/P2 rib, *K2tog*, rep from *to* 28 times, 9 sts K2/P2 rib, 1 selvage st, then bind off all sts on WS with double strand.

Sew right shoulder seam.

Set in sleeves. Sew side and sleeve seams.

(Continued on page 156)

### WOMAN'S SCHEMATICS

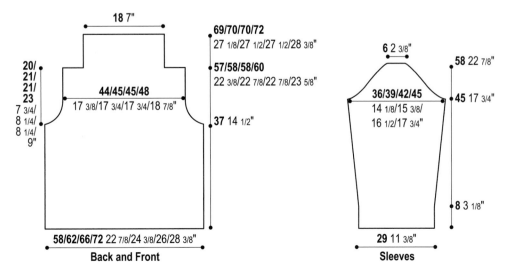

**Back and Front**

**Sleeves**

*(Continued from page 155)*

# amazone/aucuba

WOMAN'S CHART

**Cable**
Only the odd-numbered (RS) rows are shown.
Work the even-numbered rows as K the knit sts and P the purl sts.

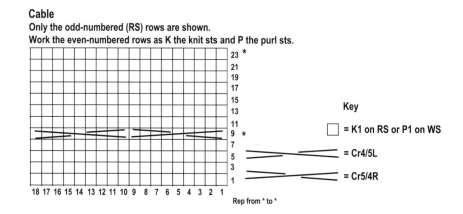

**Key**

☐ = K1 on RS or P1 on WS

⟨⟩ = Cr4/5L

⟨⟩ = Cr5/4R

Rep from * to *

MAN'S SCHEMATICS

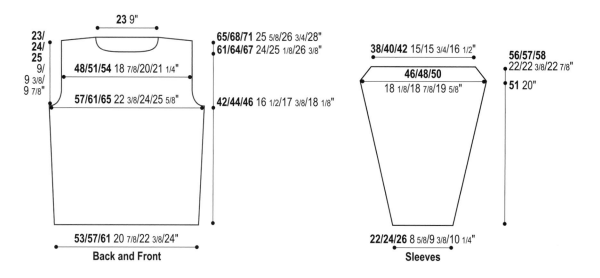

23 9"

**23/24/25** 9/9 3/8/9 7/8"

**48/51/54** 18 7/8/20/21 1/4"

**57/61/65** 22 3/8/24/25 5/8"

**65/68/71** 25 5/8/26 3/4/28"

**61/64/67** 24/25 1/8/26 3/8"

**42/44/46** 16 1/2/17 3/8/18 1/8"

**53/57/61** 20 7/8/22 3/8/24"
**Back and Front**

**38/40/42** 15/15 3/4/16 1/2"

**46/48/50** 18 1/8/18 7/8/19 5/8"

**56/57/58** 22/22 3/8/22 7/8"

**51** 20"

**22/24/26** 8 5/8/9 3/8/10 1/4"
**Sleeves**

**Fancy Pat**
Only the RS (odd-numbered) rows are shown on chart.
Work all WS (even-numbered) rows as K the knit sts and P the purl sts.

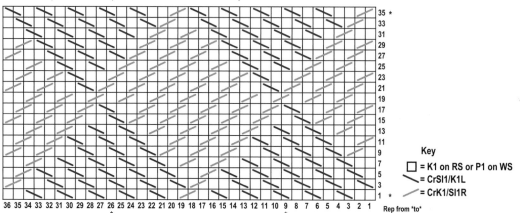

**Key**

☐ = K1 on RS or P1 on WS

╱ = CrSl1/K1L

╱ = CrK1/Sl1R

Rep from *to*

# anny blatt's advice

## Important

To ensure a perfect fit, it is ESSENTIAL to make (or knit) a swatch before starting to work. Cast on the number of stitches and work the number of rows stated in the gauge as provided in the instructions.

–If your finished piece measures *more* than 10cm or 4" square, you are knitting too loosely. Use smaller size needles.

–If your finished piece measures *less* than 10cm or 4" square, you are knitting too tightly. Use larger size needles.

–If your tension (gauge) square matches ours, you can begin by following the instructions.

**Warning to first readers:** These sweaters are made exclusively for and with Anny Blatt yarns. Each one of them is carefully created by the Anny Blatt design team taking full advantage of the unique characteristics of the yarn. Any substitution may affect the overall appearance and feel of the garment.

By using these very unique yarns, you will be sure to get the Anny Blatt legendary fine quality as well as the Anny Blatt ultimate look recognized worldwide.

**Our designs are exclusive. Commercial reproduction is forbidden without special authorization from Anny Blatt USA, Inc.**

**Jaquard Pat:** Read charts from right to left on RS rows and from left to right on WS rows. Use a separate ball for each block of color. To avoid holes in work when changing colors, twist yarns on WS. At every color change, make 1st row a K row on RS or P row on WS (to prevent color from previous row from showing through).

**Blocking directions:** Place each knitted piece on a towel over a flat surface, and pin to measurements following schematic. Steam lightly (except for Mohair, Angora and Stretch' Anny). Allow to dry, then remove pins.

## Abbreviations

*...* = Rep between *s as many times as indicated, otherwise until the end of the row.

**alt** = alternate(ly)

**approx** = approximately

**beg** = begin(ning)

**Ch** = chain

**cm** = centimeter(s)

**cn** = cable needle

**cont** = continue

**Dc** = double crochet

**Dec** = decrease(ing)

**dpn** = double pointed needles

**foll** = follow(s) (ing)

**in** = inch(es)

**Inc** = increase(ing)

**K** = knit

**K1b** = knit 1 in row below

**LHS/RHS** = left/right – hand side

**M1** = make 1

**mm** = millimeter(s)

**P** = purl

**pat** = pattern

**Psso** = pass slipped st over knitted st(s)

**rem** = remaining

**rep** = repeat

**Rev st st** = reverse stockinnette stitch

**RS** = right side

**Selv** = selvage

**Sl** = slip

**Sl 1 K** = slip 1 knitwise

**Sl 1 P** = slip 1 purlwise

**st(s)** = stitch(es)

**st st** = stockinette stitch

**Ss/sl st** = slip stitch

**SKP** = slip 1, K1, psso

**SK2P** = slip 1, K2tog, psso

**Tbl** = through back of loop

**tog** = together

**Wrh/yrh** = wool (yarn) round hook

**WS** = wrong side

**WS/RS** = wrong side/right side

**Yb** = yarn back

**Yf** = yarn forward

**Yrn/yon** = yarn round needle to make 1

**O** = work no sts

## Basic Stitches

**Garter St:** Knit every row.

**Moss St:** *K1, P1; rep from * to end. On the foll rows, K the purl sts and P the knit sts.

**Double Moss St:** *K1, P1; rep from * to end. On foll row, K the knit sts and P the purl sts.
Next row: *P1, K1; rep from * to end. On foll rows, K the knit sts and P the purl sts. Rep these 4 rows.

**K1/P1 Rib:** *K1, p1; rep from * to end. On foll row, K the knit sts and P the purl sts.

**K2/P2 Rib:** *K2, p2; rep from * to

end. On foll row, K the knit sts and P the purl sts.

**K3/P2:** *K3, p2; rep from * to end. On foll row, K the knit sts and P the purl sts.

**K3/P3 Rib:** *K3, p3; rep from * to end. On foll row, K the knit sts and P the purl sts.

**Selvage st:** A stitch worked at each end of row, either in St st or garter st, and is used to make seaming easier.

**Double Crochet (dc) (US single crochet):** Insert hook into a st, yrh,

draw loop through, yrh, draw yarn through 2 loops on hook.

**Crab st (US backward single crochet):** Work 1 row dc from left to right, instead of from right to left (as in double crochet).

**Stockinette St (st st):** K 1 row on RS, P1 row on WS.

**Treble (tr) (US double crochet):** Yrh, insert hook into a st, yrh, draw loop through, yrh, draw loop through, 1st 2 loops on hook, yrh, draw loop through last 2 loops on hook.

## Women's Measurements

To fit bust:

87-90 (93-96/99-102/105-108) cm
or
34-36 (36-38/38-40/40-42)"
or
Small (Medium/Large/X-Large)

The instructions are given for the smallest size with the larger sizes in parentheses. Where only one figure is given, it applies to all sizes.

# retailer list*

**Arizona**

Tucson | Purls 2
| 520-296-6363

**California**

Anaheim Hills | Velona Needlecraft
| 800-972-1570
| www.velona.com

Arcadia | Skeins
| 626-301-7968
| skeinyarns@aol.com

Bakersfield | Classy Knits
| 866-325-7226
| classyyarn@classyyarns.com

Bellflower | Stitches in Time
| 562-804-9341

Calistoga | Calistoga Yarns
| 707-942-5108

El Cerrito | Skein Lane
| 510-525-1828
| www.skeinlane.com

El Segundo | Slipt Stitch
| 310-322-6793

Half Moon Bay | Fengari
| 650-726-2550

Hemet | Lazy Daisy
| 909-658-8134

La Jolla | Knitting in La Jolla
| 858-456-4687

Lafayette | Big Sky Studio
| 925-284-1020
| www.bigskystudio.com
| Yarn Boutique
| 925-283-7377
| www.yarnboutique.com

Laguna Beach | Strands and Stitches
| 949-497-5648

Long Beach | Alamitos Bay Yarn Co
| 562-799-8484
| abyarn@earthlink.net

Los Angeles | Jennifer Knits
| 310-471-8733
| jenwen@prodigy.net
| Knit Café
| 323-658-5648
| www.knitcafe.com
| Suss Design
| 323-954-9637
| www.sussdesign.com

Menlo Park | Knitter's Studio
| 650-322-9200
| www.knittersstudio.com

Mill Valley | Yarn Collection
| 800-908-9276

Morgan Hill | The Continental Stitch
| 408-779-5885

Oakland | Article Pract
| 510-652-7435
| Knitting Basket
| 800-654-4887

Palm Desert | Yarn Boutique
| 760-340-3081
| Yarn Co Palm Desert
| 760-341-7734

Palm Springs | Ruth's Needlecraft
| 760-327-4464

Pismo Beach | Stitch & Pearl
| 805-473-3851

Redding | Artful Hand
| 530-221-8313

Redondo Beach | L'Atelier
| 800-833-6133
| rb@latelier.com

Rolling Hills Est | Concepts in Yarn
| 310-230-9902
| infor@conceptsinyarn.com

San Carlos | Creative Hands
| 650-591-0588

San Diego | Needleworks
| 619-296-8505

San Francisco | Atelier
| 415-771-1550
| Greenwich Yarns
| 415-567-2535
| Imagiknit
| 415-621-6642
| Cottage Yarns
| 650-873-7371

San Rafael | Dharma Trading
| 415-456-1211

Santa Barbara | BB's Knits
| 805-569-0531

Santa Monica | L'Atelier
| 310-394-4665
| sm@latelier.com
| Wildfiber
| 310-458-2748

Sherman Oaks | Needle World
| 818-784-2442
| needleworld@needleworld.com

Studio City | La Knitterie Parisienne
| 800-2BUYYAR
| laknitpar@earthnet.net

Truckee | Jimmy Beans Wool
| 530-582-9530
| www.jimmybeanswool.com

West Hills | The Craft House
| 818-999-2720

**Colorado**

Denver | Ewenique Yarns
| 303-377-6336
| ewenique@worldnet.att.net

Lakewood | Showers of Flowers
| 800-825-2569
| www.showersofflowers.com

Palisade | Cozy Knit & Purl
| 970-464-1088

**Connecticut**

Cromwell | Fabric Place
| 860-632-5744

Wallingford | Country Yarns
| 203-269-6662

**Florida**

Bellaire Bluffs | Flying Needles
| 727-581-8691

Celebration | Hopskotch
| 231-334-4044

Palm Harbor | Uncommon Threads
| 727-784-6778
| nnollett@gte.net

Sarasota | Spinning Wheel
| 941-953-7980

Winter Park | Sip & Knit
| 407-622-5648
| www.sipandknit.com

**Georgia**

Dahlonega | Magical Threads
| 706-867-8918

**Illinois**

Chicago | Knitting Workshop
| 773-929-5776
| knittingworkshop@ameritech.net
| We'll Keep You In Stitches
| 312-642-2540
| bettystitch@aol.com
| Knitters Niche
| 773-472-9276

Decatur | Enticements
| 217-422-5870

Des Plaines | Mosaic Yarn Studio Ltd
| 847-390-1013
| mosaicyarn@aol.com

Wheaton | Lizzies
| 630-690-7945

Winnetka | Caroline's Fine Yarns
| 847-441-0400
| www.carolinesfineyarns.com

**Indiana**

Indianapolis | Mass. Ave Knit Shop
| 317-638-1833

**Maryland**

Annapolis | Yarn Garden
| 800-738-9276

www.yarngarden.com

| | | |
|---|---|---|
| Ashton | Fiberworks | |
| | 301-774-9031 | |
| | www.fiberworks4yarn.com | |
| Baltimore | Woolworks | |
| | 410-337-9030 | |
| Frederick | Keep Me In Stitches | |
| | 240-379-7740 | |
| Glyndon | Woolstock | |
| | 410-363-1160 | |
| | leslyes777@aol.com | |

## Massachussets

| | |
|---|---|
| Framingham | Fabric Place |
| | 508-872-4888 |
| Newton | Fabric Place |
| | 617-965-5500 |
| Randolph | Fabric place |
| | 781-963-1100 |
| Woburn | Fabric Place |
| | 781-938-8787 |

## Michigan

| | |
|---|---|
| Ann Arbor | Flying Sheep |
| | 734-623-1640 |
| | Knit A Round |
| | 734-998-3771 |
| | knitaround@aol.com |
| Birmingham | Right Off The Sheep |
| | 248-646-7595 |
| Beulah | Yarn Market |
| | 231-882-4640 |
| Caro | Ruby's Yarn & Fabric |
| | 989-673-3062 |
| Cedar | Inish Knits |
| | 231-228-2800 |
| Charlotte | Yarn Garden |
| | 517-541-9323 |
| Clarkston | Basketful of Yarn |
| | 248-620-2491 |
| Frankenmuth | Rapunzels |
| | 989-652-0464 |
| Glen Arbor | Yarn Shop |
| | 231-334-3805 |
| Grand Haven | The Fibre House |
| | 616-844-2497 |
| Holland | Friends of Wool |
| | 616-395-9665 |
| | www.friendsofwool.com |
| Howell | Stitch In Time |
| | 517-546-0769 |
| Menominee | The Elegant Ewe |
| | 906-863-2296 |
| Mt Clemens | Crafty Lady |
| | 810-566-8008 |
| Plymouth | Old Village Yarn Shop |

734-451-0580

| | |
|---|---|
| Port Huron | Mary Maxim |
| | 810-987-2000 |
| Portage | Stitching Memories |
| | 888-805-6190 |
| | stitchingmem@aol.com |
| Royal Oak | Ewe-Nique Knits |
| | 248-584-3001 |
| Suttons Bay | Gallery 2 |
| | 231-271-4980 |
| Traverse City | Lost Art Yarn Shoppe |
| | 231-941-1263 |
| West Bloomfield | Knit Knit Knit |
| | 248-855-2114 |
| | knitknitknit@wwwnet.net |
| West Branch | Evergreen Sampler |
| | 989-345-1800 |
| Wyoming | Threadbender |
| | 616-531-6641 |

## Minnesota

| | |
|---|---|
| Minneapolis | Clickity Sticks Yarn |
| | 612-724-2500 |
| | www.clickitysticks.com |
| White Bear Lake | Sheepy Yarn Shoppe |
| | 651-426-5463 |
| | www.sheepyyarnmn.com |

## Nebraska

| | |
|---|---|
| Omaha | Personal Threads |
| | 800-306-7733 |
| | carolyn@personalthreads.com |

## New Hampshire

| | |
|---|---|
| Hancock | Green Acres |
| | 888-413-5155 |

## New Jersey

| | |
|---|---|
| Colts Neck | Knitting Gallery |
| | 888-294-9276 |
| | www.knittinggallery.com |
| Englishtown | Knit N Purl |
| | 732-536-6050 |
| Garwood | Knitter's Workshop |
| | 908-789-1333 |
| Marlton | Knitting Knook |
| | 856-985-8042 |
| | knittingknook@aol.com |
| Pitman | Karen's Needlecraft Shop |
| | 856-589-4427 |

## New York

| | |
|---|---|
| Brooklyn | Knitting Hands |
| | 718-858-5648 |
| | www.knittinghands.com |
| | M & M Yarn Connection |
| | 718-436-5262 |
| Farmington | New York Knits |

585-924-1950

| | |
|---|---|
| Larchmont | Silver Canvas Ltd |
| | 914-834-4868 |
| Middletown | Bonnie's Kozy Knit |
| | 845-344-0229 |
| New York | Downtown Yarns |
| | 212-995-5991 |
| | Knitting 321 |
| | 212-772-2020 |
| | Purl |
| | 212-420-8796 |
| | www.purlsoho.com |
| | Seaport Yarns |
| | 212-608-3100 |
| | www.seaportand.com |
| | The Lion and The Lamb |
| | 212-876-4303 |
| | The Woolgathering |
| | 212-734-4747 |
| | www.thewoolgathering.com |
| Woodstock | The Yarn Shoppe |
| | 845-679-2900 |
| | theyarneshoppe@hotmail.com |

## North Carolina

| | |
|---|---|
| Blowing Rock | Dee's Yarn Nook |
| | 828-295-5051 |
| Greensboro | Yarns etc… |
| | 336-370-1233 |
| | yarnsetc@earthlink.com |
| Huntersville | Knit One Stitch Too |
| | 704-655-9558 |
| | knitonestitchtwo@aol.com |
| Raleigh | Great Yarns |
| | 800-810-0045 |
| | www.great-yarns.com |

## Ohio

| | |
|---|---|
| Cincinnati | Fiber Naturell |
| | 513-921-7538 |
| Cleveland | Fine Points |
| | 216-229-6644 |
| | www.finepoints.com |
| Defiance | The Fifth Stitch |
| | 419-782-0991 |
| | alelupp@defnet.com |
| Olmstead Falls | Abigayle's Quiltery |
| | 440-235-7446 |
| Toledo | Fiberworks |
| | 419-389-1821 |
| Woodmere | The Knitting Room |
| | 216-464-8450 |
| | www.theknittingroom.com |

## Oregon

| | |
|---|---|
| Ashland | The Web.sters |
| | 800-482-9801 |

| | | | | | |
|---|---|---|---|---|---|
| | www.yarnatwebsters.com | Dallas | Yarn and Stitches 972-239-9665 merriman@gte.net | Winchester | Frog Eye Fiber Emporium 540-662-0717 |
| Bandon | The Wool Company 541-347-3912 | Houston | Merribee Needle Arts 281-440-6980 | **Washington** | |
| Coos Bay | My Yarn Shop 541-266-8230 | | Nancy's Knits 713-661-9411 nanknit@swbell.net | Bellevue | Skeins! LTD 866-452-5654 www.skeinslimited.com |
| Lake Oswego | Molehill Yarns 503-697-9554 | Plano | The Wooly Ewe 972-424-3163 | Edmonds | Spin A Yarn 425-775-0909 www.spinayarn.com |
| Portland | Northwest Wools 503-244-5024 | **Utah** | | Everett | Great Yarns! 888-320-6802 www.greatyarns.com |
| | The Yarn Garden 503-239-7950 theyarngarden@cs.com | Ogden | The Needlepoint Joint 801-394-4355 | Poulsbo | Wild & Wooly 360-779-3222 |
| Salem | Artistic Needle 503-589-1502 | **Virginia** | | Renton | Knittery 800-742-3565 |
| **Pennsylvania** | | Alexandria | Springwater Fiber Workshop 703-549-3634 infor@springwater.org | Seattle | Full Circle 206-783-3322 fullcircle56@msn.com |
| Lancaster | Oh Susanna 717-393-5146 | Burke | Yarn Barn 703-978-2220 www.geocities.com theyarnbarn | | Weaving Works 888-524-1221 weavingworks@earthlink.net |
| Princeton | Glenmarle Woolworks 609-921-3022 | | | | |
| Oakdale | Tonidale 412-788-8850 ingeborg1@webtv.net | Charlottesville | Art Needlework, Inc 804-296-4625 tsarto@aol.com | | Yarn Gallery 206-935-2010 yarn_gallery@yahoo.com |
| **Rhode Island** | | Falls Church | Aylin's Woolgatherer 800-775-9665 aylins@wool.com | **Wisconsin** | |
| Warwick | Fabric Place 401-823-5400 | Manassas | Old Town Needlecrafts 703-330-1846 knitwit109@aol.com | Eau Claire | Threade Bear 715-835-9006 |
| **Texas** | | Midlothian | Got Yarn 888-242-4474 www.gotyarn.com | Fond Du Lac | The Knitting Room 920-906-4800 |
| Austin | European Knits 512-345-0727 | | | | |
| | Hill Country Weavers 512-707-7396 | | | | |
| Bedford | Simpatico Yarns 817-285-6067 | | | | |

*Correct at time of printing. For more up to date info, go to www.annyblatt.com or e-mail info@annyblattusa.com.

# acknowledgments

We would like to thank the many wonderful people without whom this book could not have been created. At Sixth&Spring Books, we'd like to thank Trisha Malcolm, Theresa McKeon, Cara Beckerich and Michelle Lo. We'd also like to extend our gratitude to the staff at Anny Blatt France: Marie-Irene Garcia and Gilles Borrot. Thank you to Ronda Maddy, Ric Frievalt and Jean-Christophe Tarazona at Anny Blatt USA. And last but not least, Nancy Cheung from Nancy Knits in Houston, Texas.

All photography courtesy of Laines Anny Blatt.